Sport Funding and Finance

Books in the Sport Management Series

Sport Governance
Russell Hoye and Graham Cuskelly

Sport and the Media
Matthew Nicholson

Sport Funding and Finance
Bob Stewart

Managing People in Sport Organizations
Tracy Taylor, Alison J. Doherty and Peter McGraw

Sport Funding and Finance

Bob Stewart

ELSEVIER

AMSTERDAM • BOSTON • HEIDELBERG • LONDON • NEW YORK • OXFORD
PARIS • SAN DIEGO • SAN FRANCISCO • SINGAPORE • SYDNEY • TOKYO

Linacre House, Jordan Hill, Oxford OX2 8DP, UK
30 Corporate Drive, Suite 400, Burlington, MA 01803, USA

British Library Cataloguing in Publication Data
A catalogue record for this book is available from the British Library

Library of Congress Control Number:
A catalogue record for this book is available from the Library of Congress

ISBN-10: 0 7506 8160 8
ISBN-13: 978 0 7506 8160 5

For information on all publications visit our web site at
http://books.elsevier.com

Trademarks/Registered Trademarks

All brand names mentioned in this book are protected by their respective trademarks
and are acknowledged

Typeset by Charon Tec Ltd (A Macmillan Company), Chennai, India
www.charontec.com

Printed and bound in the Netherlands

Working together to grow
libraries in developing countries

www.elsevier.com | www.bookaid.org | www.sabre.org

ELSEVIER   BOOK AID International   Sabre Foundation

Contents

Contents

Contents

Contents

Series Editor

Dr Russell Hoye is Senior Lecturer in Sport Management, School of Sport, Tourism and Hospitality Management, La Trobe University, Victoria, Australia.

Russell has taught sport management courses since 1993 in Australia at La Trobe University, Griffith University, and Victoria University as well the University of Hong Kong and Tsinghua University in China. His main teaching areas are sport management, organizational behavior, sport policy, and sport governance. Russell serves as the Coordinator of Honours and Postgraduate Studies for the School of Sport, Tourism, and Hospitality Management at La Trobe University. He is a former Board Member of the Australian and New Zealand Association for Leisure Studies (ANZALS) and a current Board Member of the Sport Management Association of Australia and New Zealand (SMAANZ). He was the Guest Editor for the inaugural special issue of *Sport Management Review* on professional sport in Australia and New Zealand published in 2005.

Russell's areas of expertise include corporate governance, organizational behavior, volunteer management, and public sector reform within the sport industry. He has acted as a consultant for the Australian Sports Commission, Sport and Recreation Victoria, and a number of local government and non-profit organizations. His research interests focus on examining how governance is enacted with sport organizations and how volunteers engage with and are managed by sport organizations. He has published articles on these topics in journals such as *Nonprofit Management and Leadership*, *Sport Management Review*, *European Sport Management Quarterly*, *Society and Leisure*, *International Gambling Studies*, *Third Sector Review*, *Sporting Traditions*, *Managing Leisure*, *Football Studies*, *Annals of Leisure Research*, and the *Australian Journal on Volunteering*.

Sport Management Series Preface

Many millions of people around the globe are employed in sport organizations in areas as diverse as event management, broadcasting, venue management, marketing, professional sport, and coaching as well as in allied industries such as sporting equipment manufacturing, sporting footwear and apparel, and retail. At the elite level, sport has moved from being an amateur pastime to a significant industry. The growth and professionalization of sport has driven changes in the consumption and production of sport and in the management of sporting organizations at all levels of sport. Managing sport organizations at the start of the twenty-first century involves the application of techniques and strategies evident in the majority of modern business, government, and non-profit organizations.

The *Sport Management Series* provides a superb range of texts for the common subjects in sport business and management courses. They provide essential resources for academics, students and managers, and are international in scope. Supported by excellent case studies, useful study questions, further reading lists, lists of websites, and supplementary online materials such as case study questions and PowerPoint slides, the series represents a consistent, planned, and targeted approach which:

- provides a high-quality, accessible, and affordable portfolio of titles which match management development needs through various stages;
- prioritizes the publication of texts where there are current gaps in the market, or where current provision is unsatisfactory;
- develops a portfolio of both practical and stimulating texts in all areas of sport management.

The *Sport Management Series* is the first of its kind, and as such is recognized as being of consistent high quality and will quickly become the series of first choice for academics, students, and managers.

Brief Biography for Bob Stewart

Bob Stewart is Associate Professor and Chair of the Sport Management and Policy Group at Victoria University, Melbourne, Australia. Bob has taught into undergraduate and postgraduate sport management programs for 15 years, and is one of Australia's leading sport management educators. His primary responsibilities have been sport finance, sport policy, and sport and globalization.

Bob is the sole author of *The Australian Football Business*, Kangaroo Press, 1984; co-editor of *More Than a Game: An Unauthorised History of Australian Football*, Melbourne University Press, 1998; co-author of *Sport Management: A Guide to Professional Practice*, Allen and Unwin, 1999; co-editor of *Football Fever: Grassroots*, Maribyrnong Press, 2004; co-author of *Australian Sport: Better by Design? The Evolution of Sport Policy in Australia*, Routledge, 2004; co-editor of *Football Fever: Crossing Boundaries*, Maribyrnong Press, 2005; and co-author of *Sport Management: Principles and Applications*, Elsevier, 2006.

Bob is currently researching the commercial and cultural context of anti-doping policy in Australia sport. Bob also has a special research interest in the political economy of football.

Preface

This book is directed to units of study that are linked to courses in sport management and strategy. It is particularly suitable for programs that focus on accounting principles, financial management, budgeting, economic impact statements, and program evaluation. The book is also valuable for study programs where the focus is on sports' commercial and financial evolution.

This book will be relevant to readers from English-speaking countries like Australia, New Zealand, Great Britain, and Canada. Each of these countries has a mature university sector that offers a broad range of programs in sport management and sport studies. It will also be attractive to readers from the Asia-Pacific region (which includes countries like India, Indonesia, Korea, Malaysia, Singapore, and Thailand). There is a rapidly growing interest in sport management training in these countries, with sport funding and finance being integral to any program.

This book is directed to readers who wish to get both a broad and deep understanding of the commercial and financial structure of sport in various contexts. To this end, this book will provide readers with a three-tiered learning experience. The first tier will take a macro-perspective by giving readers a broad appreciation of the commercial evolution of sport, and how it has managed to move from the kitchen-table model to the corporate-boardroom model, and along the way become quite a sophisticated industry from a financial viewpoint. So, in the first tier of the book attention will be given to the commercial development of sport using USA and European pro-sport leagues as a benchmark. Changes in the funding arrangements of sport will be highlighted, and different funding sources will be examined in detail. These sources will include traditional items like membership income, income from social activities, and gate/game receipts, and the big-ticket items like gaming income, sponsorship, broadcast rights fees, merchandising income, and government grants and subsidies.

The second tier will promote a micro-analysis of sport funding and finance by giving readers a sound grounding in the principles and practice of effective financial management. Readers will be introduced to basic accounting principles and practice, and then led into more complex issues of pricing, costing, financial analysis, budgeting, economic-impact analysis, and feasibility studies. Each of these topic areas will provide considerable skill development by giving readers the core concepts and principles, and applying them to both fictitious and real-world case studies. The third tier will explore future developments in sport finance and funding, and examine how they impact on sport management knowledge and skill requirements.

Within this framework, this book will provide readers with two types of learning outcomes. The first outcome is knowledge based and will include the following:

1. A grounded understanding of the commercial evolution of sport from the 1950s to the present.

2. An understanding of the different commercial phases sport goes through to reach commercial maturity.
3. An appreciation of the major global sport events and leagues, and their financial arrangements.
4. An insight into the financial strengths and weaknesses of contemporary sport.

The second outcome is skill based, and by reading the book and completing the cases, readers will be able to do the following:

1. Identify the different legal structures of sport organizations and the financial implications of each structure.
2. Explain the main accounting conventions and how they impact on the financial management of sport organizations.
3. Identify the foundations of double-entry book-keeping.
4. Construct a simple set of accounts for a sport organization.
5. Use ratio analysis to evaluate the financial performance of sport organizations.
6. Explain how sport organizations can create profits, value, and wealth.
7. Understand different methods of constructing budgets, and use them to control the financial operation of a sport organization.
8. Set up models for identifying and managing costs.
9. Identify different methods for setting prices for sport goods and services, and to apply them to specific settings and events.
10. Undertake financial planning exercises and feasibility studies for a sport organization or facility.
11. Undertake a cost-benefit analysis for a sport organization event.

In summary, readers of this book will obtain both a broad knowledge of the commercial evolution of sport and its current financial operation, and the necessary skills both for understanding and supervising the financial operations of a sport organization.

Note on Cases, Currencies, and Exchange Rates

Many cases are provided throughout this book. In some instances the cases are taken from the real world, and in other instances the cases are fictitious. Whereas the data in the real-world cases are expressed in specific national currencies (e.g. GBP, EUR, AUD, USD, and YEN). The fictional case data is expressed through the traditional dollar sign ($).

In order to make relevant comparisons between the different data in the real-world cases, it is important to be clear about the currency conversion rates. The following exchange rates applied when the manuscript was prepared for publication in July 2006:

Australian Dollar to British Pound

1 AUD = 0.400 GBP
1 GBP = 2.500 AUD

Australian Dollar to US Dollar

1 AUD = 0.737 USD
1 USD = 1.355 AUD
1 GBP = 1.845 USD
I USD = 0.540 GBP

Australian Dollar to Japan Yen

1 AUD = 84.737 YEN
1 YEN = 0.012 AUD
1 GBP = 211.530 YEN
1 YEN = 0.0047 GBP

Australian Dollar to Euro

1 AUD = 0.581 EUR
1 EUR = 1.721 AUD
1 GBP = 1.445 EUR
1 EUR = 0.691 GBP

**PART
ONE**

Sport Funding:
Commercial
Context

1

The metamorphosis of sport

Overview

This chapter examines the progress of sport over the last 50 years. It looks at the old model of amateurism and volunteerism, and traces through its transformation into a sport system that is centered on the fan, the professional athlete, the governing board, the new generation stadium, the multifunction venue, and the paid manager. The effect of this shift on the sporting landscape, and the finance skill requirements of sport managers will be investigated. The role of government will also be noted.

Sport diversity

Sport is an enigmatic institution, and comes in many forms and shapes. For instance, the mainstay of sport in many countries is the community club which relies on the support of its members to sustain its activities. These clubs can be single-sport organizations like tennis clubs and swimming clubs, but they can also be multifunctional, and provide a range of sports under the same roof. They are nearly always managed by volunteers who pay fees for the privilege of playing. There are also sporting associations whose primary role is to provide administrative support to clubs, organize competitions, and generally develop the sport they represent, whether it is netball, table tennis, or volleyball. While these organizations have many paid employees, they also rely on volunteer staff to run their programs and manage their affairs. Then there are commercial leisure centers that provide sport services on a fee-for-service or user-pay principle. Gymnasia and swim centers often fall into this category, and can be either privately owned, or owned by local councils. There is also a raft of professional sport clubs and leagues that play in large stadia, attract thousands of spectators, and generate mass media coverage. These sport organizations are book-ended by first, government and its agencies, and second, the media and sport merchandisers who both promote sport and use its star players to attract customers. The different types of sport organizations that comprise the Australian sport system are listed in Table 1.1. While this structure will be similar for many other English-speaking nations with a strong government presence, there will also be variations that reflect different political and cultural conditions.

Table 1.1 Main Organizational Players in Australian Sport

	Government	Non-profit Organizations	Commercial Organizations
National spread	Minister for Sport Government Departments Australian Sports Commission Australian Sport Anti-Doping Authority	National Olympic Committee Australian Commonwealth Games Association National sport leagues National sport associations University sport associations	TV and radio stations The Internet National newspapers National brand name sponsors National sport good suppliers
State spread	State Minister for Sport State Sport Academies Health promotion agencies Major event corporations	State sporting associations State sport leagues Sport stadiums (outdoor) Sport arenas (enclosed)	State-based media Local brand name sponsors
Local spread	Municipal councils	Universities and schools Sport clubs Sport grounds and venues Sport and leisure centers	Sport good retailers Sport and leisure centers

Source: Oakley, R. (1999:62–63).

The role of the state, the market, and civil society

While Table 1.1 confirms the contribution government makes to sport, it also needs to be recognized that it is just one of a number of contributors to sport's ongoing development. In some societies government, or the state as it is broadly identified, may play a dominant role, but in other societies its role may be far more circumspect. A useful way of understanding the relationship between the state and society is to distinguish between three distinct but interdependent social orders (Ibsen and Jorgensen 2002). The first social order is the state and its apparatus. The role of the state is to govern members of society by establishing a bureaucracy that enforces an array of rules and regulations. It also mobilizes resources through its taxing powers, and uses them to establish an economic and cultural infrastructure that allows commerce and the arts to flourish. The second social order is the market, which is the focal point for business activity. This is the home of the private sector, which is driven primarily by the desire for market expansion and profits. The third social order is civil society which comprises a complex web of informal, non-market relationships that are mainly situated around households, neighborhoods, and local communities. Civil society is most visible in the unstructured networks that characterize the dynamics of small social and friendship groups.

The intersections of these three social orders create four different sectors and organizational forms. They are the non-profit public sector, which is driven by the state; the profit-based commercial sector, which is driven by the market; the informal sector, which is driven by civil society; and finally, the voluntary sector, which is driven by aspects of all three social orders. The organization of society between the state, the market, and civil society is illustrated in Figure 1.1.

Sport can fit into any of the four sectors depending on first, the traditions and values that underpin the sport experience; and second, the scale of resources that each sector can command. In Australia, Great Britain, and New Zealand, for example, sport has traditionally taken place in the voluntary and informal sectors, but over recent years there has been a growing interest in the sport by the commercial sector. Together with greater direct involvement by the state and public sector, this has resulted in a significant allocation of sport resources into these areas of society.

Figure 1.1 provides a useful context within which to discuss the sport funding roles of the state, the market and the volunteer sector. It indicates that while the state may have enormous influence over the structure and practice of sport in one set of political conditions, it can just as easily have minimal influence over sport in some other situation. The model also suggests that even where the state is passive in respect of sport development, there may be a flourishing sport system in one or more of the other sectors, depending on how highly sport is valued in each sector. The model also implies that there is no single or best way for society to organize its sport systems and practices. It all depends on which sector is seen to be the appropriate provider of sport facilities and activities, and what types of sport outcomes are intended. For example the state

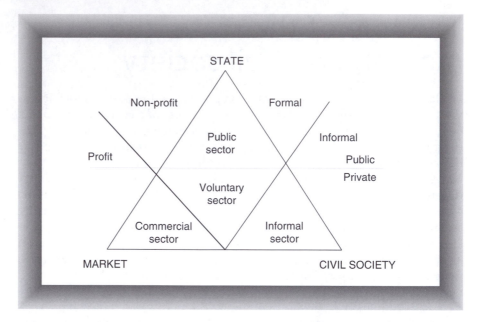

Figure 1.1 A Sectoral Model of Society (Adapted from Ibsen and Jorgensen 2002)

may be seen as the most effective provider of elite athlete training facilities and large stadia, while the voluntary sector may be used to provide community sport, and sport-for-all activities. Apart from the USA, where the private sector dominates sport funding, there has been a significant expansion of national government funding of sport. In Western Europe and the Asia-Pacific region most international-standard venues are funded by government, as are elite training facilities (Stewart, R. et al., 2004; Green and Houlihan 2005).

The practice of sport

The practice of sport can also be viewed from different perspectives. For some it is all about participation, playing the game for its own sake, and using the game to develop character and leadership. In other words sport can be a vehicle for making better people and better communities. In these instances commercialism is often viewed as a problem by its tendency to over-emphasize winning, encourage gambling, and undermine the values of amateurism. On the other hand, some people believe that sport can only achieve its potential if it is well supported and funded. In other words, commercialized sport will increase standards of play by sustaining professional sport leagues. At the same time the benefits of commercial sport are not always shared equally, since some sports are inherently more popular than others and attract more funding. As a result sports like canoeing, water polo, and rowing will always be disadvantaged so long as they are played in the shadows of popular spectator sports like the various codes of football (American football, Australian football, Gaelic football, rugby league, rugby union, and world football), tennis, and cricket.

Essentially then, sport practice comprises two distinctive but connected strands. The first strand is community sport, which comprises participant-based sport geared around the local club, the volunteer administrator, a simple organizational structure, and the recreational player. While a few talented young players will use the local club as the springboard for entry into the world of elite sport development, most club members will focus their energies on interclub competition and building their social networks. The second strand is professional sport, which is centered on the elite performer and geared around spectators who provide the catalyst for the sports' commercial development. It attracts media coverage which in turn provides a promotional impetus for further spectator interest. Broadcasting of events emerge, rights fees are negotiated, corporate sponsors see the benefits of linking their brands to a sport league or club, and all of a sudden professional sport leagues and mega-sport events begin to occupy large slabs of the sports landscape. When sport becomes commercial, rather than recreational, officials, players, and fans begin to take it very seriously.

The meaning of sport

Sport is important to people in many ways. It provides an ideal forum for expressing one's physicality; it improves fitness, and builds social networks, particularly when played in a club setting. In professional sport, team games are particularly popular because they meet a deep-seated need for tribal identity, and provide an archetypal ritual where fans can re-live ancient ceremonies and social practices. They consequently become a modern counterpart of ancient hunting patterns where different tribes compete for power, status, and recognition (Morris 1981). It provides an effective frame for understanding the relationship between fans and clubs. Team sports provide strong tribal connections that allow members to play out a variety of traditional roles and practices. In the clubs, for example, the tribal elders comprise the club president or chairperson, senior officials, coaches, fitness advisors, and medical support staff. The elders and players enact tribal rituals that both reinforce the sport's values and regulate the behaviors of its participants. Rituals include mid-week commentary, pre-game preparation, the display of signs and slogans that emphasize discipline and endeavor, and pre-match addresses that urge players to selflessly contribute to the greater good. The players are the tribal heroes, and are cheered and lauded, and perform on the field of play until their time is up, in which case they are replaced by new personalities. There are also many tribal trappings that provide color, noise, and public exposure. They include player outfits, club photos, club colors, insignia, badges, emblems, and trophies. Central to the tribal practices are the fans, or tribal followers. They provide the passion and commitment by proudly displaying their loyalty and affiliation. The fans and tribal followers accentuate intertribal rivalries through the purchase of memorabilia, dressing in club colors, and inciting the followers of other teams and rival tribes. They also

7

compose tribal chants and team songs, which are used to not only assert their identity, but to also intimidate rival tribes. However, these strong tribal connections to sport have been occasionally threatened by the growing financial sophistication of league and events and the consequent changes to sport's cultural practices.

The changing fan–club relationship

This close relationship between sport fans and their clubs is pivotal to the ongoing sustainability of professional sport competitions and leagues (Crawford 2004). In the various codes of football for example, there has been a steady growth in the fan base, particularly when television viewers of sport are added to the fans who attend the venues. The audience for major global events is no longer measured in millions of supporters, but billions of watchers. However, the relationship between clubs and fans has also been problematic in response to the many changes that have taken place in the structure and practice of many sports. Over the last 50 years, the sport–fan relationship has gone through three developmental phases, with each phase corresponding to an increase in sport's commercialization and financial expansion.

Phase 1

In many countries, sporting organizations have traditionally been member based, and as a result fans have always had a formal way of influencing the club's direction. This member-based structure meant that for the price of a membership fee, fans could vote for committee members, or alternatively seek election themselves. Clubs also depended for their survival on the contribution of volunteers. This constituted the first phase of the fan's relationship with their club, team, or event. It was engaged and local, and can be called the integration phase.

Phase 2

As sport organizations become more commercial there is pressure to develop a business dimension to the club's operations. Professional staff are hired to secure the club's future through increasing funding and membership. Decisions are made about a sport club's traditional practices in response to the claims of sponsors, conflict occurs over the distribution of revenues, and vested interests emerge. While disputes are frequent, fans still believe they can play a part in the club's progress. This can be called the negotiation phase.

Phase 3

The final phase coincides with sport's commercial entrenchment and professionalization. As sport tightens its connections with the sponsor, the merchandiser and the television networks, a number of things happen. Players' earnings increase rapidly, volunteer officials are replaced by paid staff, and many fans see sport as just another leisure experience for sale in a competitive market place. Venues are upgraded, and replaced with large scale all-seat stadiums. All of this escalates the costs of running leagues and clubs, and in turn memberships and admission charges rise dramatically. The whole fan profile changes in this phase. Traditional fans are marginalized, and their space is occupied by supporters whose focus is entertainment as well as tribal identities. This is called the commodification phase.

Consequently, by the end of phase three fans have been transformed into customers (King 1998). The fans-as-customers model has influence insofar as they have purchasing power, and provide market research data from their participation in surveys and focus groups. While fans are now consulted on all manners of things, they are generally excluded from clubs' decision-making processes, whether it is a not-for-profit or a commercial enterprise. While some fans are critical of this state of affairs, others are happy to leave it all to the clubs so long as they achieve success. When this fragmentation is combined with escalating costs, low-income fans are pushed to the margin and the privileged fans are those who are prepared to pay for an entertaining experience. The increasing emphasis on entertainment and the increasing costs of attending major sport events are most clearly evident in major sport leagues around the world. In the USA and Western Europe in particular the continual increase in player salaries and improvement in venue amenities has produced a general improvement in the quality of the contest and the fan experience. However, these changes have also led to an increase in player salaries and stadium rentals, which in turn has increased the cost of staging games (Howard and Crompton 2004). As a result admission and ticket prices have increased dramatically (in Chapter 11 a more detailed analysis of sport event pricing is undertaken). Despite this shift to the fan-as-customer, and the escalating costs of consuming sport, the tribal nature of professional sport is still strong (Crawford 2004). This neo-tribalism not only differentiates sport's consumption for other types of buyer behavior, but also explains sport's importance in a world where traditional identities and loyalties are increasingly under threat.

Money and sport

This commodification and professionalization of sport has produced many strains and tensions, but overall has strengthened its hold over the public

Table 1.2 Europe's Most Profitable Sport Clubs 2005

Club Name	Annual Revenue (EUR million)
Real Madrid	276
Manchester United	245
AC Milan	234
Juventus	229
Chelsea	221
Barcelona	208
Bayen Munich	190
Liverpool	181
Inter Milan	177
Arsenal	171

Source: Deloittes (2006).

Table 1.3 USA Pro-Sport League Average Player Salaries 1991–2003

Year	MLB (USD million)	NFL (USD million)	NBA (USD million)	NHL (USD million)
2003	2.55	1.32	4.54	1.64
1991	0.6	0.35	0.99	0.32

Source: Howard, D. and Crompton, J. (2004:40).

consciousness (Wann, Melnick, Russell and Pease 2001). Sport has established its position as a vehicle for creating personal meaning and cultural identity, and provided a lucrative career path for many people. In Western Europe and North America in particular, professional sport clubs are multi-million dollar enterprises, where players frequently earn more than corporate CEOs and senior politicians. A recent survey of European world football clubs found that 10 clubs earned more than 170 million Euros a year. The rankings for 2005 are listed in Table 1.2.

In addition, recent studies of professional sport in the USA have revealed that many players earn more than USD 1 million a year. In the National Basketball Association (NBA), for example, the average annual player salary in 2003 was just over USD 4.5 million. The sharp upward trend in player salaries in the other major USA professional sport leagues (the National Football League (NFL), the National Hockey Leagues (NHL), and Major League Baseball (MLB)) are summarized in Table 1.3.

The commercial transformation of the Olympic Games

Despite the problems arising out of sport's cultural and structural changes during the last 50 years, it has strengthened its organizational and commercial foundations enormously. Take for example the Olympic Games. In 1956 the Games were held in Melbourne Australia. While the Games were rated a success, they were nearly cancelled in 1954 when it was found that the organizing Committee could not agree on which venue was to be the main stadium. There was heated debate as to whether it was to be an inner suburban sports ground at Carlton, or the better know and more centrally located Melbourne Cricket Ground (MCG). The International Olympic Committee (IOC), the world governing body for the Olympics, was concerned that the organizing committee was poorly managed and could not make effective decisions. This organizational problem was compounded by a tight budget, although the budget deficit was ultimately filled by the generous support of the Victorian State Government and the Commonwealth (Federal) Government. It should also be remembered that there was virtually no sponsorship income, and the income from broadcasting rights were negligible. In fact there was a dispute over the extent to which radio and television station should be charged for the right to cover the Games. Television was introduced into Australia in 1956, and coincided with the staging of the Melbourne Olympic Games. The Games were immediately seized on by the television industry as a vehicle for stimulating the purchase of television sets, while the Games Organizing Committee reflected on how television could be used as a means of raising extra revenue. In 1955 the Organizing Committee considered the possibility of selling the exclusive television and newsreel rights to an English company. The Committee confirmed that such an arrangement was being considered, and, if successful, would provide much needed funds for amateur sport in Australia. However, in response to claims that such a decision would deny other television stations access to the Games, and diminish the Game's international promotion, the plan was abandoned. As a result, there was no income to be sourced from this area. In short, the Melbourne Olympic Games Organizing Committee relied exclusively on income from government and ticket sales to fund this major sporting festival.

The 1956 Melbourne Olympics provide an exemplar of how major sport events were funded and managed during the early post-World War 2 period. They were the last of the so-called amateur-Games. Most of the athletes were not paid and participated for the glory of winning a medal on the international sporting stage. Competition was intense and serious but the athletes received little material benefit. In addition the Organizing Committee for the Melbourne Games comprised a few paid officials, but many more volunteers who were involved in both Games management and operational activities.

However, this all changed over the next 50 years. The Sydney 2000 Games and Athens 2004 Games were mega-sport events that cost around USD 3500 million and USD 5500 million respectively to mount and run. By contrast the average costs of mounting and running the Games in the 1970s and 1980s was around USD 600 million, the lowest being Montreal in 1976 (Preuss 2000).

Over this period there was also a concomitant increase in revenue. The most explosive increase came through the sale of the broadcast rights to television stations. As noted previously, the fee for the Melbourne Games was negligible. However with the development of a global satellite network in the late 1960s and a consequent expansion in the global audience, the fees increased substantially over the next 20 years. For instance the rights fee for the 1968 Mexico Games was USD 46 million. A subsequent increase in competition between the US television networks led to spirited bidding for the rights, which was reflected in a USD 106 million fee for Montreal in 1976 and a fee of USD 594 million for Seoul in 1988. The broadcasting fee continued to rise during the early part of the twenty-first century. The Sydney and Athens Olympics attracted over USD 1000 million and the most recently negotiated fee for Beijing will give the Organizing Committee USD 1700 million. It should also be noted that nearly 90 percent of the total broadcast fee income comes from two sources: NBC, the major American network will contribute USD 1000 million to the Organizing Committee for Beijing, while the European Broadcast Union (EBU), a consortium of mainly government stations in Western Europe will contribute another USD 500 million (Preuss 2000; Preuss 2004).

The same explosive increase is evident in the area of sponsorship. Between 1956 (the Melbourne Games) and 1972 (the Munich Games) sponsorship did not register at all on the Organizing Committee budget scale. The only commercial support came from a few billboards around the main facilities and a number of advertisements in the Games' programs and publicity documents. However, as the global television audience for the Games expanded it became increasingly attractive for globally marketed products (e.g. Coca Cola, American Express, and Ford) to promote their products through Olympic Games sponsorship. Sponsorship made its mark at the 1984 Los Angeles Games when the Organizing Committee secured USD 250 million from the corporate sector. For the 1996 Atlanta Games, sponsorship increased to USD 658 million and at the Athens Games the Organizing Committee obtained USD 690 million of sponsorship (Preuss 2004).

The third significant expansion in Olympic revenue came through income from merchandising. At both the Munich and Montreal games, merchandising income averaged out at USD 6 million, but by Seoul in 1988 it had increased to USD 26 million. During this period it became clear that the Olympic emblems and symbols (in particular the Olympic Rings) had become a highly marketable brand. In order to protect the brand and preserve its monopoly ownership the IOC registered it as an official trademark and sought legislative support for its exclusive use of the symbols from the host nations to the Games. This monopoly control, combined with an increase in global recognition enabled the IOC to expand its merchandising income to more than USD 80 million for the Atlanta and Athens Games (Preuss 2004).

The other interesting change in Olympic Games financing relates to the balance between government funding and private commercial funding. During the 1970s, 80 percent of Games funding was sourced from government, but this figure progressively fell during the 1980s and 1990s. For the Seoul Games of 1988 only 44 percent of its costs were sourced from government, while for Sydney the percentage of government funding was around 70 percent. The two most privately financed games were Los Angeles in 1984 and Atlanta in 1996. In fact in the case of the Los Angeles Games a referendum resulted in a vote not to provide significant public finance for the Games since it was feared that a drain of resources from other state programs would lead to a deterioration of the quality of life of Californians. Nearly all the facilities were privately funded, some of the venues were named after global businesses and this led to an operating surplus of USD 381 million (Preuss 2000). The experiences of Los Angeles and Atlanta can be contrasted with the funding arrangements for the 1980 Moscow Games. Given its economic structure at the time (it was the archetypal command economy) it was axiomatic that all funding was from government. The balance between government and private/market-based funding will vary from nation to nation, depending on the relative size of each sector.

The Asian experience: the J.League

Sport has not only undergone a commercial transformation in Europe and the USA, it has also been similarly affected in Asia. A good illustration is Japan's professional world football J.League, which was established in 1991 with three primary goals. They were to first, diffuse and improve Japanese football, second, develop a sporting culture that focused on both fandom and participation, and third, use the League to build international exchanges and recognition.

Each club based its activities in a home-town area and worked in close cooperation with local residents, administrators, and corporations. The home town was not a franchise, but rather the place where stakeholders worked to improve community life through sport. The J.League was also a deliberate move away from company sports teams, which previously dominated their sporting landscape. Clubs were encouraged to diversify their ownership base so that the business fortunes of a single organization did not endanger club management, and team names were changed from those of private businesses like Hitachi, to home-city names like Kawisha.

The J.League commenced in 1993 at the Tokyo National Stadium in front of approximately 60 000 fans. It marked not only the long-awaited start of professional world football league in Japan, but also a new sporting culture based on city and community identification. The emphasis on tribal identity worked well, and stadiums were quickly packed with fans wearing their team colors. In addition, the recruitment of internationally recognized players improved

13

the skills of local players, and local volunteers provided match-day support for their local teams. Words like supporter and fan have been added to the Japanese vocabulary, and many Japanese children now dream of playing in the J.League. The number of clubs has grown to 28 playing in two divisions, and the quality of play has risen steadily. Japan qualified for the FIFA 1998 World Cup, and reached the last 16 at the 2002 FIFA World Cup, which was co-hosted by Japan and South Korea.

Aggregate season attendances briefly fell after hitting a peak of 5.6 million in 1994, but increased strongly again after 2000. In the 2003 season the aggregate attendance was just over 7 million, while average attendances were 17 000 in Division 1 (J1) and 8000 in Division 2 (J2). This compared favorably with equivalent world football leagues in the USA and South Korea, where average game attendances were just over 15 000 and 10 000, respectively. Albirex Niigata had the League's highest average attendance of just over 30 000. In fact, nearly every financial indicator improved over the first 10 years of the League's operation. The J.League website (www.j-league.or.jp) makes the following points:

1. In 2003 average annual club revenue was Yen 2800 million for J1 clubs and Yen 978 million for J2 clubs.
2. Ticket sales revenue increased by 50 percent between 1999 and 2003.
3. League sponsorship was Yen 2310 million in 1993, but had increased to Yen 4020 million in 2003.
4. Broadcasting rights increased from Yen 1093 million in 1993 to Yen 4820 million in 2003.

Sport finance hubs

The above discussion shows that sport around the world has become increasingly commercialized over the last 50 years. While the USA is commercially dominant, Western Europe also supports many professional sport leagues and circuits in car rallying, Formula 1, motor cycles, athletics, basketball and handball, with world football being dominant. At the same time a third significant sports hub has formed in East Asia and the Pacific, with a build-up of sport resources in Japan, China, Korea, Australia, and New Zealand, and to a lesser extent in India. The expanding financial strength of sport in this region is reflected in the staging of a number of mega-sport events over recent years, culminating in the 2008 Beijing Olympic Games and 2010 Delhi Commonwealth Games.

Financial literacy

Despite sport's rapid commercialization there are many gaps in the financial knowledge and skills of sport organization managers. One of the most common features of contemporary sport management is the limited training and experience in finance and funding. As previously noted, money is now the basis of sport. Sport managers can no longer get away with financial irresponsibility and financial illiteracy. Even in Australia's most professionalized sport leagues there are many examples of ineffective financial management. In the Australian Football League (AFL) for example at least three clubs are technically insolvent, with liabilities nearly double their assets, which do not reflect well on the competencies of club administrators – but more about this later. All of the above discussion though, points to the need for the training of managers who are not only good at setting strategic directions, keeping stakeholders happy, and handling a diverse group of employers, but also handling money. The finance function in sport is now an essential management task. As a result, there is now a need to ensure the following occurs:

1. Keep accurate financial records
2. Construct realistic budgets and financial plans
3. Monitor expenses and revenue
4. Ensure adequate cash flows and ongoing liquidity
5. Create income generating assets
6. Control debt levels.

The costs of poor financial management are also significant. They include the following:

1. Loss of management control
2. Inability to accurately measure performance
3. Falling asset values
4. Increasing levels of debt
5. Escalating costs
6. Lack of cash
7. Operating losses
8. Liquidation.

Sport organizations, whether they are structured as public enterprises, private companies, or non-profit entities, must have sound financial management systems embedded in the operations. Sport is now a multimillion dollar enterprise with a sophisticated funding base that demands professional management to sustain its viability and extend its global footprint.

Questions to consider

1. Explain the difference between the organization of sport 50 years ago, and how it looks today.
2. Compare the strengths and weaknesses of traditional sport with the strengths and weaknesses of contemporary sport.
3. Discuss the relative importance of the state, the market, and civil society in driving sport in your region or nation.

4. Why is sport so important to so many people?
5. Do you agree with the statement that without fans there would be no commercialized sport? And, if so why?
6. Describe the main features of professional sport, and identify the main beneficiaries.
7. Explain how the Olympic Games transformed itself financially over the last 50 years.
8. What are the two dominant, and the one emerging, financial hubs of world sport?
9. Why is good financial management so important to the viability of sport?
10. What are the main factors leading to sport's escalating costs?

Further reading

For a detailed analysis of why sport is so important to people and how the fan has become the cornerstone of commercial sport see Crawford G. (2004) *Consuming Sport: Fans, Sport and Culture*. Routledge, London, and Wann, D., Melnick, M., Russell, G. and Pease, D. (2001). *Sport Fans: The Psychology and Social Impact of Spectators*, Routledge, New York. For more discussion of sports fan as a form of neo-tribalism see Morris, D. (1981). *The Soccer Tribe*, Jonathon Cape.

A useful contrast between non-profit community sport and professional sport is contained in Hoye, R., Smith, A., Westerbeek, H., Stewart, B. and Nicholson, M. (2006). *Sport Management: Principles and Practice*. Elsevier, Chapter 3 (Non-Profit Sport) and Chapter 4 (Professional Sport).

A broad analysis of trends in commercialized sport throughout the world is provided in Westerbeek, H. and Smith, A. (2003). *Sport Business in the Global Marketplace*, Palgrave Macmillan. For a more critical stance on global sport see Miller, T., Lawrence, C., McKay, J. and Rowe, D. (2001). *Globalisation and Sport*. Sage.

For a succinct review of the evolution of sport stadia design and construction, and the associated escalation of costs, see Thompson, P., Toolczko, J. and Clarke, J. (Eds.) (1998). *Stadia, Arenas and Grandstands: Design, Construction and Operation*. E and FN Spon. See in particular Chapter 3 (Models of Costing) for an analysis of stadia costing. The most recent update of trends in sport stadia design and construction is contained in Sheard, R. and Bingham-Hall, P. (2005). *Stadium Architecture for the New Global Culture*. Pesaro Publishing.

An expansive account of the financial transformation of motor-sports is contained in Beck-Burridge, M. and Walton, J. (2001). *Sport Sponsorship and Brand Development: The Subaru and Jaguar Stories*. Palgrave Macmillan, Chapter 2 (Marketing). The transformation of English world football during the 1990s is thoroughly documented by King, A. (1998). *The End of the Terraces*. Leicester University Press. For a succinct analysis of the commercial entrenchment of the Tour de France see Reid, E. (2003) The Economics of the Tour, in H. Dauncy and G. Hare (Eds.) *The Tour de France 1903–2003*, Frank Cass.

For a good summary of how the USA has set the commercial and cultural parameters of sport around the world see Allison, L. (2005). *The Global Politics of Sport: The Role of Global Institutions in Sport*. Routledge. An excellent case-based analysis of the hyper-commercialized aspects of world sport, and how television sponsorship and the celebrity athlete mutually reinforce each other's status and prestige is provided by La Feber, W. (1999). *Michael Jordon and the New Global Capitalism*. WW Norton.

A broad-based account of the finances and commercial foundations of the Olympic Games is contained in Preuss, H. (2000). *Economics of the Olympic Games: Hosting the Games 1972–2000*. Walla Walla Press, Chapter 2 (Financing Models) and Chapter 4 (Aspects of Business Economy). For an update of *Economics of the Olympic Games* see Preuss, H. (2004). *The Economics of Staging the Olympics*. Edward Elgar.

For a detailed analysis of how government impacts on sport development see Green, M. and Houlihan, B. (2005). *Elite Sport Development: Policy Learning and Political Priorities*. Routledge. See also Stewart, R., Nicholson, M., Smith, A. and Westerbeek, H. (2004). *Australian Sport: Better by Design? The Evolution of Australian Sport Policy*. Routledge.

2

The business of sport

Overview

This chapter will cover the scale and sourcing of funds for sport. It will distinguish between the different sources of funds (e.g. memberships, sponsorships, gate takings, social events, merchandizing, broadcast rights, and government grants) and examine the strengths and weaknesses of each source. It will also distinguish between the funding of capital works (e.g. venues and grounds) and the funding of ongoing operations (e.g. the club, association, or league). The chapter will conclude with a discussion of sport's special features, and how it is both different from and similar to the world of business and commerce.

The kitchen-table model

Sport, like all other institutions in society, can only sustain itself if it has the resources to support its activities, programs, and events. Traditionally most sport was run on shoestring budgets where the energies of volunteer officials, and membership fees kept clubs and associations afloat. In short, the people who played and administered the game provided the bulk of the resources needed for sport's ongoing development. This is known as the kitchen-table approach to sport organization management, where the administration of the game was driven by a few officials making decisions from a member's home. This model of sport organization management has a number of strengths. It not only ensured the involvement of grassroots players and members, and provided a strong local community club focus, but it also nurtured a strong set of values that centered on playing the game for its own sake, and the concomitant ideal of amateurism (Hoye, Smith, Westerbeek, Stewart and Nicholson 2006). At the same time, it also perpetuated a primitive system of management driven by an administrative committee made up of a few elected members and self-appointed officials. There was a president who was the public face of the club or association, and a secretary who kept things ticking over by keeping a member register and organizing others to manage teams, run events, and maintains the clubrooms and playing facilities. There was also a treasurer who looked after the financial affairs of the organization. The treasurer was more often than not unfamiliar with the theory and principles of accounting, but made up for a lack of expertise with a mind for detail, and a desire to ensure receipts ran ahead of expenses. Transactions were usually recorded as cash entries, where cash either moved out as a payment for something purchased and services rendered, or in as a bank account deposit.

The boardroom or corporate model

The widespread commercialization of sport around the world began in the 1970s, and transformed the ways sport organizations did business (Stewart 1984). As indicated in Chapter 1, sport, particularly at the elite end of the continuum, jettisoned its amateur values, and adopted many of the features of commercial business in their attempts to increase the scale of their operations and improve the standard of their competitions. Sport entered the age of professionalism where players were handsomely paid for their services, old-time administrators morphed into general managers and chief executive officers, and a bevy of sport scientists, psychologists, and sundry hangers on provided all sorts of assistance to athletes. As sport became more commercialized, and professionalized it changed the way it did business, and in particular developed much stronger links with the corporate sector which saw sport as a great vehicle for promoting their products and attracting audiences (Slack 2004). Some of the significant commercial developments in world sport over the last 10 years are revealed in the following incidents:

1. In 1997 the Baltimore Orioles baseball team total payroll reached USD 70 million. The team's average annual player salary was USD 2.5 million.
2. In 1998 the Dallas Cowboys football team became the most valuable sports brand in the world, at USD 274 million.
3. In 1998 Nike made the biggest sponsorship deal ever; signed the Brazilian Soccer team for 10 years, and in return gave it USD 400 million.

4. In 2000 the New South Wales Supreme Court ordered boxer, Kostya Tszyu to pay damages of AUD 7.3 million to his former promoter, Bill Mordey, for breach of contract.
5. In 2001 Vodafone, a mobile phone operator, paid about AUD 7 million in a naming rights sponsor deal with Australian Rugby Union and the Wallabies national team.
6. The 2006 Melbourne Commonwealth Games cost in excess of AUD 1000 million to stage.
7. By 2006 some Australian cricketers were earning AUD 1 million a year.
8. In 2006 Manchester United secured a shirt sponsorship with the American International Group, the world's largest insurer, for EUR 20 million a year for 4 years. This is fractionally behind the EUR 22 million annual sponsorship deal that Juventus Football Club has with the Tamoil oil company.

A three-phase model of sport's financial progress

Andreff and Staudohar (2002) extended the kitchen-table/corporate boardroom model of sport's financial progress by proposing a three-phase model that begins with the amateur structure, moves into a traditional professional structure, and finishes with contemporary professional structures.

The amateur structure (phase one) is member-focused with an emphasis on participation at the community level, with a narrowly supported pathway to elite sport and the international sports arena. Its financial viability is sustained through gate receipts, members, fees, subscriptions, cash donations, and food and drink sales (or what is called concession income in the USA). This is equivalent to the kitchen-table model of sport management referred to earlier. In contrast, the traditional professional structure (phase two) is more heavily dependent on sponsorship and government subsidies, whilst maintaining its gate receipts and local support. This structure, which is primarily concerned with sport development, is alternatively viewed as a sport-centered archetype and is the forerunner of the corporate sports model. The contemporary professional structure (phase three) is more heavily geared to corporate support as it develops its brand image and network of sponsors. The focus is on revenue generation rather than sport development and is alternatively viewed as a business-centered archetype. In order to tap into the capital markets some clubs become public companies, and by listing their shares on the stock exchange, gain access to additional equity capital. The different financial arrangements for each structure are listed in Table 2.1.

The increasing financial complexity of sport is only one side of the sport management coin. The other issue to be dealt with is the escalation of player salaries and athlete assistance programs, and the ever-increasing number of full-time support staff like coaches, trainers, and sport scientists. In addition, any increase in revenue is immediately absorbed by staff and player salaries.

Table 2.1 Sources of Finance for Different Sport Structures

Revenue Item	Amateur	Traditional Professional	Contemporary Professional
Gate receipts	✓	✓✓	✓✓
Member fees and registration	✓✓	✓	✓
Cash donations	✓✓	✓	✓
Government subsidies	✓	✓✓	✓✓
Food and drink sales	✓✓	✓	✓
Sponsors and advertising	●	✓	✓✓
Merchandising	●	✓	✓✓
Television rights fees	●	✓	✓✓

●: of no importance; ✓: of some importance; ✓✓: highly important.

While the revenue side of the sport finance equation has increased exponentially, so too has the cost side of the equation. The most newsworthy has been the escalating movement in player salaries, which was briefly noted in Chapter 1. The other major cost escalation has been in the area of stadium and arena construction (Sheard and Bingham 2005). These developments have at their core the need to establish appropriate systems of financial management and control. The other point to note is that the increasing funds available to sport are not shared equally, either between sport competitions and leagues or within them (Szymanski and Kuypers 2000).

Funding sources

It is clear that the new business-based model of sport (the corporate boardroom/contemporary professional structure) involves a massive expansion of income. However, it was also important to not throw-the-baby-out-with-the-bath-water, and so traditional forms of revenue have been maintained, although in a slightly more sophisticated form. So, member fees are still important, as too are fundraising from social activities and gate receipts. However as was touched on previously, new and varied revenue stream have opened up over the last 30 years which have transformed sport and the way it operates. The funding of sport organizations begs a number of questions, the main ones being listed here:

1. Where does the money come from?
2. Where is the money spent?
3. How are the movements of money monitored?

In answering these questions it is important to distinguish between funds that are used to create infrastructure and facilities, and funds for use in managing the day-to-day activities of a sport organization. Therefore, there are two types of basic funding uses. The first is funds for investment in capital development, and the second is funds for recurrent and operating activities.

Capital funding

Capital funding, which is money to finance investment in assets, can come from a number of sources listed here:

1. Government grants which may be federal, state, or local. The point to note is that there are differences between sports which reflect not only their scale of operation but also their likelihood of generating international success. Funding may also be subject to certain conditions being met, like adopting certain policy requirements or working within a legislative framework.
2. Loans and borrowings which could be short term (up to a year), long term (up to 20 years). Loans and borrowings are known as debt finance. The points to note are that it provides ready cash for investment in facilities and income producing assets. On the other hand, it also incurs an interest burden, and may not always generate an increase in income.
3. New share issue or a public float which is known as equity finance. The points to note are that like borrowings, it provides ready access to cash, but unlike borrowing does not impose the burden of interest payment or repayment of the principle to lenders. However it does hand over control to shareholders, and there is an expectation that a dividend will be delivered.
4. Retained earnings, which is money re-invested in the sport organization. The points to note are there is no interest payment and control is retained over funds used. For non-profit sport organizations, the retention of earnings is mandatory, since this is a legal requirement.

Recurrent funding

The recurrent funding of sport involves money to fund day-to-day operations, which comes from a variety of sources depending on the type of sport enterprise. The main revenue sources are:

1. Membership fees which may be full adult, associate, family, and similar categories. The points to note here are that they are usually upfront and relatively stable and therefore provide an immediate source of cash. Membership also serves a marketing function by establishing a core customer base.
2. Spectator admission charge which includes the categories of full adult, family, special groups and premium. The points to note are that while there is a high degree of flexibility, it is subject to significant variation because of changing attendance patterns and differences in the scheduling of games.
3. Corporate facilities including boxes and hospitality. The points to note are that a large investment is required but the strengths are that business connections are made and premium rental can be charged.

22

4. Player fees and charges include entry fees, facility charge, and equip-ment hire. The points to note here are that revenue is dependent on demand, and the user pays for the experience.

5. Special fundraising efforts are another source of recurrent funding and may include a dinner dance, rage-party, auction night, a trivia night, and so on. The points to note are that the burden is on staff and members to arrange and attend functions. However, these types of events can be profitable through large markups on food and drink.

6. Lotteries and gaming such as raffles, bingo, and gaming machines. The points to note are that permits are often required, margins are low, and there is solid competition from other venues.

7. Merchandising such as memorabilia, scarves, T-shirts, jackets, and auto-graphed equipment. The point to note is that while it can produce is a significant short-run increase in revenue, it can plateau out with a fall in on-field success.

8. Sponsorships and endorsement are another good source and may include naming rights, partnerships, signage, product endorsements, and contra deals. However the points to note are that the organization can lose con-trol and become dependent on sponsor income and defer to their partner-ship demands.

9. Catering may include take-away or sit down food or drink. The point to note is that it is labor intensive, but because it is delivered in a non-competitive environment higher profit margins can be sustained.

10. Broadcasting rights such as television and radio, and more recently Internet and mobile phone streaming rights. The points to note are that it focuses on elite sports with a large audience base, and may be irrele-vant for most sports associations and clubs. At the same time it provides the single largest revenue source for professional sport leagues.

11. Investment income such as interest earned and share dividends. However the points to note are that share prices can vary at short notice, and losses can be made which increases the level of risk. In addition, interest rates may be low.

12. Government grants, which may be federal, state, or local. The points to note are that there are often marked differences between sports, they can vary from year to year, and like government capital funds are subject to certain conditions being met.

The expenses incurred in running a sport enterprise are also varied. They include:

1. Wages and salaries such as permanent, contract, or casual administration staff and players. The points to note are that it is usually the largest expense item and is subject to inflation and competitive bidding as clubs aim to secure the best playing talent.

2. Staff on-costs, which include insurance, training, leave, and superannua-tion. The points to note here are that they are legally required, ongoing, and linked to the employment contract.

3. Marketing costs include advertising, sales promotion, site visits, trade displays, and give-aways. The point to note here is that it is easy to exceed

budget estimates since there is always a tacit assumption that too much marketing and promotion is never enough.

4. Office maintenance includes power and light, phone and fax, postage, and stationery and printing. The points to note here are that it is ongoing and tight control is required.

5. Venue maintenance includes the playing area, the viewing area and member facilities. The point to note here are that maintenance expenditure is ongoing and frequently absorbs a significant amount of revenue.

6. Player management includes equipment, clothing and footwear, medical services, fitness and conditioning, and travel. The points to note are that while they constitute an essential investment in improved performance, they also require tight budgeting.

7. Asset depreciation includes facilities, buildings, cars, and equipment. The points to note here is that assets lose value and must be replaced. Also, depreciation is a non-cash expense, and it is essential that assets be amortized as expenses over their lifetime.

While all businesses, including sport businesses, must manage their finances efficiently, and be clear about how capital investments and operational activities will be funded, there are differences in the weighting of funding sources. For example, sport has a heavy dependence on human resources and their associated costs. So, what distinguishes sport from business, and what does it imply for sport's financial management. In Chapter 1 it was noted that unlike business, sport generates a strong sense of tribal identity. However, there are also many other aspects of sport that make it a unique enterprise, and they are discussed below.

Sport's special features

As noted previously, sport's commercial development and growing financial complexity has been criticized on the grounds that increasing levels of professionalization, bureaucratization, and specialization have undermined its localism and community focus on sport. The ensuing debate about the future direction of sport has challenged many views about the nature and place of sport in society, but in the end has highlighted the commercial evolution of sport and crucial importance of having it well managed (Hoye et al., 2006). Sport, even at the local or community level, can no longer operate effectively in a cultural frame which focuses exclusively on amateurism and volunteerism, and which seeks to divorce sport from work and commerce. It has not taken long for most sport organizations to adopt the processes and practices of private sector business enterprises. Players and administrators are often paid employees, plans are designed, the sport product is branded and marketed, member and customer needs are monitored, and alliances with corporate supporters are developed. But neither is sport just another form of private enterprise. Sport can be business, but it is a special form of business (Smith and Stewart 1999). In the remainder of this chapter we explore those features of organized sport that give it its special quality.

Premierships over profits

The most significant difference between professional competitive sport organizations and private business is the way in which they measure performance. While business firms have many operational goals, their underlying purpose is to optimize profits. For example, BMW and Mercedes are fierce competitors, and by generating profits, can both claim a successful year. However, large profits will do little to convince sporting clubs of their success if they finish the season at the bottom of the ladder. While the BMW and Mercedes shareholders expect continuing profits, sports club members and fans judge performance on the basis of trophies and premierships.

Sports clubs consequently face two prevailing models of organizational behavior (Sandy, Sloane and Rosentraub 2004). The first is the profit maximization model, which proposes that a club is simply a firm in a competitive product market, and profit is an indicator of success and long-term sustainability. The second is the utility maximization model, which emphasizes the desire to win as many games as possible. The utility view concedes that while sporting organizations are by nature highly competitive, they are also status conscious, and use on-field success as their primary performance yardstick.

Changes in the sporting context and changing management practices have complicated this tension between profits and premierships. Expanding sporting options, increasing competition for the discretionary consumer dollar, and the professionalization of players and officials, has forced clubs previously solely concerned with winning to focus more strongly on revenue profits and cash flow. This reinforces the need to implement quality financial management systems.

A level playing field

While sporting organizations are often prepared to do all it takes to achieve on-field success, domination of a league or competition can be self-defeating. Highly predictable outcomes can produce low attendances and diminish the match-day, media and sponsorship revenue. The ongoing viability of the competition, and the financial health of constituent clubs will be enhanced if rules are introduced which distribute playing talent equally between teams (Quirk and Fort 1992). It is no surprise that two of the most successful professional sport leagues in the world, the US National Football League (NFL) and the Australian Football League (AFL) have implemented salary caps, player draft rules, and ceilings on lists of contracted players. Outcome uncertainty and competitive balance is an important ingredient to the commercial success of team sport competitions, although as English Premier League demonstrates, dominance by a few clubs does not always diminish its public support. While contrived uncertainty comes at the cost of a competitive marketplace, it can also improve the financial health of leagues and clubs.

25

Variable quality

As the above discussion suggests, fans are more attracted to games where the result is problematic and uncertain. By contrast, in the commercial world, predictability is important because customers demand minimum quality standards (Hoffman and Bateson 2001). Consequently, this desire for uncertain outcomes in sport has its problems, since it brings with it enormous variability in the quality of sporting performances. Many factors contribute to this variability, including weather, player injuries, the venue, the quality of the opponents, the closeness of the scores, and even the size of the crowd. The tactics employed by the opposing teams can also influence the level of game quality, and is exemplified in cricket. Captains can either make the contest dull and defensive by slowing down play and designing ultra-defensive field placements, or make it exciting by attacking batting. However chronic fan boredom and unfulfilled expectations can place the financial health of a sport in jeopardy.

Fixed-supply schedules

Fixed short-run supply schedules also constitute a problem for sporting clubs (Tribe 2004). While private sector businesses can increase production to meet demand, sporting clubs have a fixed, or highly inelastic supply curves for many of their products and services (elasticity is discussed in detail in Chapter 11). Clubs can only play a certain number of times during their business cycle, or season. Where spectator demand for a game is high, the governing body may change the venue to allow a larger crowd to attend, but cannot decide to play the match twice. However, when fans are unable to gain admission, revenue is lost.

This problem of fixed supply is particularly evident in the construction of stadiums and arenas. On one hand a large seating capacity will squeeze out any unmet demand. On the other hand chronic under utilization will increase the costs per spectator of delivering games. In the end, the problem of unmet demand can be resolved by providing more seats, or playing more games. For example, the steady increase in demand for cricket over the past 30 years has resulted in more matches being played, thereby increasing productivity and supply.

Collaboration and cartels

Unlike the competitive benefits that a business firm can secure by forcing a rival out of the market, team sport clubs depend on the continued viability of their opponents (Li, Hofacre and Mahoney 2001). In short, clubs must cooperate with their rivals in order to deliver attractive sporting experiences to fans and customers. Clubs are mutually interdependent, and the division of clubs into wealthy and high performing, and poor and low performing, can damage all clubs by making the competition less interesting.

This interdependency can produce arrangements that constrain the activities of the most clubs by cross subsidizing the less powerful clubs. Such revenue sharing in the retail industry would be unthinkable, unless, of course, it was organized as a cartel. Cartel arrangements are common in sport, where clubs not only share revenue, but also prevent other clubs from entering the market, collectively fix prices, and generally limit the amount of competition. The relationship between sport cartels and financial performance is discussed in more detail in Chapter 5.

Emotions and passions

Sport and commerce are inextricably linked, and as noted in Chapter 1, sport has a symbolic significance and emotional intensity that is rarely found in an insurance company, bank, or accounting office. While profit-centered businesses seek strong commitment from their employees, their overriding concern is efficiency, productivity and responding quickly to changing market conditions. Sport, on the other hand, is consumed by strong emotional attachments that are linked to the past through nostalgia and tradition (Crawford 2004). A proposal to change club colors in order to project a more attractive image may be defeated because it breaks a link with tradition. Similarly, coaches can be appointed on the basis of their previous loyalty to the club rather than because of a superior capacity to manage players. Sports administrators frequently allow tradition and history to dictate a sport's future, but being a slave to old practices can impede the capacity to adapt to changing circumstances and exploit new revenue opportunities. At the same time, passion can be used to sustain loyalty, attract fans, sell more merchandise, and expand public support, all of which can increase revenue streams.

Product and brand loyalty

As noted in Chapter 1, sport engenders a high degree of loyalty at both the product (i.e. sport league or event) level, and the brand (i.e. team) level, and there is consequently a low degree of substitutability between competing sport leagues and competitions. Match-day fixtures provide a clutch of entertainment benefits that attract spectators and television viewers, but these benefits are usually sport specific, and the satisfactions that come from watching one sport will not easily transfer to another (Tribe 2004). Even where fans are unhappy about game outcomes, they are unlikely to change their sporting preferences. In contrast, if consumers purchased computing equipment or a medical service, and were dissatisfied with the quality, then they would immediately consider changing providers or products, even if prices were higher. In sport, no such easy substitutability occurs. At the same time, a low degree of product substitution has its drawbacks, since it can limit a sport's ability to achieve quick market penetration. The customs and habits of sport fans make it difficult to attract them from one sport to another by using incentives or price discounts. Other inducements may therefore be necessary to build a fan base.

Many businesses use the power of sporting identification to market their products via endorsement from sporting heroes (La Feber 1999). The aim is to capture some of the loyalty and charisma associated with players, rather than working through price, convenience, or quality. This symbiotic relationship between sporting heroes, player identification, and product promotion has a powerful influence on the spending patterns of consumers, and can be used by sport organizations to deepen the revenue pools.

Differences and similarities

Foster, Greyser and Walsh (2006) tackled the sport-as-business problem by compiling a list of things professional sport and business have in common, and areas where they differed. They concluded that whereas sport and business shared a common concern for value creation, branding, funding new sources of revenue product innovation, and market expansion, sport was significantly more concerned with beating rivals, winning trophies, sharing revenue, and channeling the passions of both players (the employees) and fans (the customers). Table 2.2 lists these factors.

The other important point made by Foster et al. (2006) is that athletes are now business assets, who are instrumental in attracting fans, sponsors, and media exposure. It therefore comes as no surprise that unlike business, a sport's service deliverers (the players) earn far more than their immediate supervisors (the club managers).

Table 2.2 Models of Business and Sport

Areas of Commonality	Areas of Differentiation
Leadership and strategy matters	Winning on the field central
Value creation and value sharing	Diverse owner objectives
Search for revenue growth	Managing in the fishbowl
Value chain encroachment and fluidity	Supporting the weakest
New product innovation	Handicapping the strongest
Astute and creative contracting	Revenue pools and allocation rules
Quality of the product matters	Athletes as business assets
Branding matters	Managing the badly behaving player
Fans and customers as a business pillar	Limited financial disclosures
Globalization	Sport as an entertainment cocktail

Source: Foster et al. (2006:2).

Striking a balance

To summarize, sport is not simply just another form of business enterprise, but neither is it so special that it has no connection to business. While the special features of sport referred to above suggest that it needs to be managed in ways that fit its idiosyncratic values and structure, it works best under strong business models and sound management principles. One of the weaknesses of sport at the community level is its failure to grasp management theory and best practice models, and use them to improve the performance of the sport system. At the same time, sport's unique structures and practices have important implications for the management of sport organization finances, as the following chapters show.

Questions to consider

1. Contrast the kitchen-table model of sport management with the corporate model of sport management.
2. Using the kitchen-table/corporate model of sport as a base, explain how Andreff and Staudohar (2002) have used a three-phase model of sport organization development to explain the different ways sport has been funded over time.
3. Sport can use funds for capital development or operational activities. What is the difference between these two sets of financing activities?
4. Provide three examples of where funds can be accessed for capital investment.
5. Discuss the ways in which sport's revenue-raising strategies have changed over the last 50 years. What might explain these changes?
6. Distinguish between operating revenue and operating expenses, and give three examples of each that are particularly relevant to sport.
7. In what ways is sport similar to business?
8. In what ways is sport different from business?
9. What makes the product–quality issue such a problem for sport?
10. Why is branding and image-building an important issue for sport organizations?

Further reading

For a more detailed account of the financial evolution of sport organizations see Andreff and Staudohar, P. (2002). European and US Sports Business Models. In C. Barros, M. Ibrahimo and S. Szymanski (Eds.), *Transatlantic Sport: The Comparative Economics of North American and European Sport.* Edward Elgar, pp.23–49. The distinction between the sport-centered archetype and the business-centered archetype is explored in detail in Cousins, L. (1997). From Diamonds to Dollars: The Dynamics of Change in AAA Baseball Franchises. *Journal of Sport Management*, 11, 11–30.

For an in-depth discussion of how sport organizations around the world secure funds for their operation go to Forster, J. and Pope, N. (2004). *The Political Economy of Global Sporting Organisations*. Routledge, Chapter 4 (Sources of Sport Revenue). An extensive examination of revenue sources for USA sports is provided by Howard, D. and Crompton, J. (2004). *Financing Sport*, 2nd Edition. Fitness Information Technology, Chapter 7 (Stadium Seating and Naming Rights), Chapter 10 (Broadcast Rights), Chapter 11 (Food Service and Souvenirs), Chapter 12 (Sponsorship) and Chapter 16 (Fundraising).

An overview of the differences and similarities between sport organizations and business organizations is provided in Foster, G., Greyser, P. and Walsh, B. (2006). *The Business of Sports: Texts and Cases on Strategy and Management*, Thomson, Section 1-1 (The Business of Sports: A Perspective from Stanford). See also Smith, A. and Stewart, B. (1999). *Sports Management: A Guide to Professional Practice.* Allen and Unwin, Chapter 2 (Special Features of Sport).

For an analysis of the variety of goals and motives pursued by sport organizations see Li, M., Hofacre, S. and Mahoney, D. (2001). *Economics of Sport.* Fitness Information Technology, Chapter 2 (Economic Motives of Sport Organizations). See also Sandy, R., Sloane, P. and Rosentraub, M. (2004). *The Economics of Sport: An International Perspective.* Palgrave Macmillan, Chapter 2 (Club and League Objectives).

3

Financing professional sport

Overview

This chapter will look at the financing arrangement of mega-sport events like the Olympic and Commonwealth Games and professional sport leagues like the American National Basketball League (NBA), Major League Baseball (MLB), the National Football League (NFL), the Australian Football League (AFL), National Rugby League (NRL), and the English Premier (world football) League (EPL). It will highlight the differences and similarities in funding, and in particular how revenues are sourced and distributed.

The context

As noted in Chapter 1, over the last 50 years there has been a transformation in the structure and operation of sport. Professional sport now occupies more space that it ever did, and the many hundreds of small-scale community sport activities with shallow funding pools with an emphasis on participation have been overshadowed by those sports with mass spectator appeal (Forster and Pope 2004). The demise of amateurism, particularly in those sports with a large following, has provided the space for professionalization where many more players can make a living from the game. According to Foster, Greyser and Walsh (2006) this explosion in sport's commercial development is the result of the growth in four over-arching revenue streams that have taken over from match-day receipts as the key revenue sources.

First, broadcasting rights fees are pivotal drivers of sports' commercial growth. In the USA, the NFL has recently secured multi-network and cable television agreement that provides it with USD 1800 million over 8 years. This will in turn provide each NFL team with a guaranteed base revenue of around USD 70 million for each of the 8 years of the agreement. Second, sponsorship has also become a major income source. Large multinational businesses not only provide financial support in return for the use of a team or league as a promotional vehicle, but the arrangement also allows participating organizations to create a co-branding strategy. The team or league gets the benefit of being linked to a successful business partner, while the business firm secures a promotional benefit from being associated with a high profile sport organization and its supporter and viewer base.

A third emerging revenue source is various in-stadium and arena arrangements that can be secured by sport venue managers. These range from stadium naming rights and to corporate box leasing, to preferential seat bookings, catering franchises, and car parking facilities. Finally, professional sport has, over recent times, expanded its store-based sales of team and league-related merchandise. This merchandise can take the form of branded apparel, gifts and mascots, books, magazines, and journals that provide statistics and inside-stories on fans and favorite teams. There are also videos and DVDs that provide mementos of special incidents and events. These items are listed in Table 3.1.

Table 3.1 Incremental Revenue Sources (beyond ticket sales)

1. Broadcasting rights fees (over-the-air, cable, direct)
   - national
   - local
   - Internet (as a medium)
2. Sponsorships
   - teams
   - arenas
   - in-stadium/arena (signage, "official" stadium concession brands)
   - broadcast ads
3. In-stadium
   - naming rights
   - luxury boxes
   - personal seat licenses
   - concessions
   - parking
4. Stores
   - branded retail partners
   - licensed merchandise/equipment
   - publications/videos

Source: Foster et al. (2006:12).

These trends have also been documented by Szymanski and Kuypers (2000) in their study of EPL and professional world football in England between 1972 and 2000. They found that while gate receipts has traditionally been the single most important income source, its relative importance has fallen over the last 20 years. Whereas it was anywhere between 79 and 90 percent of total annual revenue in the late 1970s, it fell as low as 40 percent in the late 1990s. This was not so much the result of falling attendances, but rather the result of the emergence of new sources of revenue.

The big leagues

The home of big-time sport is the USA where professional sport leagues have been operating since the 1960s. The four dominant professional sport leagues are the National Football (gridiron) League (NFL), Major League Baseball (MLB), the National Basketball Association (NBA), and the National (ice) Hockey League (NHL). These leagues are organized around governing commissions which coordinate the leagues' operations. They schedule games, negotiate broadcasting rights, set player salary limits, and most importantly, decide who can and cannot play in the league. That is, they control the sale of new franchises, although they allow franchise holders to move their teams to another city, and sell their franchise to a new owner. These features are common to cartels, and Chapter 5 will cover this theme in more detail. In addition, teams are for the most part privately owned by a coterie of investors, and, unlike Australian professional sport, there is little room for non-profit member-based clubs. Moreover, unlike a majority of EPL clubs, they are not listed on the stock exchange, and therefore have very concentrated ownership.

The USA professional sports leagues are some of the most commercialized sport competitions in the world. The NFL has the largest commercial support, with an average annual club revenue stream of around USD 170 million. The average annual club revenue for MLB is about USD 130 million, followed by NBA clubs with an average of USD 95 million, and NHL clubs averaging out at USD 70 million (Foster et al. 2006). As a point of contrast the average annual revenue for EPL is just over GBP 65 million, while for AFL clubs it is about AUD 25 million.

A large part of these revenue streams are used to pay player salaries. In the NFL, salaries on average account for around USD 80 million, or 47 percent of total club revenue. In MLB average salaries are USD 70 million, which is 54 percent of average club revenue. NBA average club salaries are USD 60 million, or 63 percent of revenue, while NHL average salaries are about USD 40 million or 62 percent of revenue. The most profitable league is the NFL despite, its wage bill. Its big advantage is that it has the highest capacity to pay, and success in managing the wage demands of players. Figures for a sample of professional sport league club revenues and salaries are given in Table 3.2.

While the use of average figures to highlight the commercial scale of USA professional sport leagues can be quite revealing, they can also be misleading

Table 3.2 Professional Sport League Clubs' Average Annual Revenues and Average Player Salaries 2003

	USD million				GBP million	AUD million
	NFL	MLB	NBA	NHL	EPL	AFL
Average Team Revenue	170	130	95	70	65	25
Average Team Player Salary Bill	80	70	60	40	35	8

Source: Foster et al. (2006), Howard and Crompton (2004), Stewart et al. (2005).

by hiding the differences between clubs. The differences are greatest in those leagues that do not have a broad-based revenue redistribution scheme. The NFL and NBA have had for some time regulations that provide for the sharing of major revenue items like broadcasting rights fees and gate receipts, but this has not historically been the case with MLB and NHL. As a result, MLB clubs that represented large urban centers like New York and Chicago had commercial advantages over clubs that were situated in regional America. It therefore came as no surprise to find that whereas in 2001 the New York Yankees generated revenues of USD 240 million, the Minnesota Twins and the Kansas City Royals took in USD 56 million and USD 64 million respectively (Howard and Crompton 2004). It was noted that as a result of these huge revenue disparities only one-third of all league teams had a real chance of reaching the play-offs (or World Series, as they like to be called in the USA). However, in 2002 a new MLB collective bargaining agreement provided for both a salary cap and a system for redistributing gate monies from richer to poorer clubs.

The Olympic Games

The Olympic Games is an exemplar of the financial complexity that underpins the planning and management of professional sport in general, and mega-sport events in particular. As noted in Chapter 1, the Olympic Games no longer involve the expenditure of millions of dollars, but rather the spending of billions of dollars. Moreover, they also rely on many funding sources for both the construction of facilities and stadia, and the operation of the events themselves. The other thing to remember is that the International Olympic Committee (IOC) awards the Games to a city and not a private organization. The onus is consequently on the host city and its organizing committee to raise sufficient funds to ensure a quality event. A host city contract is negotiated, which not only makes the host city responsible for all facility development

Table 3.3 Funding Mix for Olympic Games 1972–2000

Host City	Private Funding Percentage	Public Funding Percentage
Munich 1972	19	81
Montreal 1976	5	95
Moscow 1980	0	100
Los Angeles 1984	98	2
Seoul 1988	56	44
Barcelona 1992	62	38
Atlanta 1996	85	15
Sydney 2000	30	70

Source: Preuss (2000:33).

and operational activities (including the opening and closing ceremonies) but also for ensuring that every event meets the standards set by the appropriate international sporting governing body (Preuss 2000).

At the general structural level there are four possible funding sources for the host city. The first source of funds is local government and the city itself. There are good reasons to expect the city to provide either cash or in-kind support since it will be the recipient of enormous international media exposure, and for the most part it will also be favorable unless there is a major management catastrophe. In practice though, the host city only ever provides a small percentage of funds to support the Games, although in 1996 the city of Atlanta spent around USD 294 million on facility improvement. For the most part the host city will invest in facility upgrade, traffic infrastructure, and security. The second source of funds is the regional or provincial government within which the host city is located. In the case of the Sydney Olympic Games the State Government of New South Wales was the major source of funds for facility construction. The large-scale funding of facility development is defended on the grounds that the taxpayers will not only benefit directly from the Games themselves, but also benefit from the legacy of having international standard sport facilities for later use. The third source of funds is the national government. National governments have been important contributors over time, and have justified their spending on the grounds that a mega-sport event like the Olympic Games provides many broad benefits, ranging from international prestige and more tourists, to the construction of social and economic infrastructure and urban renewal. The final source is the private sector, which involves all those profit-based business that manufacture and distribute goods and services to the community. The private sector not only provides funds in the form of sponsorship, but also designs, constructs, and operates facilities for use during the Games. In short, the Olympic Games can be funded either through the public purse (i.e. the various levels of government) or through the private sector. Or, it could be a mix of both.

In practice, there has been a wide variety of funding arrangements used to finance the Olympics over the last 35 years (Table 3.3). The most heavily government funded Games were the 1976 Montreal Olympics, and 1990 Moscow Olympics whereas the most heavily privately funded Games were the 1984 Los Angeles Olympics. Table 3.3 summarizes the different funding sources for the Olympics.

The use of a private–public divide to explain the funding for the Olympics is interesting, but it only illuminates part of the funding problem. It is also important to examine the more focused questions of how much income or revenue was secured, what form it took, and what it was used for. For instance, while the Sydney Olympic Games cost around AUD 3500 million to mount and run, it is also crucially important to see if total incomes matched the costs. The next task is to identify the revenue breakdown and see, for example, what proportion came from ticket sales, and what proportion came from broadcast right fees, and how much came from sponsorships. The other interesting question to consider is how much was allocated to facility construction, and how much was allocated to the management and overall operational of the Games themselves.

The most obvious thing to note is that the Games are expensive to organize. In real terms every Game since the 1970s has cost at least USD 600 million to mount and run. The two most expensive Games were Barcelona in 1992, Sydney in 2000, and Athens in 2004. The least expensive was Los Angeles in 1984, where a large proportion of events were run in existing facilities. The capital investment and operating costs of selected Games between 1972 and 2004 are listed in Table 3.4.

In discussing the total costs of mounting the Olympic Games, the key point is to distinguish between the costs of investing in facilities and venues and overall infrastructure (i.e. the capital costs), and the costs of actually running the Games (the operating costs or expenses). The capital costs can vary significantly since there may be a need on one hand to build most of the sports infrastructure from scratch, while on the other hand it may be just a matter of upgrading and improving existing facilities. This accounts for the massive costs of mounting the Athens Games since not only did operating costs escalate mainly because of the increase in security costs, but capital costs were also high because most of the venues had to be built from the ground up. The capital costs also exploded because of their very complex architectural design requirements. The IOC bid documents guidelines make this distinction very clear in order to ensure both comparable submissions, and transparent figures on each cost dimension. Table 3.5 compares the extent to which different host cities constructed new facilities for the Games, or alternatively used existing facilities.

As far as operating expenses are concerned, the IOC also requires bidding cities to break down the expenses into the following categories.

1. In-Games venue and event operations
2. Pre-Games events
3. Opening and closing ceremonies
4. General administration of Games
5. Technology
6. Advertising and promotion

Table 3.4 Capital and Operating Costs for Selected Olympic Games 1972–2004

(USD millions)

	Munich 1972	Montreal 1976	Moscow 1980	Los Angeles 1984	Seoul 1988	Barcelona 1992	Atlanta 1996	Sydney 2000	Athens 2004
Capital	*	*	*	*	700	1500	1000	2200	2400
Operation	546	399	*	467	512	1610	1200	1300	3100
Total Funds	*	*	*	*	1212	3110	2200	3500	5500

Source: Preuss (2000:33, 197); Preuss (2004). * Figures not available.

Table 3.5 Facility Construction for Selected Olympic Games 1972–2008

	Munich 1972	Montreal 1976	Los Angeles 1984	Seoul 1988	Barcelona 1992	Atlanta 1996	Sydney 2000	Athens 2004	Beijing 2008
Main Stadium	new	new	existing	existing	existing	new	new	new	new
Swim Center	new	new	new	new	existing	new	existing	new	new
Velodrome	new	new	new	new	existing	new	new	new	new
Main Arena	new	existing	existing	new	new	existing	new	new	new

Source: Preuss (2000:203); Preuss (2004).

7. Security
8. Catering
9. Medical
10. Transport.

Again, this allows the IOC to obtain a clear and comparative picture of what the operating budget will look like, and also highlight areas where there are either very conservative estimates, or where spending seems to be extravagant.

When comparing total Games expenditures, two distinct phases emerge over the 1972–2004 period. The first phase begins with the 1972 Munich Games and ends with the 1988 Seoul Games. During this phase operating expenses plateaued. Whereas Munich cost USD 546 million to run, Montreal cost USD 399 million, Los Angeles cost USD 467 million, and Seoul cost USD 512 million. The second phase begins with Barcelona in 1992 and goes through to the present time. In Barcelona operating expenses more than doubled to USD 1610 million. The figure fell to USD 1200 million in 1996 in Atlanta, but increased to USD 1300 million at Sydney, and USD 3100 million at Athens. According to Preuss (2004) the main reasons for the increase are multi-fold. Contrary to what some critics had to say about the extravagance of the Games, it was not due to higher opening and closing ceremony costs. The real reasons had more to do with the growing complexity of Games resulting from more participants, more sport disciples, more test or pre-Games events, more technical requirements for events, and greater security.

When Games revenue is addressed it is not surprising that this figure has also increased dramatically over the last 35 years. Whereas the organizers of the Munich Games raised USD 1000 million, it had risen to USD 1300 million by Seoul, and nearly USD 3500 million at Sydney. This increase arose out of tapping into new sources of revenue while also increasing existing sources. In addition some traditional sources actually fell over this period. The most dramatic increases occurred in revenue raising from sponsorship and broadcasting rights fees.

The revenue sources for both Munich and Montreal are in stark contrast to current revenue raising arrangements. At both of these Games most of the revenue was raised from the sale of commemorative coins and stamps and the proceeds from a Games lottery. In the case of Munich it was close to 90 percent. Both television rights fees and ticket sales accounted for less than 10 percent each, while sponsorship income was less than 5 percent of total revenue. The traditional revenue-raising mould was seriously broken at Los Angeles, when broadcast rights fees accounted for 30 percent of revenue raised, while sponsorship accounted for around 20 percent. The proportion of revenue raised from ticket sales had also increased to 20 percent. The contribution of sponsorship, broadcast rights fees, and ticket income is more significant when the Atlanta Olympic Games is re-examined. In this case sponsorship accounted for 30 percent, broadcast rights fees now accounted for 30 percent (the same as Los Angeles) while ticket sales were now 25 percent of total revenue. Sydney and Athens were similarly dependent on broadcast rights fees, sponsorship, and ticket income (Preuss 2000; Preuss, 2004).

English Premier League

Another example of sport's financial and commercial transformation over the last 20 years is world football in England. During the 1980s English football faced variety of crises that ranged from falling attendances, rampant hooliganism, and decrepit, unsafe stadia (King 1998). In 1991, in an attempt to solve some of the games' structural problems the governing body of English football, the Football Association (FA) published its *Blueprint for the Future of Football*, which recommended the re-invention of its first division competition as the Premier League (EPL). One of the first things the EPL did was renegotiate the television broadcast contract, which was previously held by the independent television network ITV. Coincidently around this time Rupert Murdoch's News Limited had consolidated its pay television station BSkyB and was seeking programs that would not only rate well in the first instance, but also provide the catalyst for an expansion of pay television subscribers. After spirited bidding and legal challenges BSkyB finally secured the rights to broadcast 60 live games of EPL a year for GBP 50 million a year. This was substantially higher than the GBP 11 million annual rights fee paid by ITV between 1998 and 1991. The EPL is now one of the wealthiest sport competitions in the world (Gratton 2000). Many of its constituent clubs are public companies and listed on the stock exchange. Annual revenues for the richest clubs like Manchester United and Liverpool and Arsenal now exceed GBP 100 million, and players can earn up to GBP 1 million for a single season of play.

Like the USA professional sport leagues, EPL has been able to increase its wealth through accessing a broad base of revenue streams. At the big-end of the professional sport league spectrum Manchester United's (GBP 157 million) revenue in 2005 came principally from match-day receipts (GBP 66 million), media (GBP 48 million), and commercial sponsorship and merchandising (GBP 43 million). The main revenue items for EPL clubs are illustrated in Figure 3.1.

The same trends are evident in Australia's two major professional sports leagues, the AFL and the NRL where broadcast rights fees and sponsorship now provide a larger share of total league revenues even though gate receipts have continually increased. At the same time there are other clubs in the EPL that earn significantly less. Whereas in 2002 Manchester United generated revenues of GBP 148 million, Aston Villa could only secure GBP 47 million to fund its operations. The 2002 revenues and tangible assets for a sample of EPL clubs are listed in Table 3.6.

This earnings discrepancy can be explained by the simple fact that the wealthiest clubs are also the most successful, and have a much broader and deeper fan base. In short, commercial success breeds on-field success, which in turn generates additional commercial success, which further feeds on-field success. A study of EPL by Szymanski and Kuypers (2000) found a very close correlation between a club's average annual revenue and league performance. For example, between 1972 and 1990 the highest earning clubs were Liverpool, Manchester United, and Tottenham Hotspur. They also filled three of the top five performance spots throughout this period. This state of

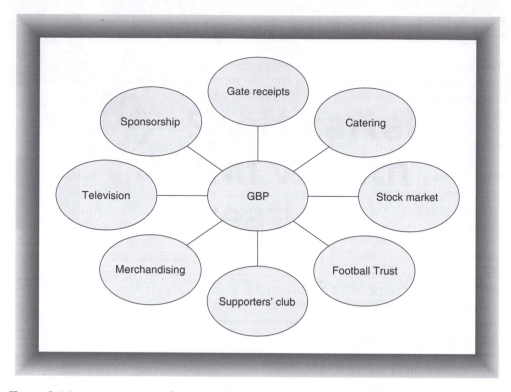

Figure 3.1 Revenue Sources for English Football Clubs. (*Source*: Szymanski and Kuypers 2000:39.)

Table 3.6 Total Revenues and Tangible Assets for a Sample of EPL Clubs in 2002

Clubs	Revenue (GBP million)	Tangible Assets (GBP million)
Arsenal	91	46
Aston Villa	47	42
Chelsea	115	180
Leeds United	99	40
Liverpool	82	43
Manchester United	148	130
Newcastle United	71	94
Tottenham Hotspur	65	46
Average	89	78

Source: Gerrard (2004b:74).

affairs is even more evident today. The only thing that has altered is that the order has slightly changed. Over the last 10 years Manchester United has taken over from Liverpool as the most financially powerful club, and not surprisingly also the best performing club. As Arsenal and Chelsea have deepened their pool of funds, so too has their performance improved. All of this begs the question as to how the EPL's financial resources might be spread more evenly to allow more clubs to share the on-field spoils.

Australian Football and Rugby League

Australia's leading professional sports leagues are the Australian Football League (AFL) and the National Rugby League (NRL). Neither league has clubs listed on the stock exchange, although some NRL clubs are owned by private consortia. The AFL comprises a majority of member-controlled clubs constituted as companies limited by guarantee. So it can be said that both leagues are essentially non-profit entities where surplus funds are reinvested in league and club development.

The AFL generates more revenue than the NFL which is the result of its larger match attendance, broader base of sponsorship, and greater broadcasting rights fee. Whereas the AFL annual television rights fee was AUD

Table 3.7 ARL and NRL Revenues and Valuations

AFL Club Finances 2005			*NRL Club Finances 2005*		
Team	*Total Revenue (AUD million)*	*Value (AUD million)*	*Team*	*Total Revenue (AUD million)*	*Value (AUD million)*
Collingwood	39	44	Brisbane	20	18
Brisbane	32	37	St George	15	14
Hawthorn	29	34	Melbourne	13	13
West Coast	29	33	Canterbury	13	12
Essendon	28	33	Newcastle	13	12
Sydney	28	32	Sydney City	12	12
Geelong	27	31	Parramatta	12	11
Fremantle	26	29	Canberra	11	11
Port Power	24	27	North Queensland	11	10
Richmond	23	27	New Zealand	10	9
Melbourne	24	26	West Tigers	10	9
Adelaide	22	25	Penrith	9	9
St Kilda	21	25	Cronulla	9	9
Carlton	20	24	Manly	9	5
Kangaroos	22	24	South Sydney	9	4
Western Bulldogs	21	23			

Source: Business Review Weekly, March 16–22, 2006, p. 39.

156 million in 2005, the NRL television rights fee was just under AUD 80 million a year in 2005. However they are both significantly in excess of the newly established world football A-League, which has recently negotiated AUD 17 million a year (for 7 years) agreement with FOX Sports the pay television network.

Table 3.7 compares the annual revenue figures of AFL clubs with those of NRL clubs. While the median revenue for AFL clubs is around AUD 25 million, it is only AUD 11 million for NRL clubs. This not only reflects the higher broadcast fee for AFL, but its much larger average game attendance figure (35 000 compared with 15 000). In fact the average game attendance for the AFL is the fourth largest for sport leagues around the world. The USA NFL is ranked first, with an average game attendance of around 60 000 followed by the German Bundesliga with 40 000 and EPL with 36 000.

Table 3.7 also contains a valuation of clubs, in which a much higher value is placed on AFL clubs. These valuation figures also beg the question as to how the valuations are calculated, why some clubs will be valued more highly than others and the relationship between a club's annual stream of revenues and its value and overall level of wealth. This will be discussed in the next chapter.

Questions to consider

1. Identify the seven most important revenue sources for professional sport teams.
2. Explain how sport stadia are used to generate revenue for stadium owners, teams, and leagues.
3. Rank North American sport leagues on the basis of their average team revenues.
4. Calculate the proportion of total team revenues accounted for by player payments.
5. Explain how the Olympic Games are funded.
6. Over the last 30 years how important has government been as a funding source for the Olympic Games?
7. Compare the capital cost of hosting the last four Olympic Games with their operating costs.
8. Explain the origins of the EPL, and the source of its commercial growth.
9. How wealthy are EPL clubs, and how do the revenue streams compare to North American professional sport teams?
10. Contrast the revenues of the main professional sport teams in Australia. How would you explain the revenue gap between AFL and NRL?

Further reading

For an extensive discussion of the finances of North American professional sport leagues see Howard, D. and Crompton, J. (2004). *Financing Sport*, 2nd

Edition. Fitness Information Technology, which provides a chapter-by-chapter breakdown of revenue sources, with special attention to ticket sales and broadcasting rights fees. See also Foster, G., Greyser, P. and Walsh, B. (2006). *The Business of Sports: Texts and Cases on Strategy and Management*. Thomson, Section 2 (Leagues, Including a Discussion on Women's Professional Sport in the USA), Section 3 (Clubs, Which Includes Comparative Studies of Sport Clubs in Different Leagues), Section 8 (Broadcasting, Media, and Sports) and Section 10 (Financial Valuation and Profitability). For an overview of the key commercial issues being addressed in North American sport see Rosner, S. and Shropshire, K. (2004). *The Business of Sports*. Jones and Bartlett.

One of the most comprehensive studies of the commercial evolution of the Olympic Games has been undertaken by Barney, R., Ween, S. and Martyn, S. (2002). *Selling the Five Rings: The International Olympic Committee and the Rise of Olympic Commercialisation*. University of Utah Press. See also Preuss, H. (2000). *Economics of the Olympic Games: Hosting the Games 1972–2000*. Walla Walla Press. For a more political analysis of the commercial expansion of the Olympics see Pound, R. (2004). *Inside the Olympics*. Wiley, Chapter 6 (Keeping Corporate Company) and Chapter 7 (Broadcasts Bonanza).

One of the most detailed analysis of EPL Finances is provided in Szymanski, S. and Kuypers, T. (2000). *Winners and Losers*. Penguin, especially Chapter 2 (Revenue). Also see and Morrow, S. (2003). *The People's Game? Football Finance and Society*. Palgrave Macmillan. Other references on the commercial expansion of EPL include Gratton, C. (2000). The Peculiar Economics of English Professional Football, in J. Garland, P. Malcolm, and M. Rowe (Eds.), *The Future of Football*. Frank Cass, pp. 11–28. An earlier critique is provided by Horton, E. (1997). *Moving the Goal Posts: Football's Exploitation*. Mainstream Publishing.

4

Wealth creation in sport organizations

Overview

This chapter will examine the ways in which profitability and wealth are generated in different leagues and clubs. It will begin with a discussion of the factors that impact upon a sport organization's revenue raising and asset building capacity. This chapter will end with an analysis of how to go about measuring the wealth of sport organizations and their real worth or value.

What makes sport profitable?

As the previous chapters show, not only has sport in general become more commercialized and professionalized over the last 50 years, but it has also become more fragmented with many other clubs and associations just managing to provide the basic services to players and members. Moreover, even within the same league or competition, a few clubs can snare more than what seems to be their fair share of funds and resources. This begs the question as to what factors and forces impact on the profitability of a league or competition, and why some clubs become increasingly wealthier, while others stagnate. An illuminating explanation is provided by Szymanski and

Kuypers (2000) who begin by making the salient point that financial success in general and profitability in particular, come about from two main sources.

The first source of financial success has to do with industry structure and conduct. Industry structure is crucially important since it includes the demand for the product or service. In sport the demand conditions vary enormously and generally speaking the higher the demand, the greater the revenue streams that will ensure.

Industry structure also includes the issues of costs and how technology is used to deliver the service to the public. In some respects, sport technology has changed little, but in other respects it has changed a lot. Industry structure also influences the barriers to entry into the industry. In sport leagues the barriers to entry are usually very strong since the governing body or central administration will have sole control over the structure of the league, and which new teams will be allowed to enter. High entry barriers will often allow existing member clubs, for example, to extract the same share from an ever increasing financial pie.

Industry conduct is also important since it establishes the competitive environment and determines the level of rivalry between businesses and what form the rivalry takes. In some sport leagues the rivalry between clubs is always strong in respect of on-field success. However, when it comes to revenue expansion and wealth creation there are a wide variety of behaviors, as well as constraints on that behavior. While sport leagues like Major League Baseball (MLB) and English Premier League (EPL) have few constraints on the behavior of member clubs and teams, the National Football League (NFL) and Australian Football League (AFL) are more severely constrained by rules about player salary caps, player recruitment and transfers, ticket prices, and the distribution of league revenues. As the following chapter shows, heavily regulated sport leagues will diminish inter-team rivalry in their off-field activities and also create more centralized control, which can in turn lead to cartel-type behavior. And, cartel behaviors are often used to restrict supply, increase prices, and increase revenue.

This structure-conduct approach to business behavior also underpins the five-force model first developed by the international business consultant, Michael Porter in the 1980s. Porter argues that an industry's potential for generating a competitive advantage and long-term profitability depends upon the degree of inter-firm rivalry, the threat of new entrants, the availability of substitute products, the power of buyers, and the power of suppliers. This means that a business operating in an industry where new firms can easily enter, substitute services are freely available, competition is fierce, buyers have a high degree of bargaining power, and suppliers can dictate prices, will only make slim profits. On the other hand where entry of new firms is difficult, key resources are scarce, and both buyers and sellers are fragmented, the potential for profit will be high (Mauws, Mason and Foster 2003).

The second source of financial success has to do with company strategy. Sport clubs can secure a competitive advantage through a number of tactical focal points. The first tactical focal point is innovation, and in the case of professional sport clubs it can take the form of improved administrative processes or the use of science and technology to improve player decision-making and performance. The second tactical focal point is access to strategic assets, which, in the case of sport, includes coaching skills and tactical know how. It can also include the recruitment of outstanding players whose abilities cannot be easily replicated. The third tactical focal point is the reputation of the club and its capacity to attract fan support outside its surrounding geography, and meet the aspirations of potential corporate sponsors. The reputation of the club can also be strengthened by a branding campaign that aims to secure a strong identity and image that has mass public appeal. The fourth tactical focal point is the strength of its architecture, which comprises its internal management structures and the relationships that a club can build with its stakeholders. This might involve a high degree of trust between club officials, players, and the players' union, or strong links between coaching staff and the sports science department at (say) a nearby university.

This company strategy approach to business behavior is encapsulated in the resourced-based view (RBV) of how a competitive edge can be achieved. According to Barney (1991) a competitive edge is most effectively gained not so much by reducing the level of intra-industry competition but by assembling resources that are valuable (i.e. generates greater efficiencies), scarce (i.e. not easily available), and inimitable (i.e. unique) and not easily copied. In short, superior performance will result from a strong endowment of resources that cannot be matched by competitors, and enables greater efficiencies to be achieved. RBV is particularly relevant to sport where access to the best player talent, quality coaches, and strong support systems can quickly secure a winning edge (Smart and Wolfe 2000; Mauws et al. 2003).

The ways in which these factors impact on league and team profitability are illustrated in Figure 4.1.

This model is instructive in the way it highlights both the context in which sport organizations operate and their scope to implement strategies which may secure a competitive advantage. However, its foundations are set in the commercial and business world, and not in sport. It is therefore important to design a more sport-specific model of profit generation and wealth creation that takes into account the special features of sport discussed in Chapter 2. Gerrard's (2005) model of sport-team ownership value provides a good explanatory framework since it has as its starting point the crucial proposition that profit and wealth creation in sport results from both on-field or sporting performance and off-field or financial performance. Gerrard also makes the important point that the two components are closely linked. That is, improved on-field success will produce a financially healthy outcome, while a sound financial base is likely to produce an improvement in on-field performance. Szymanski and Kuypers (2000) also make this point clearly in their research. So, what specifically underpins strong on-field performance, and what drives better off-field performance?

According to Gerrard the key to better on-field performance is the availability of playing talent and quality coaching, while the key to better off-field performance is a strong fan base (which includes both community and corporate support), and managerial efficiency. The strong fan base will provide a lucrative revenue stream, while managerial efficiency will contain costs.

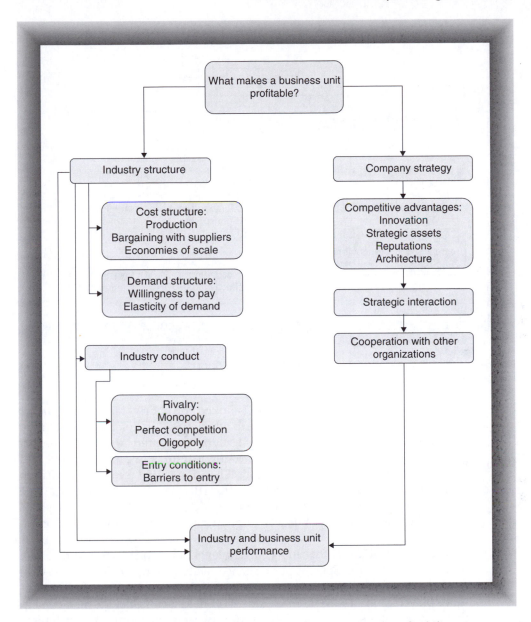

Figure 4.1 Contextual and Strategic Influences on Organizational Profitability (*Source*: Szymanski and Kuypers, 2000:132)

This sport-specific model of profit generation and wealth creation is illustrated in Figure 4.2.

This model provides a succinct picture of what drives sport club performance, what enables a competitive advantage to emerge, and why some clubs regularly outperform others.

Another explanation of what underpins a sporting club's financial sustainability is provided by Foster, Greyser and Walsh (2006). They claim that

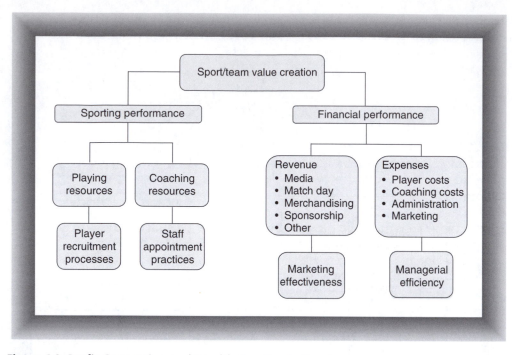

Figure 4.2 Profit Generation and Wealth Creation in Sport

the financial strength of a sport club is linked to six drivers. The first driver is the scale and strength of the league to which the club belongs. In Australia the superior financial position of AFL clubs compared to other pro-sport league clubs like world-football and rugby league is in part the result of a larger spectator base and much higher television rights fee. In Great Britain the clubs and teams that comprise the EPL have a similar advantage over teams and clubs in lower status world football leagues as well as clubs playing in the elite but less popular rugby league and rugby union competitions.

The second driver is the club's current level of performance and the scale of its supporter base. Specific performance-related factors include its on-field ranking, the quality of its coaching staff and player roster, and current marquee players. Some of the more important off-field factors include membership levels, the club's sponsor portfolio, and its capacity to control the post-game behavior of problem players.

The third driver is the club brand and its associated history and traditions. In every major sport league there are a coterie of clubs whose rich history of success give them a major branding advantage of other clubs. In EPL Manchester United and Liverpool have far and away the strongest brand, which in large part is based on their rich tradition of iconic players, on-field achievements, and fan support (Andrews 2004).

The fourth driver is the stadium in which the club plays its home matches. The stadium capacity, the quality of its facilities, and its location and accessibility all impact on the attendances and revenue. The Melbourne Cricket

Table 4.1 Financial Drivers in Professional Sport Clubs

Driver	Strong	Weak
Scale of competition	National competition	Regional competition
Level of performance	Regular appearances in final series	Regularly sits in bottom half of league ladder
Supporter base	Broad national support	Narrow provincial support
Club brand	Broad awareness, strong impact	Narrow awareness, weak impact
Stadium quality and size	New generation – all seats covered, clear sight lines	Aging – limited seating, limited cover
Scale of host city support	Single team in large city	Competing with other teams in same city
Culture and values of club	Primary concern for revenue growth	More concerned with cost containment

Source: Foster et al. (2006).

Ground (MCG) is one of the world's most well-known sport venues, and the combination of a rich history, proximity to the central business district, public transport, and quality facilities, enables it to attract more fans than any other sport stadium in Australia. Clubs which play out of the MCG consequently have an advantage over clubs that use less glamorous venues.

The fifth driver is the city or region in which the club is located. In some cities sport fandom is a peripheral cultural practice, whereas in other cities sport watching and sport participation in general are embedded within the community's social fabric. Also, a one-city team will have an advantage over teams that have to compete against other teams in the same city for the loyalty of fans, and the support of sponsors. In addition, the size of the surrounding population will affect a club's financial viability. A team that has a catchment of 500 000 potential fans, will have a significant commercial advantage over a team with 200 000 likely supporters.

The final driver is the owner's attributes and the club culture. While on one hand owners and managers may be completely committed to doing all it takes to win, on the other they may be so conservative and frugal that they will not risk excessive outlays to achieve on-field success. A summary of the drivers together with examples of strong and weak features is provided in Table 4.1.

Profits or wealth?

The above discussion raises the issues of first, how profits contribute to wealth creation, and second, the difference between profitability and wealth. The first point to note is that profitability results from the difference between flows of revenue and flows of expenses. Wealth, on the other hand has more to do with a sport organization's value at a point in time. Value is heavily dependent on the assets owned by the club or association, its levels of long-term debt, and its earnings potential although as will be noted in the following section, value is ultimately determined by how much someone is prepared to pay to secure ownership.

All things being equal, continued profitability will increase a sport organization's wealth and value. In other words, a wealthy sport organization like Real Madrid Football Club or Washington Redskins NFL team will have to build up their wealth through reinvesting their profits and increasing their revenue earning capacity over a number of years. By contrast a club that has a very low market value would most probably have a history of poor performance, a weak revenue base, and be running on deficit budgets. In the AFL at least three clubs have negative value. That is, total liabilities exceed assets and as a result the level of the accumulated funds is negative. In 2005 the Western Bulldogs' total tangible asset base of around AUD 5 million was undermined by total liabilities of AUD 9 million. The Carlton Blues exhibited a similar sluggish state of affairs over the last 5 years, and has built up debt levels well in excess of their tangible assets. It is therefore important to understand how profits are linked to wealth creation, how sport clubs and associations can be valued, and why some are highly valued, and others have much lower values.

What makes sport valuable?

As noted previously, many aspects of sport are now big business. Mega-sport events like the Olympic Games and world football World Cup have operational budgets of hundreds of millions of dollars, while professional sport leagues like the American NFL and NBA turn-over thousands of million of dollars a year. Many professional sport clubs have annual earnings of more than EUR 100 million, while the most successful clubs like Manchester United Football Club, Real Madrid Football Club, the New York Yankees Baseball Club, and the Washington Redskins Football team all generate annual earnings of more than EUR 200 million. At the other end of the professional sport club continuum, AFL clubs (which are the wealthiest sport clubs in Australia) earn between AUD 20 million and AUD 30 million a year.

Not surprisingly some leagues and clubs are much wealthier than others, and even within the same league there are significant differences in respect of revenues, profits, and wealth. It was suggested in the early part of this chapter that these differences can be explained by differences in industry structure, industry conduct, and a club or league's ability to secure a competitive advantage through access to more productive resources. It is also important to note that annual earnings provide only a very rough estimate of the wealth of a professional sport club. So how might we go beyond annual earnings and profits to secure a more reliable indicator of a club's wealth or value?

Market capitalization

The simple answer to the question "what is the real worth or value of a sporting club?" is the amount someone is willing to pay to obtain ownership of the club. In other words, it is the current market value of the club. But this immediately raises the issue as to how the market value of a sport club can be best calculated.

In the broader business world the market value of a publicly listed company (which is owned by shareholders) is found by multiplying the number of ordinary shares by their average sale price. So, if the company has one million shares trading at $10 a share, the market value is $10 million. Using this approach, which goes under the name of market capitalization, it is possible to quickly establish the value of all those Premier League clubs that are listed on the stock exchange. For example, the value of Manchester United Football Club in 2003 was GBP 610 million (Foster et al. 2006). However, this is not a feasible way of calculating the market value of most sports clubs since, with a few exceptions in European world football leagues, their shares are not traded on the stock exchange.

Market multiples

In North American professional sport leagues, where clubs (or franchises, as they are usually called) change ownership fairly regularly, the valuation of the franchise is revealed through the cost of acquisition. Over the last 10 years, for example, there has been an explosion in the valuation of NFL clubs. Whereas the asking price was around USD 150 million for a club franchise in the 1980s, it is now around USD 700 million. The record sale price for an NFL club franchise is USD 805 for the Washington Redskins in 2000, which included not only the team, but also its stadium (Howard and Crompton 2004).

Moreover, this acquisition cost can be used to estimate the market value of other clubs in the league. For example, the fictitious Little Rock Lions may have been sold to a new owner (and to be called the Long Island Lions) for $50 million, having earned an average of $25 million per annum over the previous 3 years. By dividing the acquisition price by the average annual earnings, an acquisition price-to-earnings multiple of 2.0 is calculated. This multiple of 2.0 can then be used to estimate the market value of other similar clubs. If, for instance, the Rapid Bay Rhinos annual earnings were $15 million, then by applying the acquisition price-to-earnings multiple of 2.0, the Rhinos estimated market value is around $30 million.

Book value of assets and shareholders equity

Another way of calculating a club's market value is to disect its balance sheet. One approach is to measure its total assets to determine its book value. However, this can be unreliable since it does not take into account the club's level of indebtedness. It is one thing to have a total asset base of $60 million, but the market value of the club would be severely undermined by $30 million of long-term borrowings. It is therefore more realistic to measure the club net worth which is the difference between assets and liabilities. In the case's of profit-centered sport organizations, and sport clubs that are structured as public companies, net worth is also referred to as shareholders' equity. In the case of non-profit clubs, the terms accumulated funds and members' equity are also used.

However, no matter what term is used, this can still be a fairly loose measure since it may not include some important intangibles that are not listed on the balance sheet. For example, in European world-football leagues, players are traded. They are in effect assets since they have a re-sale value. However, in many instances the real value of players is severely discounted. First, players who are recruited through the club's domestic junior development pathways are usually not listed as assets, since they did not come through the player transfer market. Second, in line with standard depreciation principles, the price paid for players on the transfer market is amortized over the contract life of the player. A player who was bought for $1 million, and contracted for 5 years could have his value reduced by around $200 000 a year until the player has, technically, no value when the contract is up for renewal. In reality this is false. Indeed, if players are competing at their peak by the end of the 5th year, their trading value could be in excess of the $1 million purchase price. While the balance sheet has the player valued at zero at the end of 5 years, the player's market value could be anything between $1 million and $2 million. Another problem resulting from using the book value of assets to establish a club's value is that many assets are listed as the purchase price. In reality many property-based assets are undervalued. A revaluation would provide a much higher set of figures.

The impact of expected future earnings

The other complicating thing about a professional sporting club's market value is that it is not only a function of past successes and earnings, but also about future successes and earnings. So, if a club is expected to perform at a high level, and this increase in performance will strengthen its profile, and attract additional resources, its market value is likely to increase. A simple method for linking earnings to market value is to calculate an average rate of return on capital invested. If, for example, the current market value of $20 million is based on annual earnings of $5 million and an average rate of return of 25 percent, then an increase in earnings to $8 million with the same expected rate of return of 25 percent will produce a revised market value of $32 million.

Club and team comparisons

Table 4.2 provides valuation data for a sample of professional sport clubs. The compounding successes of Manchester United, together with its strong

Table 4.2 Valuation of Sporting Clubs

Club Name	League	2003 Valuation (USD million)
Manchester United	EPL	1200
Washington Redskins	NFL	1100
New York Yankees	MLB	832
Juventus	Italian "A"	828
Bayern Munich	Bunduslige	617
Atlanta Falcons	NFL	603
Los Angeles Lakers	NBA	447
Chicago Bulls	NBA	356
Toronto Maple Leafs	NHL	263
Collingwood Magpies	AFL	44

Source: Foster et al. (2006:440–441).

global presence and massive support base has allowed it to accumulate profits and build up its asset base, hence its great wealth is not surprising. The Washington Redskins' substantial wealth reflects a similar set of circumstances. Moreover, like Manchester United it is a one-city team, and occupies a stadium that offers quality facilities and more than 60 000 seats a game. While the value of the Collingwood Magpies is relatively low by international standards, it is Australia's wealthiest professional sport team, which is largely due to its strong brand name, and large and loyal supporter base.

The market value of clubs, events, and leagues will continue to grow so long as they can secure stable profits and re-invest them in the improvement of player quality, venue quality, and the overall public attractiveness of tournaments and leagues. While market value can be quite different from profitability levels, continued profits through revenue growth and cost containment will increase the asset base of a club, enhance its reputation, and generally increase its financial sustainability.

Questions to consider

1. A profitable sport organization is not the same as a wealthy sport organization. Please explain.
2. Profitability in sport can come from a number of factors. One factor is the sport's surrounding industry structure and conduct. Please explain.
3. According to Szymanski and Kuypers (2000) some sport organizations are more profitable than others because they have a superior competitive strategy. Identify four tactical focal points that can be used to establish a competitive advantage.

4. Another way of looking at how sport organizations can secure a continuing profit is to examine the contributions made to sporting performance and financial performance. Explain how Gerrard (2005) goes about linking sporting performance to improved financial performance. Also identify how other factors identified by Gerrard can improve financial performance.

5. Foster et al. (2006) have listed six drivers that impact on sport clubs' financial sustainability. What are they, and how do they influence revenues and costs?

6. How is profitability linked to value and wealth?

7. Compare the use of market capitalization and market multiples as tools for estimating a sport organization's market value.

8. How can asset values and shareholder's equity be used to measure a sport organization's market value?

9. To what extent is a sport club's market value affected by expected future earnings? Give an example.

Further reading

For more details on models for examining the market value of sport organizations see Szymanski, S. and Kuypers, T. (2000). *Winners and Losers*. Penguin, Chapter 2 (Revenue) and Chapter 8 (The Future). See also Gerrard, W. (2004b). Why Does Manchester United Keep Winning? In D. Andrews (Ed.), *Manchester United: A Thematic Study.* Routledge, pp. 55–86.

For further discussion on the drivers of sport club finances see Foster, Greyser and Walsh (2006). *The Business of Sport.* Thomson, Section 10 (Financial Valuation and Profitability).

To get a detailed explanation of the background to how industry structure and conduct and company strategy affects profitability in sports organizations go to Gerrard, B. (2005). A Resource Utilization Model of Organizational Efficiency in Professional Team Sports. *Journal of Sport Management*, 19(2), 143–169; Mauws, M., Mason, D. and Foster, W. (2003). Thinking Strategically About Professional Sports. *European Sport Management Quarterly*, 3, 145–164; and Smart, D. and Wolfe, R. (2000). Examining Sustainable Competitive Advantage in Intercollegiate Athletics: A Resource-Based View. *Journal of Sport Management*, 14(2), 133–153.

The link between the theory and practice of wealth creation in English world football is extensively examined by Szymanski, S. and Kuypers, T. (2000). *Winners and Losers*. Penguin, Chapter 6 (Competitive Advantage in Football). Rosner, S. and Shropshire, K. (2004). *The Business of Sports.* Jones and Bartlett, Chapter 12 (Sport Franchise Valuation) has a useful discussion on the valuation of intangible assets like player contracts and acquired goodwill.

For a succinct introduction to sports' branding and how brand equity can be used to increase a sport organization's value see Ferrand, A. and Torrigiani, L. (2005). *Marketing of Olympic Sport Organizations*. Human Kinetics, Chapter 1

(Branding). See also Amis, J. and Cornwell, T. (2005). *Global Sport Sponsorship*. Berg, Chapter 4 (Global Brand Equity, FIFA and the Olympics).

For an analysis of how the video-game industry might be used to enhance the value of sport clubs see Rosson, P. (2005). SEGA Dreamcast: National Football Cultures and the New Europeanism, in M. Silk, D. Andrews and C. Cole (Eds.), *Sport and Corporate Nationalism*. Berg, pp.167–185. See especially p. 175 where it is put into the context of a value-chain for football business.

For an explanation of how the discounted cash flow (DCF) technique can be used to calculate the value of a sport organization's assets see Beech, J. and Chadwick, S. (Eds.) (2004). *The Business of Sport Management*. Prentice Hall, Chapter 7 (Sport Finance).

5

Sport cartels and wealth creation

Overview

This chapter examines the ways in which sport cartels can use their monopoly power to increase revenue, constrain costs, and generally ensure their long-term financial viability. Specific attention will be given to the Australian Football League (AFL) and how it went about increasing its revenue streams and wealth over the last 20 years. Using the models of profit-making discussed in the previous chapter, it will be shown that the AFL created a cartel structure that allowed it to regulate the sale of the football product, control its supply, manage its pricing, give clubs a minimum guaranteed income, and restrict the entry of new clubs.

What is a sport cartel?

Many professional sport leagues (especially those in the USA and Australia) operate as a joint venture or cartel. A cartel is a collective of firms who by agreement, act as a single supplier to a market, and in doing so, pursues a number of joint policies. As a result, cartels are able to minimize competition, restrict the entry of new firms, control the supply and cost of their products, coordinate advertizing and promotion, set prices, and most fundamentally, protect the interests of member organizations. In order to secure member

Table 5.1 Features of a Generic Cartel

Feature	Business Application
Decisions on cartel composition	Erection of high-entry barriers in order to control competition
Decisions on the spread of the cartel	Relocation/merger of firms to expand markets and reduce competition
Control over input and labor costs	Exclusive arrangements with suppliers and internal labor markets
Control over prices	Fixed wholesale and retail prices to guarantee markup
Decisions on growth maximization	Enter new markets in order to expand sales
Decisions on revenue sharing and income distribution	Guaranteed minimum income for cartel members to secure compliance

Source: Stewart, Dickson and Nicholson (2005:97).

compliance, cartels will normally impose sanctions and penalties for the violation of its rules and regulations.

In most countries cartels are illegal, since they act against the public interest by increasing monopoly power and limiting competition. Trade practices legislation aims to break up cartel behavior by prohibiting collusive behavior by firms in the same industry. It prohibits conduct that denies new firms entry into an industry, prohibits mergers and takeovers that will substantially reduce competition, and prohibits suppliers agreeing to fix prices. The main features of cartels are listed in Table 5.1.

Sport leagues have a natural tendency to adopt cartel-like behavior since they depend on the cooperation of many teams to ensure a viable competition (Quirk and Fort 1992). This is evident in the evolution of professional sport leagues in basketball, baseball, ice hockey, and football in the USA. While member teams will be highly competitive, and primarily concerned with on-field dominance, they also understand that their long-term viability depends on a high-quality competition where teams are of comparable strength and ability. Therefore, for a sport cartel to operate effectively, it must enforce policies that constrain member behaviors and maximizes the league's public appeal and long-run sustainability (Fleisher, Goff and Tollison 1992). This means that the league will formulate rules that control the conduct of teams, administrators, players, and coaches. Sport cartels will therefore aim to:

1. have a centralized decision-making organization that regulates constituent teams and clubs, and disciplines members who breach the league's rules and regulations. This is a core requirement, since cartels will maximize their returns only if they act as single enterprises.

2. expand profits by imposing cost-minimization regulations. These regulations include rules that restrict competitive bidding for players, and set ceilings on total player wage payments.

3. expand the market by admitting new teams to the league, extending the playing season, or playing games at different times of the week.

4. enhance their product in order to improve the absolute quality of the game. This may involve the development of player skills, making stadiums more comfortable, and securing safer and more predictable playing surfaces.

5. enhance their product in order to improve relative game quality by providing uncertain game outcomes, which is often referred to as competitive balance. This can be achieved by drafting the best recruits to the worst performing clubs at the end of the season, and redistributing league income so that all member teams can afford minimum standard of administration, coaching, and sport science support. The additional imposition of salary caps can also improve competitive balance in some situations.

6. heighten the league's reputation and status through centralized promotion campaigns that aim to improve the public image of the sport. Rules are put in place to regulate the conduct and behavior of team administrators, coaches, and players.

7. use their monopoly power to maximize broadcast rights fees. This will involve negotiating as a single entity, and avoiding any arrangement that allocates the rights to individual teams.

The policies and rules that characterize sport cartels are listed in Table 5.2.

Unlike more traditional industries, the sport industry is often allowed by government to pursue what are effectively anti-competitive practices. This occurs because there is tacit agreement that restrictive practices are essential for the sport league to sustain its public interest and long-term viability. In other words, a completely unregulated sport league will be unsustainable since a few clubs will use their superior fan and revenue base to capture the best players and dominate the premiership race. This argument is supported by the claim that while the resulting conduct may be anti-competitive or a restraint of trade, it is not unreasonable, or against the public interest. It is claimed, therefore, that unlike the world of commerce and industry, sport leagues often perform poorly under free-market conditions, and some form of self-regulation is essential to produce the outcome uncertainty that attracts fans, sponsors, and media interests (Sandy, Sloane and Rosentraub 2004).

The case of the AFL

In the following section the recent performance of the AFL will be examined through the prism of cartel structure and conduct. In doing this, the sport cartel template illustrated later in this chapter in Figure 5.2 will be used to address the following questions. First, to what extent has the AFL established structures that enable it to govern its affairs, and regulate the conduct of member teams as if it was a single entity? Second, how successful has the

Table 5.2 Policy Features of a Sport Cartel

Policy Feature	Examples and Cases
Policies for managing league structure, composition, and team location	Admit new teams into league, provide incentives for clubs to merge or relocate, set league fixtures and playing schedules
Policies to prevent the entry of rival leagues	Establish long-term contracts with media organizations, stadia owners, and star players
Policies for increasing relative game quality and improving competitive balance	Establish recruiting zones, create player draft, and implement salary caps and player wage ceilings
Policies to regulate league costs	Design regulated player transfer market, implement salary caps and wage ceilings for member club staff
Policies to regulate league prices	Control admission prices, set prices for league merchandise and publications
Policies for increasing absolute game quality and improving general appeal of game to public	Develop programs to optimize player skill and abilities, improve spectator facilities and stadium design, refine rules of game
Policies to ensure the reputation of the game/league	Design rules to protect the good name of the game, implement codes of conduct for players, and rules to restrict public comments of officials
Policies for expanding the market for the game	Conduct centralized promotional and advertizing campaigns, manage player participation and game development programs
Policies for maximizing broadcast right agreements	Be the sole supplier of broadcast rights to television and radio stations
Policies for redistributing revenue	Pool television rights and redistribute to member clubs, implement income equalization schemes
Policies for increasing revenue streams	Sell brand name and logo to merchandizers, sell advertizing and promotional space to sponsors

Source: Stewart, B et al. (2005:99).

AFL been in reorganizing the competition so that it can capture new markets, and attract new fans? Third, has the AFL been able to increase its revenue base by both broadening and deepening its income steams? Fourth, in what way has the AFL been able to control costs by fixing player wage bills and operational expenses, and to fix prices by setting common admission and merchandise prices? Fifth, in what ways has the AFL managed demand by influencing game quality, where quality had both an absolute dimension (the competition has many star players and comfortable venues) and a relative dimension (games are exciting where the outcome is uncertain)? Sixth, what schemes have been put in place to pool income and redistribute it to ensure a guaranteed minimum income for member teams? Finally, to what extent has the AFL used rules, agreements, and threats to manage the behavior of administrators, coaches, and players, and to protect the good name and reputation of the game?

Centralized governance

The Victorian Football League (VFL), from which the AFL emerged, was formed in 1897. It expanded during the 1920s, and by 1980 had become a competition of 12 teams based in Melbourne. Throughout this period the VFL was governed by a Board of Directors that comprised delegates from each of the 12 clubs, with the day-to-day management conducted by a central administration. During the early 1980s the VFL faced many threats and problems. The South Melbourne Club, which relocated to Sydney in 1982 in order to avoid liquidation, was finding it difficult to attract a viable fan base, attendances were falling, and 8 of the 12 clubs were technically bankrupt.

Two task-force reports commissioned by the VFL in the mid-1980s were the catalysts for a major restructuring of the League. It was clear that a system of governance that relied on member clubs nominating delegates to the Board was inappropriate in such a turbulent environment. In late 1985 the VFL Board of Directors was replaced by a commission elected by member clubs. This commission structure has continued to the present day, and has been used to provide centralized decision-making and a set of rules and regulations by which the clubs have to abide.

League expansion

During the 1980s world football was considered a threat to Australian football, and the new Commission also became aware that the New South Wales Rugby League (NSWRL) competition, after many years of neglect, had increased its public support and reach. It had already admitted teams from the Australian Capital Territory (ACT) and Wollongong, and was investigating the possibility of admitting teams from the Gold Coast and Brisbane, which it did in 1987. The AFL Commission report *Establishing the Basis for Future Success* recommended interstate expansion as a way of both managing the threats from world football and rugby league, and extending the reach of the VFL beyond Melbourne and Sydney. It was agreed to establish VFL clubs in Brisbane and Perth, thus producing a 14-team competition covering four of Australia's seven states.

The Commission's national ambitions led to the Adelaide Crows being admitted in 1991 and the Fremantle Dockers in 1995. These were strategically

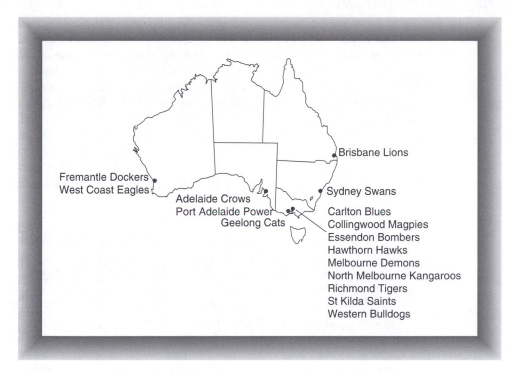

Figure 5.1 Location of AFL Teams 1997–2006. Adapted from Hess and Stewart (1998:236)

important decisions, since they provided a better national balance, curbed the growing financial dominance of the West Coast Eagles, and reduced the impact of rugby league decisions to locate teams in Adelaide and Perth. In 1997 Port Power, a second Adelaide club, was admitted to the League which coincided with the merger of Fitzroy and Brisbane. This created a 16-team competition covering five states, which continues through to the present day. The national spread of the AFL competition is illustrated in Figure 5.1.

The AFL's cartel structure allowed a more centralized management model to emerge, in which the interests of the League as a whole were of primary concern. Support for the national expansion from existing member clubs was reinforced by the distribution of the AUD 4 million licence fee paid by newly admitted clubs.

Flexible scheduling of games

The Commission's centralized control also allowed further restructuring to occur at the end of 1990 when the VFL changed its name to the AFL. This national expansion strategy was accompanied by a plan to improve the quality of the competition by rationalizing the use of playing venues, upgrading facilities, and playing games over the whole weekend as a way of giving

61

broadcasters greater programming opportunities. By 1989 Sunday football received State government approval, and the Melbourne Cricket Ground (MCG) progressively became the home venue for most Melbourne-based clubs, and with the construction of the Docklands stadium in 2000 (which was renamed Telstra Dome) further relocations and rescheduling occurred, and in 2006 the MCG and Telstra Dome became the only Melbourne venues to regularly host AFL fixtures.

Creating a level playing field

The AFL also used its cartel structure and monopoly power to implement a raft of policies to achieve a balanced competition. In the early 1980s players were regulated by rules that tied them to their club until such time the club decided to grant a transfer. This master–servant relationship was reinforced by a geographic zoning system that tied all likely recruits to a specific club. In 1983 the VFL's player transfer policy was challenged in the Victorian Supreme Court, where it was concluded that the clearance, transfer, and zoning rules were an unreasonable restraint of trade and that they be replaced by a system of player drafts and contracts. Player transfer rules were amended so that by 1986 a national player draft was in place. Player transfer fees were removed, and player lists were reduced, all of which stabilized the cost structure of clubs, but gave players little choice as to where they would like to play.

Controlling player costs

Player payments have also been a vexing issue for the AFL. Rules for containing player payments were first established by the VFL in 1930, when a maximum wage was implemented. However, the rule was flouted so often during the 1970s that escalating player wages had undermined the financial viability of many clubs.

To protect the league against a wage–cost explosion a salary cap was introduced in late 1984, which was modeled on the American National Basketball Association (NBA) wage ceiling policy of 1983. The cap not only constrained the player wage costs of member clubs, but also helped redistribute playing talent more evenly. The salary cap subsequently became the pivotal strategy for controlling player payments. In 1983 it was set at AUD 0.5 million per member team, but since then has steadily increased. In 1996 it was AUD 2.5 million and is now AUD 8 million per team. The Commission sets the salary cap, which it recently retitled Total Player Payments, based on movements in broadcast rights fees, revenue from finals games, and club membership income. This means that the salary cap will increase in line with the League's revenue, and by implication, the club's capacity to pay. The scale of the expansion in player payments is illustrated in Table 5.3. The salary cap dampened the bargaining

Table 5.3 Payments to AFL Players: 1980–2005

Year	Salary Cap (AUD Million)	Average Player Earnings (AUD Thousand)	Percentage of Players Earning More Than AUD 100 000 Per Year
1980	Not applicable	11	0
1985	1	15	0
1990	2	45	2
1995	2.5	75	18
2000	5	127	62
2002	6	167	68
2005	8	203	75

Source: AFL *Annual Reports* 1981–2005.

strength of recruits, and eliminated the player hoarding by rich clubs that occurred in the 1970s and early 1980s.

The AFL Commission has also implemented sanctions that impose penalties on clubs that breach the salary cap provisions. In 2002 Carlton, Richmond, Fremantle, and St Kilda were all found to have breached the salary cap, and were penalized through a combination of fines and denial of national draft choices.

Improving absolute game quality

The AFL Commission also developed policies and strategies for improving the overall quality of the game. From the 1990s the AFL used sport science and improved technologies to develop the skills and athleticism of players. Just as there had been an increase in the corporate logic that dominated decision-making in the off-field AFL, a similar logic underpinned the development of the on-field side of the AFL. The game became faster with the players being taller, heavier, and possessing a greater aerobic capacity than previously. Sport science, underpinned by physiology, biomechanics, and psychology, became an integral part of the AFL landscape. Tactically, the game advanced considerably, which resulted in an increase in the number of fulltime assistant coaches.

The same innovative approach was applied to stadium development. The pivotal place of the MCG in the national league was reinforced in 1992 when its AUD 150 million Great Southern Stand was completed. The comfortable new seating and improved sight lines were instrumental in increasing the average MCG attendance from 25 000 to more than 40 000 during the next few years. Stadium redevelopment peaked in the late 1990s when the AFL helped construct a new generation stadium in Melbourne's inner west Docklands precinct complete with retractable roof.

Strengthening the brand

Although the AFL expanded its fan base substantially during the 1980s and early 1990s, it was aware of the growing national presence of rugby league. It was particularly aware of how rugby league's cleverly constructed marketing campaigns during the early 1990s had increased the game's national profile. The Australian Rugby League's Tina Turner promotional campaign, which began in 1989, aimed to soften the game's hyper-masculine, blue-collar image by selling the game's sociability and excitement to a white-collar audience.

By contrast, the AFL had historically let the media promote the game through its game reporting. But all this changed in 1993 when it contracted the leading advertizing agency, Campaign Palace, to design a promotional campaign that would not only update the game's public image, but also capture the attention of people with little exposure to the traditions of Australian football. The campaign brief was to promote the AFL as a national game, and gear it heavily to New South Wales and Queensland. To this end it was decided to feature overseas athletes and celebrities who would express congratulatory amazement about some aspect of the game using the tag line "I'd like to see that". In one feature Russian cosmonaut, Sergei Avdeev, said "Australia launching men into space every few minutes? I'd like to see that".

The campaign ran from 1994 to 1998, and by the fourth year had achieved a national recall rate of 97 percent. It also coincided with an increase in total season attendance from 4.7 million in 1994 to 6.1 million in 1998. This was followed by the "I was here" campaign in 1999 and the "For the Love of the Game" campaign in 2002. The "For the Love of the Game" highlighted the community roots of Australian football, and how the AFL was assisting community football throughout the nation.

Improving the League's reputation

For a cartel like the AFL, it is not enough to strengthen the brand and extend its exposure. It is also important to use its monopoly power to improve the League's overall standing and reputation in the sport world. This standing and reputation is not only a function of the quality and balance of the competition, the skill of players, and the standard of stadiums. It is also a function of the behavior of the League's administrators, coaches, and players.

The lengths the AFL has gone to in order to protect its reputation is revealed in the collective bargaining agreement (CBA) between the Commission and the AFL Players Association (AFLPA), which covers issues related to players and their performance. The most recent CBA includes sections on player payments, injury and veteran lists, contracts, use of player images and, choice of player footwear. The Commission helped fund the implementation of CBA programs, and in 2003 allocated AUD 5 million to support professional development and player welfare programs, including the provision for players in their retirement.

The CBA also incorporates a code of conduct, which has been jointly formulated by the Commission, AFLPA, and member clubs. The purpose of the code is to promote the good reputation of Australian football, the AFL competition, AFL clubs, and players by establishing standards of performance and behavior for AFL footballers. In addition, it seeks to deter conduct which could have an adverse effect on the standing and reputation of the game. The code of conduct also incorporates rules and regulations related to doping and racial vilification, which reinforces the AFL's desire to maintain a clean image, as well as provide positive role models for children.

The AFL introduced an anti-doping code in 1990 as a result of a growing public awareness of the effects of performance-enhancing drugs on both the health of athletes and the image and appeal of the competition. The Justin Charles case of 1997, where he tested positive for anabolic steroids, provided the catalyst for entrenching the League's anti-doping policy. In 2005 the AFL extended its policy by introducing penalties for the use of illicit recreational drugs. Any player who tests positive for cocaine or ecstasy on match day can now expect a 12-match suspension for the first offence and a 2-year suspension for the second.

Expanding participation

Throughout the 1990s the AFL had used its monopoly power to expand the market, substantially increase its annual revenue and net worth, maintain control over player wages and transfers, achieve competitive balance, and establish codes of conduct that guided the behavior of players. However, there was a growing concern that while it had managed the national competition very well, it had been less successful in pursuing its role as the keeper-of-the-code, and developing the game in the northern markets of New South Wales, Queensland, and the Northern Territory.

AFL administrators were acutely aware that Queensland and New South Wales would soon be home to more than half of Australia's population. The northern markets were considered integral to a national competition, and the AFL developed a three-pronged approach to sustain its dominant position in the sporting marketplace. The first prong aimed to ensure that the Brisbane Lions and Sydney Swans were both financially stable and successful on the field, the second prong aimed to ensure greater television exposure of the AFL competition, while the final prong involved heavy investment in game development and junior participation.

Managing the sale of broadcasting rights

Television has always had a strong relationship with the AFL, and throughout the 45 years of negotiating broadcast rights, the VFL/AFL always acted on behalf of member clubs. The AFL was the jewel in the crown of the Seven Network's programming, and their relationship created significant corporate synergies. While the AFL praised the breadth and quality of Seven's football coverage, the Seven Network provided saturation levels of promotion for the AFL. The Seven Network valued the relationship so highly that in 1998 it agreed to pay the AFL AUD 40 million a year until the end of 2001 for 4 weeks of pre-season competition and 26 weeks of the premiership league. However, the Seven Network's relationship with the AFL was severed in December 2000, when a consortium headed by Rupert Murdoch's News Limited secured the broadcast rights to all AFL fixtures for a fee of AUD 500 million over 5 years. In a complex arrangement, the rights were spread across one pay television and two free-to-air providers, namely Foxtel, the Nine Network, and the Ten Network, respectively. In the latest round of negotiations held in early 2006 the Seven and Ten networks colluded to outbid the Nine Network. They secured the rights to broadcast the AFL's fixtures for 5 years in return for a record payment of AUD 750 million. The growth in television broadcast rights income is illustrated in Table 5.4.

In the aftermath to the 2001 and 2006 agreements there were rumblings from member clubs and venue managers like the MCG that it may be possible to challenge the monopoly power of the Commission over broadcast rights. In Major League Baseball in the USA, member teams negotiate their own local free-to-air and cable television broadcast rights. However, this resulted in some clubs obtaining up to a USD 50 million advantage over rival teams. The AFL Commission declared its intention to be the sole negotiator so that the competition as a whole will benefit, rather than a few powerful clubs.

Table 5.4 Trends in Broadcasting Rights Fees 1980–2007

Agreement Year	Fees (AUD Million)	Fee As Percentage of Total Commission Revenues
1980	1	4
1985	4	22
1990	8	27
1995	17	24
2000	40	36
2002	100	63
2007	150	70

Source: AFL, *Annual Reports* 1981–2005; and Stewart (1984).

Redistributing the pool of revenue

The VFL and AFL have a history of pooling part of the league revenue and redistributing it, through a system of cross-subsidization, to member clubs in equal amounts. In the early 1980s, 20 percent of net match proceeds was put into an equalization fund together with broadcasting rights income as well as the net proceeds from the final series. Over the following 20 years the revenue pooling policy was strengthened, and by 2006 included all broadcasting rights fees, all corporate hospitality income, the net income from the finals series, and the profits from the *Football Record*, the match-day publication. Overall, around 40 percent of all League revenue is now pooled and redistributed to member clubs. The AFL's revenue pooling policy is a powerful tool for controlling the behavior of member clubs. While the AFL claims it is not a banker to the clubs and does not guarantee club debts, its pooling policy has allowed a number of member clubs to survive serious financial crises. Consequently, the AFL's policy, by protecting weaker clubs, has been able to preserve the viability of the League.

Cumulative financial impact

As a result of the above practices the AFL's revenue base (comprising both Commission and club income) has exploded exponentially. This reflects its ability to set admission prices, attract large at-ground crowds, and generate high-rating television audiences. In 1990 total Commission revenue was AUD 30 million, by 2003 it had increased to AUD 171 million, and by 2006 had reached around AUD 220 million. A large part of this growth came from broadcasting rights fees. Whereas it contributed just under AUD 8 million in 1990, it had increased to AUD 17 million in 1995, AUD 100 million in 2003 and is expected to generate around AUD 150 million a year between 2007 and 2010. Sponsorship and merchandising income also increased rapidly over this period, although on a much smaller scale. Club incomes grew at a similar rate. In 1990 average member club income was AUD 4 million, had increased to AUD 8 million in 1995, and escalated to AUD 25 million in 2005. By 2006 total annual League revenues exceeded AUD 450 million, with broadcasting rights fees accounting for 30 percent of total League revenues. The growth in AFL income and at-ground attendances from 1980 to 2005 are listed in Table 5.5.

Overall, the establishment of a centralized Commission enabled the AFL to better control its member clubs, regulate fixtures, and pursue its national expansion agenda. It continued to regulate the movement of players by replacing its zoning rules with a national player draft. The draft not only ensured an even spread of playing talent across the teams, but because it reduced the competition for players, dampened the ability of young recruits to negotiate a starting salary commensurate with their abilities. The Commission also extended

Table 5.5 AFL Income and Attendances 1980–2005

Year	Commission Revenue (AUD Million)	Average Club Revenue (AUD Million)	Total Season Attendance (Million)
1980	15	1.2	3.7
1985	18	1.5	3.1
1990	30	4.0	4.1
1995	72	8.2	5.9
2000	111	12	6.6
2002	160	17	6.4
2005	220	25	6.5

Source: AFL *Annual Reports* 1981–2005.

its reach over player payments by introducing a salary cap, which established a ceiling on the total player wage bill. It used its monopoly power to enhance game quality by improving stadium facilities, rationalizing venues, and developing player athleticism and skills. It continued to negotiate broadcasting rights as a single entity. It also introduced an array of coercive agreements and codes of conduct that increasingly constrained the behavior of administrators, players and, coaches as a way of maintaining the reputation of the League. Finally, it increasingly pooled league income and redistributed it to member clubs to ensure they had a guaranteed minimum income to sustain their financial viability. There is no doubt the AFL's financial success, in large part, resulted from its cartel structures and behavior, which is illustrated in Figure 5.2.

Figure 5.2 confirms that profit-making in professional sports leagues is a function of both the drive to expand revenue and the need to control costs. In the case of a sport league cartel both revenue expansion and cost-containment strategies can be secured through a centralized body that regulates its member clubs by a combination of incentives and coercion.

Questions to consider

1. Identify the main features of a cartel.
2. In what ways is a cartel similar to a monopoly?
3. What do cartels do in order to restrict competition, contain costs, and increase revenue?
4. What are the main features of a sport cartel, and how might it go about constraining the conduct of its member clubs in order to secure its financial future?
5. What cartel-like features does the AFL possess?

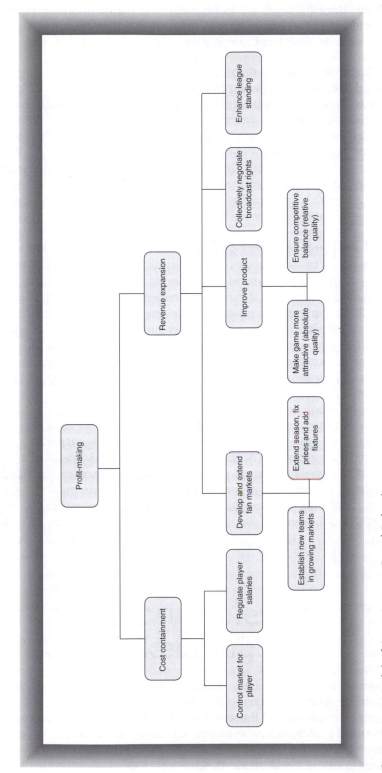

Figure 5.2 A Model of Sport League Cartel Behavior

6. How does the AFL go about restricting competition, constraining its costs, and increasing revenue?
7. Why is the concept of competitive balance so important in the AFL, and what does it do to secure a more balance competition?
8. Why is reputation and brand image important to the AFL, and how does it use its monopoly power to improve it?
9. How does the AFL use its monopoly power to maximize its income from broadcasting rights fees?
10. Contrast the cartel-like conduct of the National Football League (NFL) with the operation of English Premier League (EPL).
11. How would you rank the AFL, EPL, and NFL in terms of their cartel structure and conduct?

Further reading

An instructive introduction to cartel behavior in sport is contained in Fleisher, A., Goff, B. and Tollison, R. (1992). *The National Collegiate Athletic Association: A Study in Cartel Behavior*. The University of Chicago Press, Chicago. See also Downard, P. and Dawson, A. (2000). *The Economics of Professional Team Sports*. Routledge, Chapter 3 (League Structures).

For a succinct coverage of how professional sport leagues go about restricting competition and regulating member clubs see Leeds, M. and von Allmen, P. (2005). *The Economics of Sports*, 2nd Edition. Pearson, especially Chapter 4 (Monopoly and Anti-trust) and Chapter 5 (Competitive Balance). Also see Sandy, R., Sloane, P. and Rosentraub, M. (2004). *The Economics of Sport: An International Perspective*. Palgrave Macmillan, Chapter 7 (Sports Teams and Leagues: From a Business Necessity to Dominating Cartel).

One of the most detailed accounts of the long-term effects of sport league regulation in the USA is Quirk, J. and Fort, R. (1992). *Pay Dirt: The Business of Professional Team Sport*. Princeton University Press. See especially Chapter 5 (The Reserve Clause and Anti-Trust), Chapter 6 (Why Do Pro Athletes Make So Much Money?) and Chapter 7 (Competitive Balance).

For an expansive analysis of the economic organization of professional world-football leagues in Europe and England see Dobson, S. and Goddard, J. (2001). *The Economics of Football*. Cambridge University Press, especially Chapter 2 (Professional Football), Chapter 3 (Competitive Balance) and Chapter 9 (Current Issues and Future Prospects).

For a discussion of the benefits and costs of highly regulated leagues on one hand, and unregulated leagues on the other see Rosner, S. and Shropshire, K. (2004). *The Business of Sports*. Jones and Bartlett, Chapter 2 (Leagues: Structure and Background) Chapter 3 also takes a critical look at revenue sharing in professional sport leagues.

A concise comparison of the structure and conduct of European and North American professional sport leagues is made by Szymanski, S. (2004). "Is there a European Model of Sports?" In R. Fort and J. Fizel (Eds.), *International Sports Economic Comparisons*. Praeger, pp.19–38.

PART TWO

Sport Funding: Financial Management

6

Sport finance foundations

Overview

This chapter will discuss the principles underpinning the effective financial management of sport organizations. It begins with a brief history of book-keeping and accounting systems, and the ways in which the financial affairs of organizations were managed. Students will then be introduced to the different financial entities relevant to sport organizations, and the special financial features of each entity. They include sole traders, partnerships, non-profit incorporated associations, companies limited by guarantee, and public companies. The remainder of the chapter will focus on the importance of good financial management, and the steps required to establish appropriate systems and structures.

A brief history of accounting

There has always been a need to manage the financial affairs of groups and organizations. In ancient Greece and Rome the use of money in the form of coins enabled rulers of states, the leaders of communities, and the owners of businesses to calculate their wealth by listing the money they owned, and comparing it with the money they owed. It led to establishment of banks, which set up account books, and loaned money to its citizens. Around 600 BC the ancient Greeks also used systems of accounting to assess the efficiency of government programs. The civil servants of the time were required to keep a list of their receipts and expenditure, which could be examined by an appointed group of so called public accountants. Ancient Rome had a similar system of controls over government spending. Auditors were used to verify spending by the treasury, and in particular review spending on public works and the operation of the Roman Army.

During the eleventh and twelfth centuries in England financial management focused more on the feudal manor and the local tradesperson. Subsequent to his invasion of England, William the Conqueror conducted a survey of every estate from which taxes to be paid were calculated. This led to the creation of the Doomsday book which provided information for annual listing of rents and taxes payable to the King of England from 1130 to 1830. This list was called the Pipe Roll. County sheriffs were appointed to collect the rents and taxes, and the monies paid to the King were recorded through the marking of a hazel wood stick. These tally sticks were notched and marked to indicate how much income had been received from each estate or business, and when it was paid. When Sheriffs had collected their money, they would meet with the King's treasurer where the money would be taken, the Pipe Roll entry marked accordingly, and a receipt issued. This occurred at a table covered by a checkered cloth, hence the term exchequer to describe the treasurer's role.

However, it was not until the fifteenth century that what we now know as double entry book-keeping was invented. The Italian Renaissance was a period of enormous artistic and commercial vitality, and one of its many innovations was the introduction of double entry book-keeping. In 1494 Luca Pacioli, a mathematician and monk, published a book titled *Everything About Arithmetic, Geometry and Proportion* (or *Summa*, its abbreviated Italian title). One of his chapters (called Reckonings and Writings) was on the topic of accounting, and in it he described the fundamentals of an accounting system that we still use today. Pacioli identified the journal as the foundation document that lists the details of every financial transaction. It includes the date it occurred, the nature of the transaction, and whether it was a payment or a receipt. He also invented a system of ledger entries. The ledger provided a radical departure from previous book-keeping systems since it enabled the compiler of the books to include an offsetting entry for every transaction. That is, for every entry on the left side of the ledger (a debit entry), there had to be an equivalent entry on the right side of the ledger (a credit entry). Pacioli also discussed the concept of the trial balance where all the debit entries were tallied and compared with summary of all the credit entries. His double entry system required that the debits would equal credits. The Venetian System, as it was subsequently called, allowed Italian merchants to do business efficiently because of its superior book-keeping outcomes. As trade expanded it spread across Europe and became the standard model for keeping the books thereafter. The Pacioli accounting model will be discussed in more detail in the next chapter.

Another major book-keeping development occurred in England during the Industrial Revolution in the eighteenth century. This time it revolved around the management of costs in the manufacturing industry. Josia Wedgwood, one of England's major pottery producers, found that he could better manage his production costs by calculating detailed costings for materials and labor. He also distinguished between overhead costs, fixed costs, and variable costs. He identified the ways in which these costs changed as production levels changed, and explained how unit costs would fall as total production increased. He could then calculate the saving from large production runs and economies of scale.

In the nineteenth century accounting became a profession through the establishment of the Institute of Chartered Accountants in Edinburgh, and as the Industrial Revolution accelerated, the demand for accountants increased exponentially. During the twentieth century the globalization of commerce, increasing inter-firm competition, the increasing complexity of corporate taxation, and stringent government regulation have all increased the demand for accounting systems that allow businesses to manage their financial affairs efficiently, ensure a competitive advantage, and provide appropriate information to owners and regulators.

Accounting and sport management

Unfortunately, sport has for many years lagged behind the business sector from a financial management perspective. This is due to a number of reasons. First, it has a history of amateurism, which meant that money management was not as important as participation and the pleasure of competition. Second, most sport organizations were traditionally run on a small scale where budgets were constrained by membership income. Third, sport was seen as something different from business, and as result, there was no crucial need for sophisticated systems of financial management. However, this has all changed over the last 50 years as Chapters 1 and 2 explain. Even small-scale sports now have to ensure their financial viability in the face of competition from other sporting activities. Moreover, government now requires sport associations to manage their affairs efficiently to qualify for grants and subsidies. And, there has been a massive growth in professional sport around the world, which in turn requires sound financial management for their overall sustainability.

For the most part sport management education has centered on planning, strategy, and marketing. While this approach has fostered the emergence of many sophisticated development and marketing plans for sport organizations, it has undervalued the importance of good financial management competencies. There are still many sport managers who have difficulty reading balance sheets and profit and loss statements, and who would be unable to distinguish between the investing section of a cash flow statement and the financing section of the statement.

75

There are a number of facets to being a good financial manager. The first is to be systematic in the way one runs the organization, and provide resources for the proper keeping of the books. The second is to understand the difference between the reporting function of the accounts (which is to provide financial summaries to stakeholders) and the management function of the accounts (which is to generate data that can be used to monitor and control the financial affairs of the organization). The third is to become financially literate, which means being able to not only understand and speak the language of accounting and book-keeping, but also being able to accurately interpret financial documents including budget papers, economic impact statements, project evaluation reports, cash flow statements, profit and loss statements, and finally, balance sheets.

The need for financial management skills is increasingly important when having to accommodate a range of legal and reporting requirements. In most nations around the world there are generally accepted accounting principles that go under the acronym of GAAP. The aim of GAAP is to make financial statements consistent and comparable, and consequently allow investors and other stakeholders to make judgments about the relative performance of businesses. This principle applies equally to sport organizations. Attempts have also been made to develop international standard accounting principles, and in recent times an International Accounting Standards Board (IASB) has been established. The Board has set International Financial Reporting Standards (IFRS) for the format and content of balanced sheets, the definition and valuation of assets, the classification of liabilities, and how profits should be defined and calculated.

Key accounting principles

There are a number of accounting principles that underpin financial management and reporting around the world. These principles allow for a standard framework by which accounting records are created and displayed. Unless otherwise noted, the following principles will apply to accounting documents discussed in subsequent chapters of this book.

The business entity

The first principle is that for legal and financial purposes the business is separate from its owners or proprietor. This means that even where the owner of the business and its management may be the same people, there is a clear distinction between the business or organization as an entity, and the ownership. This also means that even in an owner-operated business, all transactions involving the owner are designated and recorded. So, if the owner injects her own funds into the business, this is recorded as an increase in the owner's equity, and an increase in the cash assets of the business. Alternatively if the owner decides to take money out of her business, it is recorded as a decrease in the owner's equity, and a fall in the cash assets of the business.

The going concern

The second principle is that the business or organization has a life of its own independently of what happens to the owner or proprietor. So, the business continues to operate and is a going concern until it is wound up, or liquidated. This means also that assets will be valued at their purchase price or market value, and not at a forced sale price.

The accounting period

The third principle is that the business life of the organization is divided into distinct accounting periods. For each period, usually of 1 year in length, accounts are prepared and made available to all stakeholders. Under this principle the aim is to include all transactions that occur in the period, and not to exclude relevant items of revenue and expenditure.

Historical cost

The fourth principle is that unless designated otherwise, all transactions will be recorded at their historical cost. This applies to not only all recurrent expenses like wages and overheads, but also assets like merchandise, buildings, machinery, and other equipment. Assets will be valued at their historical cost, unless there has been a revaluation, in which case notes about their depreciation or increase in value will be provided in the financial statements.

Conservatism

The fifth principle is that financial information will be reported conservatively. This means that expenses and liabilities will never be underestimated, and where there is any doubt, the higher figure will prevail. The opposite applies to revenue and assets. Being conservative means that where there is any doubt, they should be underestimated. That is, in this instance the lower figure will prevail.

Materiality

The sixth principle is that financial reports should contain everything that is significant and relevant. In particular, any significant shifts or changes in assets, liabilities, revenues, and expenses should be noted. This principle, which is called the doctrine of materiality, also means that where there is variability between annual reports, these differences be made clear and transparent.

Reliability

The seventh principle is that the same methods and practices should be used in constructing the accounts. This also called the principle of consistency, and it means that methods for distinguishing between different types of assets and liabilities should be the same, depreciation should be calculated on a uniform basis, cash flow statements should follow the same format, and the processes for calculating operating and net profits should be consistent.

Organizational contexts

As the above discussion shows, there is a concerted attempt around the world to standardize the accounting and financial management functions, and ensure that statements and reports adhere to a common set of rules and guidelines. At the same time it should be remembered that accounting and financial management will take place in many different settings and contexts. In particular, organizations can take on different legal forms.

Single proprietor

The simplest business entity is one which is owned and operated by a single person. They are known as sole traders. The owner supplies the cash and other assets to establish the business, and is also able to draw money out of the business, which is effectively the profits. The owner can also borrow funds to build up the asset base of the business. At the same time, the personal affairs of the owner are kept separate from the financial transactions of the business. While from an accounting viewpoint the owner is separate from the business, from a legal viewpoint the owner is not. This means the owner or operator is liable for all debts of the business.

Partnership

A partnership has a similar structure to that of single proprietor. The key difference is that it can be owned by two or more people. No specific legal requirement is needed to form a partnership other than a written agreement to say that a partnership has been organized. Like a single proprietor business, the partners are liable for the debts of the business. Single proprietorships and partnerships are easy to establish, although they must be registered as a business, and provide for a unique business name. However, they provide little legal protections for the owners, and in situations where large debts have been accumulated the claims of creditors may have to be met in part from their personal assets.

Company

In order to provide a stronger business structure and greater legal protection a company can be formed. A company will cost more to form than a single proprietorship or partnership, but it has the benefit of creating a legal separation between the owner or owners and the business. Because the business is a separate legal entity the owners are not liable for its debts. However the owners are the designated shareholders in this form of business, and their shareholding or equity in the business may be used to meet creditors' demands. However their losses cannot exceed their shareholdings. This feature is known as limited liability.

There are different types of companies. The first is a proprietary company, which is allowed no more than 50 shareholders. In addition it cannot raise funds from the public. However, its shares can be transferred to some other person. It is also allowed to pay dividends to shareholders. A second type of company is the public company. A public company has no limitation on the number of shareholders, and can raise capital by inviting the public to subscribe to an issue of shares, debentures and loans. Public companies are listed on the stock exchange, and their shares can be traded at will. In the English Premier League (EPL) world-football competition most clubs are registered as public companies, their aim being to ensure access to a larger funding base. Like a private company, it can distribute dividends to shareholders. The benefit of the public company structure is that it allows access to large amounts of funds or capital. The cost is that it is subject to stringent reporting requirements, and must provide detailed reports for both its shareholders and appropriate government agencies.

A third type of company is the company limited by guarantee. In this case the investors in the business are liable only for the funds they have contributed. This structure is often used in situations where an entity is established to undertake a specific mission to generate revenue, but does not wish to distribute profits. While there are no restrictions on the ability of the company limited by guarantee to earn profits, (which is why commercially-oriented sport clubs find it an appropriate legal structure) it is not able to distribute its surplus to members, or issue shares. Companies limited by guarantee must use the word "limited" or the abbreviated "ltd" after their name. In addition the setup costs are high, and, because they must be registered under the *Corporations Act* in Australia, are required to disclose significant financial information. A majority of Australian Football League (AFL) clubs have adopted this legal structure.

Non-profit associations

The above business structures may be suitable for people wishing to either make money from sports, or to distribute the profits to its owners or shareholders. However the majority of sport organizations, unlike the privately owned professional sport teams in the USA, or most of the public-company-based football clubs in the EPL, are not interested in maximizing profits for their owners. Rather, they are more concerned with servicing their members, developing the sport, and improving their on-field performances. These types of organizations are consequently interested in having an organizational or business structure that gives non-profit status while at the same time protecting their members from creditor demands and litigation.

Governments now have in place legislation which allows community sport organizations to register as incorporated associations. This allows the members to be legally separated from the entity whilst allowing tax-free status by virtue of their non-profit operations whereby operating surpluses are reinvested in the development of its facilities, improvement in its service to members, and general development of the sport.

Profit or non-profit?

Sport organizations consequently take on a number of different legal forms, depending on what their aims are, and how structured and extensive they want their business to be. The most basic structure is to be a non-profit organization that has no legal identity separate from its owners. Small community sport clubs traditionally took on this form. In another instance, the organization

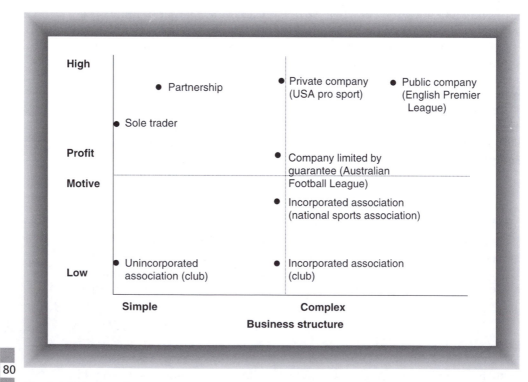

Figure 6.1 Legal Structures for Sport Organizations

may be profit-centered, but also a small sole trader or partnership. While sports clubs do not fit this model, it is particularly suitable for sport consulting firms, player agents, and sport retailers. The third possibility is to have an incorporated structure, but operate as a non-profit entity and therefore not be required to pay company tax. Most sport clubs and associations have adopted this structure, and some clubs in professional football leagues have also taken on a variation of this form by registering as companies limited by guarantee.

The final possibility is to adopt a company structure which enables an extension of funding options, and allows the club to optimize revenue and return dividends to shareholders. As noted previously this model characterizes most European and USA professional sport clubs. In Europe many are public companies, while in the USA most are small private businesses with only a few independent shareholders. The possibilities are illustrated in Figure 6.1.

Each of the structures in Figure 6.1 has its strengths and weaknesses, but as sport becomes more complex and commercialized there is growing pressure to become incorporated, and where the need to access a larger funding base is strong, to change to a private or public company structure.

Questions to consider

1. What is book-keeping all about and where and when did it originate?
2. From a commercial perspective why is it important to have a good set of books?
3. What makes for an effectively organized financial management system?
4. How does the reporting function differ from the management function when it comes to the financial management function?
5. What is the primary role of the International Accounting Standards Board?
6. Identify four important accounting principles and how they can be used to frame accounting structures and systems.
7. The financial management function can take place in many types of organizational settings. Identify the different legal forms an organization can take, and indicate which forms are most used in the sport industry.
8. Why are so many sport organizations set up as non-profit entities?
9. What are the strengths and weaknesses of setting up a sport organization as a company limited by guarantee?
10. Under what circumstances would it be appropriate to have a sport organization set up as a public company?

Further reading

For a discussion of the origin and evolution of accounting theory and practice see Giroux, G. (1999). *A Short History of Accounting and Business*, accessible at http://acct.tamu.edu/giroux/Shorthistory.html

For a more general historical study of the role of money in business and commercial affairs see Davies, G. (2005). *A History of Money from Ancient Times to Present Day*, 3rd Edition. University of Wales Press.

For a detailed examination of the formation and operation of partnerships and companies see Hoggett, J., Edwards, L. and Medlin, J. (2006). *Accounting*, 6th Edition. John Wiley and Sons, Chapter 15 (Partnerships) and Chapter 16 (Companies). The strengths and weaknesses of incorporating as an association or a company are discussed in Healey, D. (2003). *Sport and the Law*, 3rd Edition. University of New South Wales Press, Chapter 3 (The Legal Nature of Sporting Organisations).

For a sport-specific discussion of legal structures for sport organizations see Fried, G., Shapiro, S. and Deschriver, T. (2003). *Sport Finance. Human Kinetics*, Chapter 4 (Business Structure).

For a concise review of generally accepted accounting principles see Horngren, C., Harrison, W. and Bamber, L. (2002). *Accounting*, 5th Edition. Prentice Hall, Chapter 1 (Accounting and the Business Environment).

7

Setting up the accounts

Overview

This chapter will introduce the theory and practice of double entry book-keeping, making sure to distinguish between cash and accrual accounting. Financial data from fictitious sport club examples will be used to establish a simple set of accounts.

Sport and finance

As the earlier chapters have noted, significant segments of sport are now big business. At the same time it was also noted that most sport organizations are relatively small, and depend on the support of club members, volunteer officials, community businesses, and local government to sustain their operations. While high-profile professional sport leagues turn over hundreds, and in some cases, thousands of millions of dollars a year, the majority of sport clubs and associations are lucky to secure anymore than a million dollars to fund their operations. A majority of sport is really a form of small business. A suburban supermarket turns over more money than most sport clubs and associations.

Questions to ask

However, no matter what the scale or size of sport organizations, they all need to be managed in a sound and responsible manner. Many sport administrators do not feel comfortable handling money, or planning the financial affairs of clubs and associations, which often arises out of poor background knowledge and a lack of experience in managing complex financial issues. In practice, there are many financial questions that sport managers need to answer. They include:

1. What do we own?
2. What do we owe?
3. What did we earn?
4. What did we spend?
5. Did we make a profit?
6. Do we have enough cash to pay debts when they fall due?
7. How big is our interest bill?
8. Are we borrowing too much?
9. Did we improve upon last year?
10. How do we compare with other similar sport organizations?

There is also the problem of making sense of the vocabulary of accounting. The distinction between assets and liabilities is mostly clear, with assets amounting to all those things we own, and liabilities being all those things we owe to others. However, the distinction between tangible and intangible assets, and current and non-current liabilities may often be less clear. The concepts of owner's equity and shareholder's funds can also cause confusion, while further difficulties can arise when contrasting operating profit with net profit. When listening to how financial ratios operate the confusion may be compounded. The distinction between a working capital ratio and a debt to equity ratio usually needs careful explanation. A further spanner-in-the-works arises when the terms depreciation and amortization have to be explained and operationalized.

Financial records

A good first step in improving financial management skills is to become familiar with the fundamental data used to create financial records. While most sport organizations may not be as big as the average commercial business enterprise, they still engage in hundreds of exchanges and transactions every day. These transactions include the payment of wages and salaries to staff, the purchase of equipment, the sale of merchandise to members and fans, the refurbishment of offices, the ordering of stationery, and the receipt of monies from members, government, and sponsors. Also, these transactions are embedded in specific documents that include the following:

1. the purchase order, which is a statement requesting supply of a good or service in which payment is now (cash) or later (credit).
2. the invoice, which is a statement requesting payment for sale of a good or service.
3. the receipt, which is a statement that confirms payment for a good or service (this can also take the form of a paid invoice).

4. the bank statement, which is a statement of the trading account transactions that summarizes the movement of cash in and out of the business, and the amount of cash held in the cash account at a point in time.

While the above transactions are external to the organization (i.e. they involve an exchange with an outside entity), transactions can also be internal. A good example of an internal transaction is the depreciation of assets, where the wear and tear on computer equipment, and the speed with they become obsolete, make them less valuable as time goes on. This needs to be accounted for, and internal transactions provide a visible way of revealing these changes.

It is one thing to identify the transactions that will impact on the financial position of a club or association, but it is another thing to put a value on them. For the most part this issue is easily resolved since transactions involve the exchange of products (including tangible goods and less tangible services) for money. Money is both a medium of exchange and a store of value. It is the common currency by which all sorts of items (the services of a physiotherapist, or the purchase of sport equipment) can be priced and valued.

Once the transaction has been identified, priced, and valued, the next step is to record and classify these transactions. Without a system of recording and classifying the organization is left with a mass of data that means nothing more than things were either busy or slow. It is therefore crucial to set up systems for sorting transactions on the basis of some common themes or types. A simple first step is to distinguish between assets and borrowings, and revenue and expenses, and then to further divide them into sub categories or specific accounts. The final step is to compile the different accounts and create summary financial statements that reveal how the organization is going. Two sorts of reporting can occur here. First, it can be an internal report, which includes an analysis of specific issues like trends in salary costs, merchandise sales, membership income, maintenance expenses, and equipment costs. Second, it can be an external report, which is more general, and can take the form of a set of accounts comprising a profit and loss statement, balance sheet, and cash flow statement. These concepts will be covered in more detail in the following chapter.

Foundation principles of sound book-keeping

An additional thing that financial managers of sport organizations need to understand is the basics of double-entry book-keeping (briefly discussed in the previous chapter, and examined in more detail here). Once this step has been taken, the issues of how accounts are compiled, and how they can be used to construct a financial statement can be addressed. However, before this is done it is appropriate to look at the difference between a cash method of accounting and keeping the books, and the accrual method of keeping the books.

Cash method

Traditionally, most small sport clubs and associations operated using the cash accounting method where revenue and expenses are reported when they are actually received or paid. As a result, with the cash-based system, the revenue and expense patterns of the organization are an exact match with their cash flow pattern. So, under this approach, when a cheque is banked it is recorded as revenue, and when a cheque is written as payment to a creditor, it is recorded as an expense. The same goes for all cash-based transactions. As a result, the cash method of accounting is just a matter of recording all receipts and payments to the club or association over a period of time, and calculating the difference to see if there is a surplus or deficit. However, while the cash method is uncomplicated and appeals to our common sense, it does not accurately measure an organization's financial performance over specific time periods. Because the cash system is based on cash as it is spent or received, it can lead to quite inaccurate summaries of a sport organization's overall financial performance.

It can be quite misleading to record all payments or receipts for the period in which they actually occur, and then use them to measure current financial performance. Only those transactions directly relevant to the period under consideration should be included in the accounts for that period. In short, a list of cash receipts and cash payments is not a good measure of income earned and expenses incurred for that period. For example, using the cash method of book-keeping, if an organization were to pay a professional indemnity insurance premium of $5000 in advance (i.e. for the following year) it would be recorded as part of the current years' transactions (cash payment) despite the fact that the benefits would be obtained next year. Similarly, under the cash method of book-keeping, the purchase of a $6000 computer system would be recorded in the year it was bought (as a cash payment), even though it would provide benefits in many subsequent years as well. According to the cash method, expenses for the year would now total $11 000, although most of the benefits from these transactions would not be realized until the following years. On the revenues side, if club members paid $10 000 of their registration fees in advance (i.e. for next year), then, under the cash method, these monies would be recorded as cash received for the current year. The same result would occur if a sponsor wrote a $90 000 cheque for a 3-year arrangement commencing this year, and it was received and recorded in the current period. Under the cash method these two transactions produce an addition to revenues for this period of $100 000. But again this is misleading since only $30 000 was directly relevant to the current period. The cash method of book-keeping can therefore distort the real financial position of a sport organization by overstating the profit position if receipts are bunched in the current year, or understate it if payments are bunched in the current year. There must be a way of adjusting for these distortions.

Accrual method

In contrast, the accrual system is based on the notion that the real issue to be addressed is how to measure revenue earned for the current period, and to compare it to expenses incurred for the current period. This approach highlights two important principles. First, revenues and expenses need not involve the payment or receipt of cash at the immediate moment of transaction. Second, not all receipts and payments will relate to revenues and expenses for the current period. Instead, it is all about the use of resources to deliver a benefit or to impose a cost. So, under the accrual model of book-keeping, revenue is recognized when it is earned instead of when it is collected, and expenses are recognized when they are incurred instead of when they are paid for. The accrual system consequently provides more accurate details on the financial status of a sport organization than the cash-based system, and therefore is of more effective use for management decision-making.

However, it is also more complex than the cash accounting method. As already explained, with the accrual method expenses and revenues are identified independently of when cash is received or paid out. So, in the case of the $5000 insurance premium paid in advance, there needs to be a way of ensuring this $5000 is not recorded as an expense for the current year. Similarly, with the member income and sponsorship funds received in advance, there needs to be a way of making sure that it is not treated as an increase in revenue for the current year. The resolution to this problem is addressed in the following section on double-entry book-keeping. It will be shown that the insurance premium will be recorded as an asset under the heading of prepaid expense, while member and sponsor income will be recorded as a liability under the heading of income received in advance. But, more about this later.

In addition, under the accrual system revenue earned during a specific period must be matched with the expenses linked with that revenue, thus making revenue the driving force dictating the documentation of expenses. The chief purpose of the matching procedure is to ensure that an accurate picture of profit or loss for the period under review is reported. In order for the matching process to be as accurate as possible, recording adjustments are made prior to the preparation of financial statements. Consequently, a good initial step in improving financial management skills is to first understand how accounts are compiled, and second, identify the ways in which double-entry book-keeping can be used to construct a set of financial statements.

Processing transactions

To repeat, there are two basic reasons why it is important to keep records on a sport organization's financial transactions. The first is to monitor the organization's ongoing performance to ensure that costs are properly managed, and that income is sufficient to cover costs and pay bills when they fall due. The second provides a summary of its financial affairs to its stakeholders. For small sport clubs and associations there are few financial transactions,

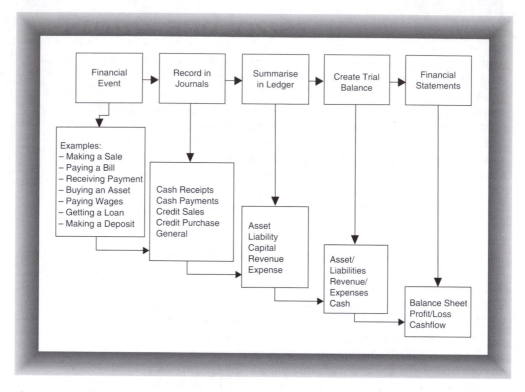

Figure 7.1 The Book-Keeping Process. (Adapted from: Smith and Stewart (1999))

leaving summaries of total receipts, and total payments as the only details to consider in calculating overall financial performance. However, other sport organizations are faced with a large number of daily transactions that influence both their profitability and wealth. They include not only commercial enterprises like fitness centers and gymnasiums, but also non-profit professional sporting clubs such as those in sport leagues. In these situations, transactions are recorded on a daily basis in journals which are subsequently totaled into ledgers, which in turn are compiled to form trial balances which form the basis for financial statements. The flow chart (Figure 7.1) illustrates this process.

Journals

To get the accounting process off the ground, transactions are recorded in chronological order, which are compiled as books or electronic files. Although financial events can be documented in a single all-encompassing journal, there are typically several subdivisions that can be used to record specific transactions. They include:

1. cash receipts journal which records all cash received;
2. cash payments journal which records all cash paid;
3. credit sales journal which records all sales of goods or services that are paid for by credit;

Table 7.1 Sample Journal Entry – Cash Payments. South Wales Indoor Polo Association

Item	Details	Amount ($)
1	Office stationery	25
2	Advertising	150
3	Postage paid envelopes	1500
4	Staff T-shirts	225
5	Promotional caps	300
		2200

Table 7.2 Sample Journal Entry – Cash Sales. North Shore Swim Center

Item	Details	Amount ($)
1	G. Hackett – full membership	550
2	L. Lenton – swim suit	50
3	T. Blair – gym membership	300
4	Ocean View City Council – corporate membership	20 000
5	J. Howard – protein powder	100
		21 000

4. credit purchase journal which records all purchases of goods or services bought with credit;
5. general journal which records purchase of assets other than stock on credit, and any other transaction that is not entered elsewhere.

These subdivisions are not always necessary, but the need for systematic record-keeping remains a fixed principle. Some simple examples of journal entries are listed in Tables 7.1 and 7.2.

Ledgers

The totals from journals are transferred to ledgers, which comprise a database of transactions grouped under a number of account categories. Moreover, for each account type there are two columns. The left-side column is designated as the debit column, while the right-side column is designated as the credit column. These accounts of credit and debit are typically represented by a T-account. The T-account includes debits on the left side and credits on the right side, as can be seen in Figure 7.2. It is important to note that debits and credits have nothing to do with gains and losses, or positive or negative balances.

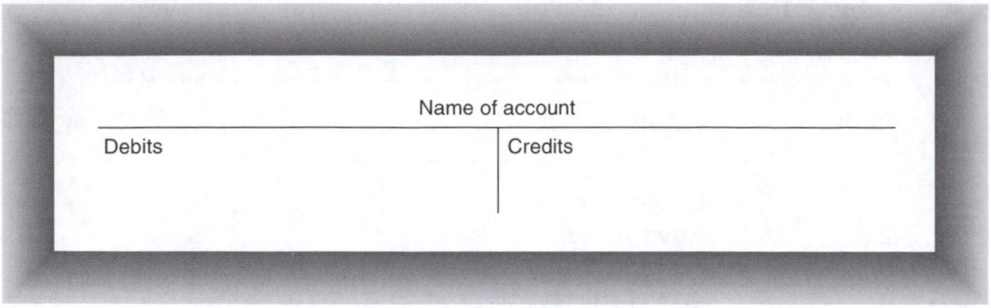

	Name of account	
Debits	Credits

Figure 7.2 The T-account

In order to understand how transactions are recorded in the T-accounts, it is necessary to understand the foundation principles of double-entry book-keeping. As indicated previously, it is built around the concept of debits and credits where a debit entry involves locating it on the left side of a ledger account, while a credit entry involves locating it on the right side of the account. In other words, debit equals a left-side entry, and credit equals a right-side entry. The other important thing to remember about double-entry book-keeping is that there are five standard groups of accounts. They are asset accounts; liability accounts; capital accounts; revenue accounts; and finally, expense accounts. The main features of each of these account types are listed below.

Account group 1: Assets

Assets are items of value owned by the business. They constitute a benefit to the business, and are categorized as follows:

1. Cash or money held in trading bank account.
2. Debtors or people who owe money to the business (e.g. purchased branded T-shirt but yet to pay) also known as accounts receivable.
3. Prepaid expense (e.g. paid for property insurance in advance).
4. Stock and merchandise (e.g. branded T-shirts for sale to members).
5. Furniture and equipment.
6. Investments.
7. Motor vehicle.
8. Land and buildings.

Assets can also be current or non-current (fixed).

Account group 2: Liabilities

Liabilities comprise the amounts owed to others by the business. They constitute a claim against the business and are categorized in the following manner.

1. Creditors or people who are owed money (e.g. purchased computer on credit) also known as accounts payable
2. Accrued payments or monies earmarked to pay future claims (e.g. provision for superannuation or employee sick leave)

3. Bank overdraft whereby the business is able to overdraw on its trading account
4. Short-term loans
5. Long-term loans.

Like assets, liabilities can be current or non-current.

Account group 3: Capital

Capital is the amount of funds invested in the business and is otherwise known as proprietorship or owners' equity.

1. Comprises the owners' contribution to the business.
2. Includes start up capital, retained profits and additional cash injections.

Owners' equity can change due to an injection of capital into the business, profits, losses, or when the owner draws money out of the business.

Account group 4: Revenue

Revenue comprises the amount earned through the business' trading activities, and includes sales, charges, and fees.

1. Can be cash and/or credit.
2. Focuses on earned revenue.
3. Monies received in advance are not included.

Account group 5: Expenses

Expenses comprise the costs associated with earning the revenue.

1. Focuses on incurred expenses, even when not yet paid for.
2. Expenses paid in advance are not included.

The most important rule in transferring records to the above ledger accounts is that for every debit entry there must be a corresponding credit entry, and for every credit entry there must be a corresponding debit entry. In other words, for every left-side entry there must be equivalent right-side entry. This means that the left-side totals must equal the right-side totals: hence the term double-entry book-keeping. All financial recording can be summarized using the equation $A = L + P$ where P is $[C + R - E - D]$. That is, assets or items of value owned (A) is always equal to liabilities or amounts owed to others (L), plus proprietorship (P) or the owner's investment. Proprietorship, or owners equity as it is often called, includes invested capital (C), revenue or amounts earned from trading (R), expenses or costs associated with earning revenue (E), and drawings that the owner may take out of the business (D). The equation can be rewritten as:

$$A = L + C + R - E - D$$

Table 7.3 Financial Recording Rules

Account	Increase	Decrease
Asset	Debit	Credit
Liability	Credit	Debit
Capital	Credit	Debit
Revenue	Credit	Debit
Expense	Debit	Credit

This states that assets will increase when borrowings, revenue and investment in the business increase, but fall if expenses increase and capital is drawn out of the business.

It is one thing to understand the above equation, and to appreciate how different transactions impact on each of the five different groups of accounts. However, it is another thing to know if that account should be debited or credited. For example, what happens to the cash-in-the-bank account when a sponsor's cheque arrives on the desk? The answer is contained within the internal logic of the double-entry book-keeping system, which provides a set of rules by which to process any transaction. These rules are listed in Table 7.3.

In using this table, two questions must be asked about each transaction that is being recorded. The first is what category of accounts does the transaction belong? For instance, will it impact on a liability account, or will it impact on an asset account? The second question to ask is will it be a debit entry or a credit entry? These rules confirm that whenever the transaction produces an increase in the level of assets and expenses it is debited (i.e. placed on the left-side of the ledger). On the other hand, when the transaction leads to an increase in liabilities, capital and revenue, it will have a credit (or right side of the ledger) entry.

The case of the Rolling Plains Tennis Club

These rules are used in recording transactions in the sample ledger for the fictitious Rolling Plains Tennis Club, which has been constructed from a single general journal. These journal entries are listed in Table 7.4.

These 10 journal entries must now be posted to the ledgers using the double-entry book-keeping rules listed above. As noted previously, the ledgers are

Table 7.4   Journal Entries for Rolling Plains Tennis Club

Transactions – July

1	Deposit of $20 000 from member-joining fees in business cheque account	11	Received payment for previous week's coaching clinic, to the value of $6000
3	Bought computer and printer for $2000 on credit	20	Paid for advertising in local paper for $400 in cash
4	Purchased office supplies (staplers, toner, etc.) on credit for $500	25	Sold photocopier for $200 cash
5	Paid insurance for members of $10 000 in cash	29	Bought new photocopier for $2500 on credit
7	Invoiced members for racquet re-stringing to the value of $600	30	Paid utilities bills totaling $1500 and rent of $2500

constructed around each of the five basic account types, which are assets, liabilities, capital, revenue and expenses. It is also important to note that every transaction will have equal and offsetting entries in the ledger account. That is, they will not only be debited into one account, but also credited into another account. This is why the accounts will always balance.

Table 7.5 identifies the ways in which each transaction will be processed. In the first instance member-joining fees has been treated as an injection of capital into the club. By applying the double-entry book-keeping recording rules, the capital account is credited (because it represents an increase) while the cash (asset) at bank account is debited (since the rules say this is done whenever an asset account increases). The office equipment and office supplies transactions both involve the purchase of assets on credit. Consequently, the office equipment (asset) account is debited in each case, but instead of crediting the cash at bank account, the accounts payable account is credited. This is because the items have been purchased on credit rather than cash. When payment is finally made, the accounts payable account will be debited, while the cash account will be credited.

The racquet re-string service constitutes earned revenue, even if the payment is late. In this case the revenue account is credited, while the accounts receivable (asset) account is debited. Had the invoice been immediately paid, then the cash account would have been debited instead of accounts receivable. When all of the journal entries have been transferred to the ledger under the double-entry method, the account balances will result (Table 7.6).

The next step is to create a trial balance, which is simply verification that equivalent debits and credits have been recorded in the accounts. Once this is done they form the basis for the construction of the financial statements. An example follows.

Table 7.5   Rolling Plains Tennis Club – Summary of Postings to Ledger

Date	Particulars	Debit ($)	Credit ($)
July 1	Cash at bank (A – increases) Capital from member-joining fee (C – increases) (member-joining fees)	20 000	20 000
3	Office equipment (A – increases) Accounts payable (L – increases) (purchased computer and printer on credit)	2000	2000
4	Office supplies (A – increases) Accounts payable (L – increases) (purchased office supplies on credit)	500	500
5	Insurance (E – increases) Cash at bank (A – decreases) (paid members' insurance)	10 000	10 000
7	Accounts receivable (A – increases) Service revenue (R – increases) (invoiced members for racquet re-stringing)	600	600
11	Cash at bank (A – increases) Service revenue (R – increases) (payment received for coaching clinic)	6000	6000
20	Advertising (E – increases) Cash at bank (A – decreases) (newspaper advertisement)	400	400
25	Cash at bank (A – increases) Office equipment (A – decreases) (sale of photocopier)	200	200
29	Office equipment (A – increases) Accounts payable (L – increases) (purchase of photocopier on credit)	2500	2500
30	Utilities bills and rent (E – increases) Cash at bank (A – decreases) (utilities expenses)	4000	4000

The trial balance

Trial balances are generally completed at the end of each month, and form the basis for financial statements. In this case, some simple calculations can be made to establish the profit and losses incurred by the club, and in addition the balance of assets and liabilities.

So, once the trial balance has been completed we are left with a set of accounts that provides a picture of the Rolling Plains Tennis Club's performance (Table 7.7). The revenue account shows an aggregate figure of $6600,

Table 7.6 Rolling Plains Tennis Club – Ledger

Date	Particulars	Debit ($)	Credit ($)	Balance ($)
	Assets			
July 1	Cash at bank (*A* – increases)	20 000		20 000
5	Cash at bank (*A* – decreases)		10 000	10 000
11	Cash at bank (*A* – increases)	6000		16 000
20	Cash at bank (*A* – decreases)		400	15 600
25	Cash at bank (*A* – increases)	200		15 800
30	Cash at bank (*A* – decreases)		4000	11 800
3	Office equipment (*A* – increases)	2000		13 800
4	Office supplies (*A* – increases)	500		14 300
25	Office equipment (*A* – decreases)		200	14 100
29	Office equipment (*A* – increases)	2500		16 600
7	Accounts receivable (*A* – increases)	600		17 200 Dr
	Liabilities			
3	Accounts payable (*L* – increases)		2000	15 200
4	Accounts payable (*L* – increases)		500	14 700
29	Accounts payable (*L* – increases)		2500	12 200
	Capital			
1	Members' equity (joining fee) (*C* – increases)		20 000	−7800 Cr
	Revenue			
7	Re-stringing (*R* – increases)		600	−8400
11	Coaching clinic (*R* – increases)		6000	−14 400 Cr
	Expenses			
5	Insurance (*E* – increases)	10 000		−4400
20	Advertising (*E* – increases)	400		−4000 Cr
30	Utilities bills and rent (*E* – increases)	4000		0
		46 200	46 200	

while expenses are $14 400, thereby creating an operating deficit of $7800. Over the same period the asset groups of accounts has a balance of $17 200 comprising cash in bank $11 800 ($26 200 less $14 400), office equipment ($4800), and accounts receivable ($600). Liabilities totaled $5000 and invested capital owners' equity was $2000. The accounting equation will therefore contain the following figures.

$$A(17\,200) = L(5000) + C(20\,000) + R(6600) - E(14\,400)$$

In summary, the Rolling Plains Tennis Club has made a loss on its operations so far, and its asset value has fallen from $20 000 (the initial injection of funds) to $17 200, its current balance. This is not a good trend, and it may be reason to secure more revenue to improve its position.

Table 7.7 Rolling Plains Tennis Club – Trial Balance

Account Title	Debit ($)	Credit ($)
Assets		
Cash at bank	26 200	14 400
Office equipment	5000	200
Accounts receivable	600	
Liabilities		
Accounts payable		5000
Capital		
Members equity (joining fee)		20 000
Revenue		
Re-stringing		600
Coaching clinic		6000
Expenses		
Insurance	10 000	
Advertising	400	
Utilities bills and rent	4000	
	46 200	46 200

The next step

Once the accounts have been systematically compiled it is then possible to produce a set of financial statements that provide a clear picture of how the club, association, or league is performing from a monetary perspective. The three key financial statements that need to be examined are the profit and loss statement, the balance sheet, and the cash flow statement. They will be discussed in more detail in the following chapter.

Questions to consider

1. Why is sound financial management so important to all sport organizations, no matter how large or small?
2. What are the key financial questions that all sport organizations need to ask in order to understand their overall financial well-being?
3. What financial records are the building blocks of all accounting systems?
4. What are three core financial statements, and what do they aim to measure?

5. Distinguish between the cash method of accounting and the accrual method of accounting. Why is the accrual method a superior system of book-keeping and accounting?
6. Describe the flow of a financial transaction from raw data to its absorption into a financial statement.
7. Explain the accounting equation.
8. Identify the five core account types and their relationship to the accounting equation.
9. What is meant by the term double-entry book-keeping and explain how it is linked to the accounting equation?
10. Construct a table that explains how transactions will be recorded using the double-entry book-keeping system.
11. Succinctly review the current financial position of the Rolling Plains Tennis Club. What has it done well, and not so well? How might it go about improving its financial performance?

Further reading

For an easy to follow discussion of basic accounting systems and processes and the basics of double-entry book-keeping see Hoggett, J., Edwards, L. and Medlin, J. (2006). *Accounting*, 6th Edition. Wiley. Another useful reading on the application of double-entry book-keeping is Horngren, C., Harrison, W. and Bamber, L. (2002). *Accounting*, 5th Edition. Prentice Hall, Chapter 2 (Recording Business Transactions).

A text that distils the basic accounting concepts is Hart, L. (2006). *Accounting Demystified: A Self Teaching Guide*, McGraw Hill. A good starting point is Chapter 8 (Debit or a Credit) which covers debits and credits. Chapter 9 (A Few Simple Transactions) puts the double-entry book-keeping principles into practice.

A sport-specific discussion of foundation financial management concepts is contained in Fried, G., Shapiro, S. and Deschriver, T. (2003). *Sport Finance*. Human Kinetics, Chapter 2 (Basic Financial Concepts).

8 Understanding the accounts

Overview

This chapter will provide a detailed discussion of three key financial statements. They are the Balance Sheet, Profit and Loss Statement, and the Cash Flow Statement. This will be followed by three fictitious cases on the issue of setting up and interpreting accounts. These cases will be used to highlight the key features of balance sheets, profit and loss statements, and the cash flow statements. Model answers are supplied at the end of each simulation.

Introduction

As indicated previously, the effective management of any sport organization requires not only a sound knowledge of the principles of financial management, but also the support of a financial recording and reporting system that allows a quick and easy reading of the club or association's financial health. It is now taken for granted that a professionally managed sport organization will produce three integrated annual financial reports. The first document is a statement of performance, or profit and loss, which reports on the revenues earned for the period, and the expenses incurred. The second document is a statement of position, or balance sheet, which reports on the current level of assets, liabilities, and equity. The third document is a statement of cash flows, which identifies the cash movements in and out of the organization. The cash flow statement is divided into activities related to day-to-day operations, activities that involve the sale and purchase of assets, and activities that involve the securing and borrowing of funds and their repayment. Each of the above three statements provides an important perspective on the financial operations of the organization, and they are discussed in more detail below.

The balance sheet

We are now in a position to say more about the balance sheet and what it means. In Chapter 7 it was noted that the accounting equation is the foundation of the balance sheet. Assets are placed on the left hand side of the balance sheet, while liabilities are placed on the right hand side. Proprietorship or owners' equity is also located on the right hand side. And, as demonstrated in Chapter 7, it will always balance. In short, the balance sheet gives a clear picture of a sport organization's wealth by contrasting its assets (things it owns) with its liabilities (things it owes). The difference between assets and liabilities is known as the net worth of the business, and in the balance sheet the term net assets is also used to identify the difference between assets and liabilities. The balance sheet can therefore be seen as a snapshot of the wealth of a sport club or association at a point in time.

The balance sheet also indicates how the assets of the organization have been funded. It can be through equity (i.e. the capital of the owner/s) or from borrowed funds from some other organization or individual. However, not all assets are the same. They can be broken down into a number of categories. So too can liabilities. As a result a balanced sheet will be set up to provide a clear picture of the level of both current and non-current assets, and current and non-current liabilities. The level of owners' equity or shareholders' capital (or accumulated funds as it is usually called in non-profit organization statements) will also be identified in the balance sheet since it is effectively the difference between the two. This is because assets can be accumulated through either the owners' capital, reinvested profits, or borrowed funds.

Assets

As noted above, assets are all those things owned by an organization. To put it more technically, they constitute resources owned and controlled by an entity from which future benefits are expected to flow. The assets of a balance sheet are not only broken down into their various categories, but they are also listed according to their degree of liquidity, with the most liquid coming first and the less liquid coming later in the statement. The measure of an asset's liquidity is the ease with which it can be converted to cash, and all those assets which can easily be converted are listed under the current assets heading. The most frequently cited current assets are cash in bank (which is stating the obvious), accounts receivable or creditors (which as we noted in Chapter 7 include those short-term invoices or bills for which payment has not yet been received), investments in the share market (which can be converted to cash through quick sale), and stocks of material and merchandise (which at a pinch can be sold for cash). Items like prepaid expenses (i.e. bills paid in advance) can also be included here. The level of current assets is an important indicator of the financial health of a sport organization since it is the means by which bills are paid, and creditors' demands for payment are met.

Assets are also listed as fixed or non-current. These assets include everything that cannot be easily and quickly converted to cash. Some stock and materials will be listed here when they do not have high turnover. The main items will be all those tangible or material assets that are essential for generating revenue, but are difficult to sell at an appropriate price in the short term. These items include office furniture and equipment (including all sorts of sports equipment), motor vehicles, buildings and land. Building improvements (e.g. a stadium upgrade) are also examples of fixed assets. The main categories of assets are listed in Table 8.1.

The balanced sheet of a sporting organization can be complicated by a number of other factors. For example, assets can either increase in value over time (i.e. appreciate) or decrease in value over time (i.e. depreciate). Property, stocks and shares, and various scarce artifacts and memorabilia are particularly prone to increase in value. On the other hand, there are other assets that can lose value quickly, and includes those things that incur constant use and wear and tear, or become obsolete, or both. Moreover, there are assets that, while not tangible, clearly add value to the organization, and should be accounted for. Accountants have recognized these financial facts of life for many years, and have consequently devised strategies for managing these phenomena.

Table 8.1 Balance Sheet – Types of Assets

Asset Category	Degree of Liquidity	Example
Cash in bank	High (current)	Trading account balance
Accounts receivable	Medium (current)	Monies owed by club members
Prepaid expense	Medium (non current)	Payment of next year's insurance
Company shares	Medium (current)	Ownership of shares
Inventory	Medium (current)	Stock of sport equipment
Office equipment	Low (non-current)	Computer system
Other equipment	Low (non-current)	Office furniture
Motor vehicle	Low (non-current)	Ownership of vehicle
Property	Low (non-current)	Ownership of office building
Building improvements	Low (non-current)	Stadium renewal

Depreciation

Depreciation is based on the principle that all non-current assets represent a store of service potential that the organization intends to use over the life of the asset. Assets therefore have a limited life as a result of their ongoing wear and tear and probable obsolescence. Accounting for depreciation is the process whereby the decline in the service potential of an asset, such as a motor vehicle, is progressively brought to account as a periodic charge against revenue. That is, the asset is devalued in response to its purchase price or market value, and offset against income. In order to allocate the cost of the asset to the period in which it is used, an estimate must be made of the asset's useful life. This will usually be less than its physical life. For example, in the case of a motor vehicle, it may be decided that after 3 years it will not be operating as efficiently and therefore will be worth less after this period, even though it is still running. If an asset has a residual, or resale value, then this amount will be subtracted from the asset cost to establish the actual amount to be depreciated.

The simplest method for depreciating an asset is the straight-line or prime-cost method. This method allocates an equal amount of depreciation to each full accounting period in the asset's useful life. The amount of depreciation for each period is determined by dividing the cost of the asset minus its residual value by the number of periods in the asset's useful life. Take for example, a computer system that was purchased for $11 000. It is anticipated that the system will have a resale value of $1000 after 5 years. Using the straight-line method of depreciation the annual depreciation will be $2000. This figure is obtained by dividing the difference between the purchase price and the residual value ($10 000) by the 5 years of anticipated useful life. This annual depreciation will then be posted as an expense in the profit and loss statement for the following 5 years. This process of spreading the cost of an asset over a specific period of time is called amortization. The idea behind this process is that there needs to be a clear way of showing the relationship between spread of benefits from an asset's use and the costs involved in creating those benefits.

Asset valuation

Asset values can also be changed to reflect current conditions and prices. Unless otherwise stated, assets are valued at their purchase price which is known as historical cost. However, many assets particularly land and buildings can increase in value over time. Unless this is periodically done, the true values of assets can be seriously understated. This problem can be overcome by a revaluation of the assets by a certified valuer, with a note to this effect accompanying the annual statement of financial operations and standing.

Intangible assets

For sporting clubs there is also the issue of how intangible assets should be treated, and how they can be valued. Intangible assets are by their very nature difficult to quantify, and their definition as non-monetary assets without

101

physical substance merely confirms their ambiguity. A good starting point is to note that there are two types of intangible assets. They are first, identifiable intangibles that include things like trademarks, brand names, mastheads, franchises, licenses, and patents. Some of these intangibles like franchises, licenses, and patents have a purchase price, and they can be amortized over their expected life. The second type of intangible assets is labeled as unidentifiable, the best example being goodwill. Goodwill arises from a combination of things like superior management, customer confidence, and a favorable location. Goodwill is seen to possess value since it can produce future economic benefits that cannot be directly attributable to some other material asset. Goodwill is relevant to sport organizations, since the ability to attract fans often originates from often vague, but strong historical attachments between club image and fan identity. While few clubs have attempted to identify a goodwill value, it is often visible when a privately owned team is sold to a new owner. The difference between the sale price and the asset value of the team will in large part be attributable to the goodwill factor.

Players as assets

Professional sporting clubs are also confronted by the issue of how players might be counted as assets, and, if they can, how they will be valued. This problem arises in professional sport leagues where teams are able to trade players through a transfer market. In English Premier League (EPL), where large transfer fees are par-for-the-course, this issue is dealt with by listing the transfer fee as an asset, and amortizing the fee over the contract life of the player. Take for instance Manchester United Football Club (MUFC) player Ronaldo, who transferred from Portugal in 2003. His transfer fee was just under GBP 12 million, and he signed with MUFC for 5 years. Using the straight-line method of depreciation his fee would be amortized at around GBP 2.4 million a year, and charged as an expense for each of the 5 years of his contract. After 2 years he would therefore be valued at GBP 7.2 (i.e. 12 less 4.8) million. At the end of his 5-year contract his value would be technically zero. However, in practice his transfer price would still be positive, unless he was cut down by injury. Indeed, if he improved over this time, his transfer fee could even be higher than his purchase price of GBP 12 million. The value of a sample of MUFC players is listed in Table 8.2.

Under this arrangement MUFC can therefore allocate a proportion of players' transfer fees as an annual expense, thereby reducing its taxable income. The bonus here is that unlike other assets that lose value over time and are depreciated, many players will in fact have increased in value. However, the balance sheet will show them as having zero value at the end of their contract. Under these conditions clubs assets will be seriously undervalued.

Liabilities

Simply put, liabilities are those things that an organization owes others. To be more exact, they are the present obligations of an entity which, when settled,

Table 8.2 Manchester United Football Club – Player Valuations 2005

Player	Contract period (years)	Transfer fee cost (GBP million)	Annual expense charge (GBP million)
Ferdinand	7	31	4.5
Howard	6	2.5	0.4
Smith	5	7	1.4
Rooney	6	25	4.2
Ronaldo	5	12	2.4

Source: Manchester United Football Club (2005: 13).

involve the outflow of economic resources. Like assets, liabilities can be categorized into current and non-current. Current liabilities included monies that are owed to people in the immediate future for services and goods they have supplied. For example a club may have purchased some sporting equipment on credit for which payment is due in 30 to 60 days. This is called accounts payable or debtors. Other current liabilities include short-term borrowings, member income received in advance, and taxes payable in the short term. Income received in advance is an interesting case because it is often intuitively viewed as revenue or assets and not a liability. However, under the accrual accounting model it is clearly not relevant to the current flows of revenue and expenses. But as monies received it has to be accounted for. So, what happens is that it is debited to cash in bank and credited as something owed to members in the future. That is, it is a liability which is listed as income received in advance.

Non-current liabilities include long-term borrowings, mortgage loans, deferred tax liabilities, and long-term provisions for employees like superannuation entitlements. The accumulation of liabilities is not of itself a problem, so long as the debt is used to build income-earning assets. However, if increasing debt is associated with losses rather than profits, then the gap between assets and liabilities will increase. In some Australian Football League (AFL) clubs the level of liabilities exceeds the value of their assets. For example in 2005 the net worth of the Western Bulldogs and Carlton Blues clubs was both negative and in excess of AUD 5 million in each instance. These figures indicate a lengthy period where expenses constantly exceeded revenues, and assets were used to pay debt. In the long run these sorts of trends are unsustainable.

Balance sheets can say a lot about a sport organization's financial health. In the following chapter this will be discussed in more detail. However, balance sheets do not tell us much about a sport club's earnings, profits and losses over the course of a month, quarter, or year. For this information we must turn to the profit and loss statement, or as it is often called in the non-profit area of sport, the income statement.

Profits and losses

It is not just a matter of examining a sport organization's assets and liabilities at a point in time in order to diagnose its financial health, it is also crucial to shift one's attention to the financial operation of sport clubs and associations over time. There are two types of financial statements that look at the movement of cash and earnings in and out of the organization. They are first the profit and loss statement, and second the cash flow statement.

The first thing to be said about the profit and loss statement is that it can go under a number of names. It can also be called an income statement, which is the non-profit sector terminology, and is also referred to as a financial statement of performance. The point to remember about most sport organizations is that they do not focus on profits and losses, but rather surpluses and deficits. In any case, it does not alter the fact that these statements look at the revenue earned during a period (say 3 or 12 months) and compare it with the expenses incurred in generating the revenue. Profit and loss statements are straightforward to compile, and moderately easy to understand, but there are some tricky areas that need to be discussed.

The first point to make is that while profit and loss statements contain many cash movements, they do not accurately represent the total cash movements in and out of the organization, since they are essentially about earned income and incurred expenses. As a result they will include many transactions that do not include the movement of cash. As noted in Chapter 7, revenue can be earned, while the cash may come much later. But it is still a revenue item that needs to be identified in the profit and loss statement. For example, a sport consulting business may have completed a strategic planning exercise for a large national sport association, and invoiced it for $50 000. If, at the end of the accounting period, the invoice has not been paid, it will still be included in the profit and loss statement as income. The adjustment or offset in the accounts will be an equivalent (i.e. $50 000) increase (or debit) in the accounts receivable asset account. If the invoice had been immediately paid, the adjustment would have been made as an increase (or debit) of $50 000 to the cash in bank asset account.

Revenue, or income as it is frequently called, is typically divided into operating and non-operating items. Operating items include all those revenues like member income and merchandise sales that provide the funds to support the day-to-day running of the club or association. Non-operating items include funds that are irregular, or even out of the ordinary. An asset sale, a special government grant or a large donation are examples of non-operating income. As indicated in Chapters 1 to 3, sport organization revenues have expanded dramatically over recent years, but for the non-professional clubs the main sources are member fees, gate receipts, government grants, fundraising activities, and sponsors.

Expenses should also be treated cautiously. The profit and loss statement should include all incurred expenses rather than just paid expenses. Buying something on credit or by cash is an expense. On the other hand, paying for something that will not be used until next year, for example, should not be listed as an expense for the period under consideration. It is an asset (i.e. a prepaid expense). For example, rental or insurance paid in advance involves a movement of cash out of the club or association, but does not constitute an expense incurred for the current period. From an accrual accounting perspective it is credited to cash account (money goes out) but will be debited as a prepaid expense since it constitutes a benefit for later use.

Depreciation

Depreciation is another expense issue that has to be dealt with. As indicted in the early part of this chapter, depreciation is an estimate of the wear and tear of working assets. In an office setting, computers are quickly depreciated for two reasons. First, they are heavily used, and second, they quickly become out of date and obsolete. Depreciation is therefore recognized as an expense and should be included in a profit and loss statement. Depreciation can be calculated in a number of ways, the most simple being the straight-line method. If, for example, a motor vehicle is purchased for $30 000 has an estimated life of 5 years, and no residual value, then the depreciation expense for the following 5 years will be $6000 per annum. Some sporting club finance managers make the mistake of listing the full cost of the motor vehicle in year 1 as an expense, but this is clearly misleading. The correct way to treat this transaction is to list it as an asset, and then depreciate (i.e. amortize) it over its estimated lifetime. Interest-paid and interest-earned also appear on profit and loss statements. Interest paid will be classified as an expense while interest received will be classified as revenue.

Operating versus net profits

As already noted, when analyzing profit and loss statements it is important to distinguish between operating profit (or surplus) and net profit (or surplus). The differences between these two terms comprise abnormal revenue and expenses, and extraordinary revenue and expenses. A transaction will be classified as abnormal if it is a regular occurrence, but in a specific case is significantly higher than normal. In the case of a sporting club an abnormal item might be an accelerated depreciation of office equipment, or a supplementary government grant. A transaction will be classified as extraordinary if it is a significant transaction, and does not regularly occur. A sporting club example includes a fine for breaching a salary cap regulation (this happens frequently in the Australian Football League (AFL) and the National Rugby League (NRL)), or the sale of an asset (this occurs in the English Premier League (EPL), where players can be traded under certain conditions).

Operating profit does not include the abnormal and extraordinary items, and is confined to those transactions that are directly related to day-to-day activities that regularly recur over the standard accounting cycle. So, operating profit is the difference between operating income and operating expenses. Net profit is something else again, and will take into account all abnormal and extraordinary items. If the sport club happens to be part of a profit-making entity, then it may be required to pay tax on its profits. This item will be subtracted from operating profit to get to a net profit figure.

Table 8.3 Profit and Loss Statement Template

Item	Amount ($)	Total ($)
Operating income		
Member fees	50 000	
Events	10 000	
Grants	30 000	
Total operating income		90 000
Operating expenses		
Administration	50 000	
Events	20 000	
Insurance	10 000	
Total operating expenses		80 000
Operating profit		10 000
Non-operating income		
Special government grant	10 000	
Non-operating expenses		
Depreciation	20 000	
Net profit		0

Depreciation is also frequently listed as a non-operating item and can also make a significant difference to the level of profit. An operating profit can be transformed into a net loss by the inclusion of depreciation as a non-operating expense. Sometimes claims are made that depreciation can distort the real profit of a sport organization, but in fact the opposite is the case. Depreciation is a legitimate expense since it takes into account that amount of assets used up to generate revenue. In the context of the above discussion a typical profit and loss or income statement is illustrated in Table 8.3.

Cash flow

We can now move on to the cash flow statement. It should be apparent that profit and loss statements do not give a clear picture of the movement of cash in and out of a sporting club or association. Cash flow statements aim to fill this gap by listing all movements of cash under three main headings. These headings are operating activities, investing activities, and financing activities. The aim here is to get a picture of the net inflow and outflow of cash, and the extent to which a club or association is able to meet its cash payment obligations. This is an important issue, since without sufficient cash to pay bills when they fall due, there is the lingering possibility that creditors will take legal action to ensure payment. This may result in insolvency and bankruptcy.

Table 8.4 Cash Flow Statement Template

	Cash In	Cash Out
Operating activities		
Member fees	X	
Sponsor income	X	
Payment of salaries		X
Investing activities		
Sale of shares	X	
Purchase of computer		X
Financing activities		
Long-term bank loan	X	
Repayment of loan		X

The transactions that are included in the operating activity section include all those day-to day activities that are required to keep the organization running. They include wages and salaries (cash out) and payment for supplies (cash out) on one hand, and membership income (cash in) and government grants (cash in) on the other. Good financial management will aim to ensure that the cash coming from operating activities will exceed the cash going out, although a short-term net cash outflow may not be all that serious.

Investing activity transactions include all those things that involve the purchase and sale of assets. The sale of assets will be associated with cash inflow, while the purchase of assets will produce an outflow of cash. The purchase and sale of office equipment and property of various sorts will fall under the investing heading, and so too will the purchase and sale of stocks, shares, and debentures. While the sale of assets can generate a quick supply of cash, it will also deplete the organization of income earning resources, so a balance needs to be struck to ensure that crucial assets are not depleted. On the other hand, the purchase of assets immediately absorbs cash, and it is therefore important to monitor the amount of cash being used for this purpose.

Financing activities involve all those things that involve the procurement of equity and borrowing of funds on one hand, and the withdrawal of funds and repayment of borrowings on the other. An increase in cash holding can come from loans, bonds, mortgages, debentures, and other borrowings, while a fall in cash holding will come from the repayment of loans and the redemption of debentures. A typical list of cash flow items is listed in Table 8.4.

A cash flow statement provides a clear and concise picture of how cash is used internally, and where it goes externally. It also signals the level of liquidity and the ease with which cash payments are supported by cash reserves. A chronic net cash outflow on operating activities is cause for concern, since it is likely to lead to asset sales or borrowings being used to finance the cash deficit. And, as was noted previously, this can lead to a fall in club or association net worth, and threaten its long-term viability.

The case of Global Sport Enterprises

The following fictitious case provides for the construction of a simple balance sheet. It starts with a series of transactions which have to be ordered and sorted. The final requirement is to construct a simple set of accounts that reveals how much was earned, and how successful the business has been. The case revolves around Derek Deadpan, an entrepreneurial young man, who saw the opportunities that were emerging in the sport industry, and after completing a short course in *Visionary Decision Making* at the local technical education college, decided to set himself up as a sport management consultant and retailer. He had saved $20 000 from his job as a chef at the local railway hotel, and put it all in his newly established trading account under the modest business name of Global Sport Enterprise (GSE).

Derek was aware that image was everything, and therefore set about setting up an office with the latest computer technology and office furniture. He spent $5000 on a personal computer and color-last printer, and another $4000 on an elegant teak desk, Italian-designed workbench, and lounge chairs. Derek paid cash for these items.

Derek quickly got some work with the newly formed Wombat Downs Men's Synchronized Swimming Association (WDMSSA) in which he was required to promote its programs in regional schools and sporting clubs. Derek was able to attract interest and support from local bowls clubs, where many of the men wanted something more athletic and aesthetically pleasing. WDMSSA paid him handsomely for his promotional services. The only problem was that he would not be getting any payment until early in the following year. The promotional work was priced at $10 000.

The constant traveling by bus began to irritate Derek, so he decided to purchase a motor vehicle for the business. An Audi was the obvious choice, since it provided the status that Derek was keen to project to his clients. However he could only afford a small second-hand van. Derek's bank manager was generous, and lent him $20 000 over 5 years to help finance the purchase of a van, which was ready to drive away. Derek used $5000 of his trading account funds to allow him to purchase the $25 000 van.

Derek also decided to get into the merchandising field, and bought $2000 worth of branded T-shirts. The T-shirt purchase was done on credit, and did not have to be paid for until the following year. That was the good news. The bad news was that Derek was not able to sell any of the T-shirts. He had a quality garment, but no sales. Derek also found out that the van needed maintenance to the tune of $5000. He did not have to pay cash for this work since his brother, who was a mechanic, gave him 6 months to pay. It was not a good time for Derek.

However, Derek's luck changed when he was offered a job organizing the Darts Grand Prix Series for the Regional Darts Association. This was Derek's most exciting task to date, and involved running events in the saloon bars of suburban hotels. This was a successful operation, since he was able to negotiate a sponsorship deal with a weight-loss center. He secured a healthy commission from the deal, and from this point on things got progressively better. Derek went on to organize a triathlon for non-swimmers, and an indoor beach volleyball competition. Overall, Derek earned revenues of $90 000 for the year from the darts, triathlon, and beach volleyball programs. He also incurred expenses of $30 000 in running the programs. All the revenues were received as cash payments, while all expenses were paid for in cash at the time they were incurred.

Derek decided that in view of his ordinary year and his declining cash reserves, he would deposit most of the profits in the trading account, and therefore keep it in the business. At the same time, he creamed off $20 000 from the profit (in the form of drawings) for his personal use. Derek has asked you to help him diagnose the financial health of GSE. He wants you to draft up a balance sheet in order to decide what his asset base is, and if his sport consulting business is better off than at the end of his first year of operation than it was at the beginning.

The model answers are listed in Tables 8.5 to 8.11. They are organized around each of the five core-account categories where each transaction has the appropriate debit and credit entries.

Table 8.5 Model Answer – GSE Asset Accounts

Account name	Debit ($)	Item	Credit ($)	Item	Balance ($)
Cash	20 000	Invoice	5000	Computer	
	90 000	Consulting	4000	Desk	
			5000	Vehicle	
			30 000	Consulting	
			20 000	Drawings	46 000
Accounts receivable	10 000	Fees			10 000
Prepaid expenses	0				0
Office equipment/	5000	Computer			
supplies	4000	Desk			9000
Motor vehicle	25 000	Vehicle 1			25 000
Other assets	2000	T-shirts			2000
Total assets					92 000

Table 8.6 Model Answer – GSE Liability Accounts

Account Name	Debit ($)	Item	Credit ($)	Item	Balance ($)
Accounts payable			2000	T-shirts	
			5000	Maintenance	7000
Short-term loan			0		0
Long-term loan			20 000	Vehicle	20 000
Other liabilities			0		0
Total liabilities					27 000

Table 8.7 Model Answer – GSE Revenue Accounts

Account Name	Debit ($)	Credit ($)	Balance ($)
Merchandise		0	0
Coaching		0	0
Consulting		90 000	90 000
Promotions		10 000	10 000
Total revenue			100 000

Table 8.8 Model Answer – GSE Expense Accounts

Account Name	Debit ($)	Credit ($)	Balance ($)
Office supplies	0		0
Wages and salaries	0		0
Advertising	0		0
Consulting	30 000		30 000
Maintenance	5000		5000
Total expenses			35 000

Table 8.9 Model Answer – GSE Capital Account

Account Name	Debit ($)	Credit ($)	Balance ($)
Investment		20 000	
Drawings	20 000		
Total capital			0

By applying the accounting equation to the above balances, the following relationships will result.

Assets ($92 000) equals liabilities ($27 000) plus revenue ($100 000) minus expenses ($35 000) plus capital ($20 000) minus drawings ($20 000). This can be expressed as:

■ A (92 000) = L (27 000) + R (100 000) − E (35 000) + C (20 000) − D (20 000).

In other words Derek produces an operating profit of $65 000, which is the difference between the revenue ($100 000) and expenditure ($35 000). This can be shown as:

■ OP (65 000) = R (100 000) − E (35 000).

Coincidentally a net worth of $65 000 resulted. Net worth is the difference between the total assets ($92 000) and total liabilities ($27 000). This can be expressed as:

- NW (65 000) = A (92 000) − L (27 000).

The case of Hot-Shot Events

This fictitious case requires the construction of a profit and loss statement. It looks at earned revenues and incurred expenses, and makes a distinction between operating and net profit. It focuses on Claudia Cakebread who has been managing her own event management business, Hot-Shot Events (HSE) for 5 years, and reckoned that this year was pretty good for her.

Claudia's first event was a sport management seminar that she held at the new multi-million dollar Convention Center at the Blue Lakes campus of Twin Peaks University. The five speakers were paid $200 each, and the cost of hiring the Convention Center ended up being $1000 a day. It was a 2-day conference, and this also involved having to arrange catering which cost another $2000 per day. Other incidental costs amounted to $1000. The conference was a raging success. One hundred people attended, and each paid $100 for the privilege of hearing Tiger Woods talk about golf being the new world game. Claudia was laughing all the way to the bank.

Her next event was the annual Blue Lakes community fun run and triathlon. She paid $20 an hour for casual staff, who put in a total of 100 hours for the day. Drink stations and various other participant support services cost another $2000. She was relieved to know that 200 participants had paid $50 each to enter the event. However it was not at all good news, since the sponsor, Trustme Real Estate withdrew at the last minute, and the $2000 promise did not eventuate. She also had to pay the St Johns Ambulance Brigade and a security company $5000 for their services.

At the beginning of the year, Claudia also purchased a new computer system for $8000. She was advised that the computer would have a useful life of 4 years and a resale value of zero. She was also advised to depreciate the computer using the straight-line method. Claudia also employed a contract office administrator who was paid an hourly rate of $20. The administrator's total working hours amounted to 300 over the year.

During the year Claudia received a one-off $4000 grant from the government to assist the development of junior sport in the local district. She also got a letter from the Blue Lakes Convention Center manager, advising that a $4000 penalty was imposed for damages to the facility. It had to be paid immediately. Around the same time, Claudia also received an advance payment of $5000 from the Desert Springs Underwater Hockey Association for a strategic planning job she was contracted to do next year. She was very happy to get this payment since she had a bit of a cash flow problem.

Claudia continued to act as a player agent, and had a stable of basket-ballers, baseballers, and footballers. She charged 1 percent commission on all contracts, and during the year she negotiated contracts to the value of $500 000, which gave a return of $5000. Toward the end of the year Claudia decided to pay the next financial year's professional indemnity insurance of $20 000. She had forgotten to take it out this year.

Claudia wants help in putting together a consolidated profit and loss statement using a number of line items. You have been invited to construct a profit and loss statement for HSE making sure that it includes only revenue earned and incurred expenses. Claudia also wants the statement to distin-guish between operating profit and net profit. The model answers are sum-marized in Table 8.10. It compares earned income with earned expenditure, whilst also differentiating between operating and net profits.

Table 8.10 Model answer – Hot-Shot Events Profit and Loss Statement

Item	Amount ($)
Operating income	
Seminar admissions	10 000
Agent fees	5000
Sponsorship	0
Triathlon/fun run event entry fees	10 000
Grants and subsidies	0
Social functions	0
Consulting fees	0
Other income	0
Total operating income	25 000
Operating expenditure	
Wages for general administration	6000
Wages for triathlon/fun run	2000
Seminar guest speakers fees	1000
Seminar facility hire	2000
Safety and security charges	5000
Triathlon/fun run event support	2000
Seminar catering charges	4000
Indemnity insurance	0
Incidentals	1000
Depreciation on office equipment	2000
Other expenses	0
Total operating expenditure	25 000
Operating surplus/profit	0
Non-operating abnormal items	0
Non-operating extraordinary items	
Government grant	4000
Damages	4000
	0
Net surplus/profit	0

The final result is a net profit of zero, which is the same as the operating profit. Although there are two extraordinary items, they offset each other. Depreciation is included under operating expenses, although in some sport association accounts it is listed as a non-operating item.

The case of the Springfield Meadows Bocce Association

This fictitious case requires the completion of a cash flow statement. It involves the compilation of a statement that distinguishes between cash from operating activities, cash from investing activities, and cash from finance activities. It centers on the task given to Margaret Moonface who is the finance director of the Springfield Meadows Bocce Association (SMBA).

Margaret has been advised that she needs to precisely monitor the cash flows of SMBA on a monthly basis. Margaret has identified a number of transactions that appear to involve cash movements for the previous month. She needs your expert guidance in presenting a proper cash flow statement to the Board of Management. Margaret would like to identify a systematic set of net inflows and outflows. All cash transactions are listed below. Can you help?

SMBA – cash movements for month ending 31 December

1. Short-term borrowing from ANZ Bank for office refurbishment: $10 000
2. Sale of shares in News Corporation: $5000
3. Government operating grant received: $10 000
4. Payment to ACE Office Supplies for office equipment: $10 000
5. Annual sponsorship from Oceania Pasta Supplies: $50 000
6. Sale of used office furniture: $2000
7. Late receipt of affiliation fees from clubs: $3000
8. Promise by New Naples Traders Association for national championships: $10 000
9. Income from intensive strategic planning workshop for affiliated clubs: $5000
10. Payment for next years' professional indemnity insurance: $10 000
11. Interest payment on NAB loan to upgrade rink: $5000
12. Free supply of promotional T-shirts from Department of Ethnic Affairs: value $3000
13. Income received in advance for gold-pass memberships: $2000
14. Part repayment of medium term loan from NAB: $20 000
15. Payment of player expenses for international travel: $25 000
16. Proceeds from sale of historic painting titled *Bocce Game At Yarra Park*: $3000

113

Table 8.11 Model Answer – Springfield Meadows Bocce Association Cash Flow statement

	Cash In ($)	Cash Out ($)	Net Cash Flow ($)
Cash flow from operating activities			
Govt Grant	10 000		
Sponsor (Oceania)	50 000		
Fees (affiliation)	3000		
Workshop (Planning)	5000		
Gold pass	2000		
Interest received (NAB)	2000		
Prize money (Milan Masters)	10 000		
Fees (Sussex Downs)	18 000		
Total cash in	100 000		
Insurance (prof indemnity)		10 000	
Interest paid (NAB)		5000	
Travel		25 000	
Sports science		5000	
Wages		15 000	
Total cash out		−60 000	
Net cash flow from operating activities			40 000
Cash flow from investing activities			
Shares sale	5000		
Furniture sale	2000		
Painting sale	3000		
Total cash in	10 000		
Equipment		10 000	
Share purchase (Barclay)		10 000	
Printer purchase		5000	
Multi-media purchase		15 000	
Total cash out		−40 000	
Net cash flow from investing activities			−30 000
Cash flow from financing activities			
AN2 borrowings	10 000		
Total cash in	10 000		
Loan repayment (NAB)		20 000	
Total cash out		−20 000	
Net cash flow from financing activities			−10 000
Net increase/decrease in cash held	120 000	−120 000	0

17. Payment to Know-It-All Sport Science Consulting Services for intensive team psychological counseling: $5000
18. Purchase of shares in Barclay Bank: $10 000
19. Purchase of color laser printer: $5000
20. Interest received on interest bearing deposits with NAB: $2000

21. Wage payments to casual staff: $15 000
22. Prize-money for winning International Teams Trophy at Milan Masters event: $10 000
23. Additional registration fees received from Sussex Downs Branch: $18 000
24. Purchase of multimedia IT package to provide desktop publishing facility: $15 000

The model answers are compiled in Table 8.11. The statement is broken into operating, investing, and financing activities and for each item the impact on cash inflow and cash outflow is designated.

The above statement signals a healthy cash flow situation. In particular the operating activity net cash inflow of $40 000 indicates the capacity to maintain a highly liquid position. In particular, the strong cash flow operating activities is able to easily cover the loan repayment.

Questions to consider

1. What does a balance sheet aim to show?
2. How are assets categorized in a balance sheet?
3. On what basis are assets re-valued over time?
4. What is the principle that underpins depreciation and amortization?
5. What is the difference between tangible and intangible assets?
6. Identify some intangible assets that are particularly important for sport organizations.
7. Contrast current with non-current liabilities.
8. What does a profit and loss statement aim to show?
9. Give examples of how net profits can be different from operating profits.
10. Explain why a profit and loss statement is a weak indicator of movements of cash.
11. What does a cash flow statement aim to show, and how is it constructed?

Further reading

For a simple introduction to the structure and function of balance sheets, profit and loss statements, and cash flow statement see Hart, L. (2006). *Accounting Demystified: A Self Teaching Guide*. McGraw Hill, Chapter 2 (The balance sheet), Chapter 3 (The Income Statement), Chapter 4 (The Cash Flow Statement) and Chapter 5 (How the Financial Statements are Related). For a more detailed and technical review of financial statements and what they say see Hoggett, J., Edwards, L. and Medlin, J. (2006). *Accounting*, 6th Edition. Wiley, Chapter 25 (Analysis and Interpretation). See also Atrill, P., McLaney, E., Harvey, D. and Jenner, M. (2006). *Accounting: An Introduction*,

Pearson Education Australia, Chapter 3 (Measuring and Reporting Financial Position), Chapter 4 (Measuring and Reporting Financial Performance) and Chapter 5 (Measuring and Reporting Cash Flows).

For a succinct discussion of financial statements of non-profit organizations see Anthony, R. and Young, D. (2003). *Management Control in Non-profit Organizations*, 7th Edition. McGraw Hill, Chapter 3 (Published Financial Statements).

A useful sports-specific review of financial statements is contained in A. Gillentine, and R. Crow (Eds.), (2005). *Foundations of Sport Management, Fitness Information Technology*, Chapter 6 (Sport Finance).

9

Financial analysis

Overview

This chapter provides a detailed discussion of the ways in which the financial performance of sport organizations can be analyzed by examining the balance sheet, profit and loss statement, and cash flow statement. It will focus on the measures for gauging profitability, liquidity, long-term indebtedness, and net worth. Customized measures to suit the special requirements of different sport organizations will also be discussed.

Introduction

It is one thing to compile a few accounts, keep an eye on how much credit a sport club or association has built up, and monitor revenue and expenses from time-to-time. It is another thing to understand and calculate precise measures of a sport club's financial performance over time. This second task requires exposure to a number of tools for measuring profitability, short-term financial stability, long-term financial stability, and finally the club or association's level of net worth or wealth. A discussion of these four approaches to financial analysis will follow.

The first thing to note is that in order to make sense of financial information it is necessary to establish some sort of reference point or benchmark. At first glance the revelation that a club has secured $20 million in annual revenue may seem to be a good result. However, it may be only 5 percent more that the revenue earned 5 years ago when the economy was depressed. In addition, annual expenses may have increased by 10 percent over the same time period, thereby cutting into club surpluses. Moreover, it is found that a majority of clubs in the same sport league are earning in excess of $25 million, with two clubs earning more than $30 million. This immediately places the club or association's financial performance into a specific context. In other words, it is important to measure a club's financial position using reference points and benchmarks which gives a stronger sense of relative financial well-being.

There are three reference points that need to be identified before any effective analysis can take place. The first reference point is a sport club's previous performance. In this instance the questions to ask are what happened last year, 5 years ago, or even 10 years ago. This is called horizontal analysis, but is also referred to as longitudinal or trend analysis. Trend analysis can highlight significant increases or falls in broad items like annual revenue and total expenses, or even more specific items like sponsorship income, merchandise sales, player payments, and advertising expenses. The second reference point is a base figure in the accounts like total assets or total revenue. In this instance it is possible to examine one figure in relation to another. So, instead of just identifying a profit or surplus, it will be possible to view it in relation to some other item. A profit of $2 million, for example, can be viewed as a proportion of total revenue of $50 million to give a profit ratio of 4 percent. If the asset base is $25 million then the return on assets calculation will be 2 over 25, which is 8 percent. The final reference point is the performance of similar clubs. In this instance the question to ask is: did the club do better or worse than the one in the next suburb or local competition, or indeed a similar club in another region or country? For example, a county or state cricket association may have just posted a record level of annual revenue, and made a handsome surplus, and smugly concluded that it had done very well. However, if all other county or state governing bodies had exceeded its bottom line results, then its comparative performance would be viewed as dismal.

Each of the above three reference points can be used to strengthen the analysis by providing comparative data, and encouraging a more contextual examination of the figures. However, whatever approach is taken, it is crucial to understand the variety of measures that can be used to assess both broad and specific financial issues within a sport club or association. This involves undertaking some form or ratio analysis that has as its focus profitability, short-term financial stability, long-term financial stability, and finally the club or association's level of wealth or net worth.

Measures of profitability

Profit (or surplus) is superficially easy to measure since it is straightforward to calculate the difference between aggregate income and aggregate expenditure.

However, we need to clearly distinguish between operating profit and net profit. There can sometimes be a substantial difference between the two since, as was noted in the previous chapter, depreciation, abnormal, and extraordinary items on both the income and expenditure side need to be taken into account. Moreover, the relationship between revenue (or aggregate income), expenses (or aggregate expenditure), and profits can be examined from a number of perspectives.

Return on revenue

First we can look at profit in relation to revenue, earnings, or income. For example, if aggregate income for the year was $4 million and expenditure was $3.6 million, the profit or surplus is $0.4 million. If profit is expressed as a percentage of income it comes out as 10 percent. So, the return on revenue is 10 percent. For a not-for-profit organization like a sporting club this would be good result, since profit making is not its prime goal, and in any case, additional earnings are retained the club. A club can end up with a high or small ratio, a high or improved ratio being an indicator of good performance.

It is also possible to compare expenditure to income with a view to producing an expenditure to income ratio. Using the above example the ratio is calculated by dividing the $3.6 million expenditure into the $4 million revenue. The ratio is 1.1 and can be expressed as 1:1.1. That is for every dollar of expenditure the club earned 1.1 dollars of income. A ratio less than 1 would be unsatisfactory, since losses will be made, while a figure in excess of 1 would indicate the capacity to operate profitably (for another example see Table 9.1).

Return on assets

We can also link income or profits to assets. In this case we are finding out how productively we use our assets to generate revenue to ensure the sustainability of our operations. For example, one club may have tangible asset backing of $2 million, and generate revenue of $500 000. The revenue return on assets is consequently 25 percent. Another club may have earned $1 million, but on a much higher tangible asset base of $5 million. In this case the revenue return on assets is 20 percent which may suggest a poorer use of its

Table 9.1 Example of Return on Revenue Ratio

Profit ($)	Revenue ($)	Return on Revenue Ratio (Profit/Revenue)
20 000	500 000	0.4 (4%)

Table 9.2 Example of Return on Assets Ratio

Profit ($ million)	Tangible Assets ($ million)	Return on Assets (Profit/Assets)
0.5	10	0.5 (5%)

revenue generating capacity. Again, all other things being equal, the higher the ratio, the better the performance.

The same calculations can be made for profits and assets. In this case either the operating or net profit can be compared to the assets of the club or association. If the operating profit is $200 000 and the value of the tangible assets is $5 million then the profit return on assets is $200 000 divided by the $5 million which is 0.4 or 4 percent (for another example see Table 9.2).

Measuring short-term financial stability

We also need a measure of how well we can service our short-term debts when they fall due. For example, sport clubs will usually build up their accounts receivable item by buying things on credit. There is no problem with this so long as the club has the funds to pay these short-term debts at the appropriate time. And, of course, it has to be paid for in cash. If a sport club or association regularly fails to pay its bills then when they fall due creditors can take legal action to force them to pay, this can lead to insolvency and bankruptcy whereby the club or association must sell off all its assets and stop operating. Consequently all sport clubs and associations need a way of monitoring their capacity to pay bills when required. The key issue here is to have enough cash, or assets that can be easily and quickly converted to cash, to cover all short-term debts.

Working capital

The best indicator of a sport club's ability to pay its short-term debt is its working capital, or level of liquidity, which is the difference between current assets and current liabilities. Current assets include items like cash (which is axiomatic), accounts payable (which includes those transaction where payment is imminent), inventory (which is merchandise for sale), and stocks and shares that can be converted to cash in a matter of days. Current liabilities include mainly those transactions for which payment to a creditor is due in the

Table 9.3 Example of Working Capital (Current) Ratio

Current Assets ($ million)	Current Liabilities ($ million)	Current Ratio (Current Assets/Current Liabilities)
3	3.2	0.94 (0.94:1)

30–90 days, and are called accounts payable. The ideal situation is to have current assets exceed current liabilities. This indicates the capacity to cover all short-term debt. For example, one club may have current assets of $1.9 million and current liabilities of $2.2 million, while another club may have current assets of $1.5 million and current liabilities of $1.2 million. In the case of the first club its working capital is −$0.3 million, which would be cause for concern. In the case of the second club, the working capital is +$0.3 million, which provides a solid buffer from which to comfortably pay its short-term debts when they become due. These raw figures can also be converted to a ratio by dividing current assets by current liabilities. In the above case the first club has a working capital ratio (or current ratio, as it is often called) of 0.86, or 0.86:1. This means that for every dollar of current liabilities the club has only 86 cents of current assets which is not a satisfactory position to maintain for any length of time. On the other hand the second club has a working capital/current ratio of 1.25 or 1.25:1. This means that for every dollar of current liabilities the club has $1.25 in current assets, and it can therefore comfortably pay its short-term debts when they fall due (for another example see Table 9.3).

Cash flow

The cash flow statement can also be used to identify the strength of a club or association's cash reserves. A useful tool here is the cash flow adequacy ratio, which assesses the capacity of an organization to provide sufficient net cash inflow from its operating activities to cover its repayment of long-term borrowings and any assets it acquired. It can also include dividends paid, but for most sport clubs this will not be relevant. For example, a club may have generated a net cash flow from operating activities of $900 000, but at the same time repaid $600 000 of long-term debt, purchased property for $450 000, and installed a computer system worth $50 000. The cash flow adequacy ratio is calculated by adding up the loan repayment and asset purchases ($1.1 million), and dividing it into net cash flow from operating activities ($900 000). This will produce a ratio of 0.82, or 0.82:1. That is for every dollar of aggregated loan repayment and asset purchases it is only supported by 82 cents of cash from its operating activities. This may not be a problem for 1 or 2 years, but would signal the need to better manage investing and financing activities. This trend would clearly need to be reversed over the longer term to ensure appropriate levels of net cash inflow (for another example see Table 9.4).

Table 9.4 Example of Cash Flow Adequacy Ratio

Loan and Asset Payments ($)	Net Cash from Operating Activities ($)	Cash Flow Adequacy Ratio (Cash from Operations/ Loans and Assets Purchased)
90 000	70 000	0.71 (0.71:1)

Measures of operating efficiency

It is also important to have some way of identifying how well club or association revenues and resources are being managed, and how effectively they are being used. In professional sport there is an assumed link between total revenue received and successes delivered. In other words, the greater the revenue generating capacity of a club or association, the greater the likelihood of on-field success. This is particularly evident in English Premier League, where the four richest clubs (Manchester United, Chelsea, Liverpool, and Arsenal) inevitably occupy one of the top-five positions in the League table. However, the correlation is not perfect and there are many instances of relatively wealthy clubs who underachieve, and a few poorer clubs who, in boxing parlance, punch above their weight.

Revenue efficiency ratio

One important indicator of a club's efficient use of revenues and resources is its ability to generate revenue from its supporter and fan base. While it is important to cultivate a broad supporter base, it is equally important to create a level of fan loyalty whereby they contribute consistently and intensively to the club's revenue steam. Whereas one club may have a large fan catchment (i.e. it has a large surrounding population, or possesses a strong brand image which attracts people from all over the place) many of their fans may be only marginally attached to the club, and attend games and take out memberships only when the club is playing well, or the weather is fine.

For instance, it might have a revenue base of $50 million and an average home attendance of 25 000. This relationship between total revenue and average home attendance is called revenue efficiency, and measures the ability of the club to attract financial support from it fans. The ratio is calculated by dividing average home attendance into total revenue, and measured the revenue received for each fan who attends a home game. In the above example the revenue efficiency ratio is 50 million divided by 25 000 which is 200 000 or 200 000:1. That is, for every fan who attends each week, the club generates

Table 9.5 Example of Revenue Efficiency Ratio

Total Annual Revenue ($ million)	Average Home Attendance	Revenue Efficiency Ratio (Annual Revenue/Average Home Attendance)
2	25 000	80 (80:1)

$200 000 in revenue. Without any benchmark it may seem a reasonable outcome. However, another club with a much smaller support base, and consequently a much lower average game attendance of 15 000, may have an annual revenue of $45 million. In this case the revenue efficiency will be 300 000:1. The club is consequently able to extract an average of $300 000 from each fan who attends on a weekly basis. So even though the second club has a lower revenue base, it is able to better utilize its fan base. This could be the result of a stronger merchandising program, more effective member servicing, or a more passionate and committed relationship between fans and their club (for another example see Table 9.5).

Wage efficiency ratio

Another indictor of a club's efficient use of revenues and resources is its ability to win games without incurring huge wage bills. As indicated earlier, there is a close correlation between revenues earned and games won. This is close to being axiomatic, since clubs with large revenue streams can lure the best players with the bait of more money. However, there are also many instances where rich clubs who can afford to buy the best players do not perform at the level they expect, while less wealthy clubs can often compete successfully on much smaller budgets. Let us assume for example that Club 1 has an annual wage bill covering players, coaches, and support staff of $15 million and last season it won 15 out of 20 games. Club 2 on the other hand, won 18 games, but had a wage budget of $22 million. To calculate a wage efficiency ratio total wage costs is divided by league wins. The wage efficiency ratio for Club 1 is 1 (or 1:1). That is, it cost an average $1 million in wages to win each game. On the other hand, even though it won more games, Club 2, had a higher wage efficiency ratio. It was therefore less efficient than Club 1 since it needed $1.2 million on average to win each game (for another example see Table 9.6).

Table 9.6 Example of Wage Efficiency Ratio

Total Wage Bill ($ million)	Games Won	Wage Efficiency Ratio (Total Wages/Games Won)
5	20	250 000 (250 000:1)

Measuring long-term financial stability

We also want to get a clear picture of how much long-term debt a sport club has built up. It does not automatically follow that a large amount of borrowed money is going to be a problem, but is does present a potential for later difficulties if profit levels fall, and it becomes difficult to pay back both the loan or principal and the interest on it. The Melbourne Cricket Club (MCC), one of Australia's largest sport organizations, is a good example of this as can be noted in its balance sheet. On the other hand, the Moonee Valley Racing Club, another large sport organization, has virtually no long-term debt that reflects little long-term borrowing of money over 10–30 years.

We can use the financial leverage ratio or the debt to equity ratio to measure the relative levels of long-term indebtedness. Both measures are comparing the amount of borrowed money in the business compared with the amount of invested funds from either the owners in the form of their own capital or profits that have been ploughed back into the business. For example, the Wessex South Horse Racing Club finds that it has $2 million of debt (both current and long-term) and $500 000 in equity or accumulated member funds. Its debt to equity ratio is therefore $2 million divided by $500 000 which is 4 or 4:1. That is for every dollar of equity the club has $4 of debt. This indicates a high level of debt dependency (for another example see Table 9.7).

It is also appropriate to contrast the total assets with total long-term liabilities. This identifies the proportion of the total funds in the club or business that comes from long-term borrowings and bank loans. The bigger the proportion, the greater the risk.

Measuring wealth

Finally we need to have some way of deciding if a sport club is any more or less wealthy than it was 5 or 10 years ago. A sport organization that has become less wealthy over the years would be cause for concern. A quick look

Table 9.7 Example of Debt to Equity Ratio

Debt ($ million)	Equity ($ million)	Debt to Equity Ratio
5	10	0.5 (0.5:1)

at the Australian or British Olympic Committees suggests that it might just be in this situation, since they will accumulate assets for the early part of the 4-year Olympic cycle only to liquidate a large slab of them in the later part of the cycle in order to fund athletes' participation at the Games. On the other hand, it would hard to see Tennis Australia or the All England Tennis Club being worse off now than they were in 1996, given the overwhelming success of the Grand Slam tennis championships.

Measuring wealth is relatively easy. It is merely a matter of comparing total assets with total liabilities. The difference is the net asset of the organization, which in fact usually designated at the bottom of the balance sheet. This is also referred to as the net worth, which is also equal to the level of accumulated surplus or members' funds, which is the non-profit sector name for shareholders' funds.

The case of the MCC

The Melbourne Cricket Club (MCC) is one of Australia's oldest sporting clubs. It is also one of the wealthiest. It has the advantage of managing the Melbourne Cricket Ground (MCG) one of the world's great sporting icons. Its great financial strength is its capacity to attract thousands of members who are prepared to pay a hefty annual fee (around AUD 600) to secure the right to attend sporting events and use the Club's extensive hospitality and facilities. It is also the home of cricket and Australian football. At the same time it has borrowed heavily over the past 15 years to upgrade the stadium. This begs the question as to just how financially healthy the MCC is.

The following table summarizes its key financial indicators for the last few years. The table begins in 1990 when the MCC began its major redevelopment and ends in 2005 when stage two of the redevelopment was completed in time for the 2006 Commonwealth Games (Table 9.8).

The indicators show that the MCC has increased its scale of operations significantly over the last 15 years. Operating income has increased from AUD 14 million to AUD 69 million, and expenses have been constrained to ensure the generation of continuing surpluses. The great strength of the MCC is its membership income which has increased from AUD 8 million to nearly AUD 31 million. On the expense side, one of the most revenue-absorbing items is interest paid, which in 1997 comprised nearly 30 percent of operating income. This resulted from the MCC's heavy borrowings, which were used to fund its stadium redevelopment. This heavy dependency on debt is reflected in its high debt to equity ratio, which was 5:1 in 2002. The MCG is one of the world's great sport stadiums, and while its redevelopment was underpinned by debt finance, it has given the stadium enormous revenue generation capacity. Its long-term sustainability is strong so long as it continues to attract quality sport events throughout the year.

Table 9.8 MCC Financial Indicators 1990–2005

Indicator	1990 (AUD million)	1997 (AUD million)	2002 (AUD million)	2005 (AUD million)
Operating income	14.1	41.6	62.3	69.4
Members fees	7.9	16.8	22.6	30.5
Events	1.7	7.6	16.2	12.5
Sponsors and marketing	3.5	9.5	17.8	17.5
Operating expenses	10.3	30.1	57.9	61.3
Administration	2.2	6.4	18.1	16.5
Arena operations/maintain	3.7	5.1	10.4	11.3
Interest paid	1.8	13.4	10.7	7.9
Operating profit	3.8	11.5	4.4	8.1
Depreciation/amortization	−1.6	−9.7	Included in administration expenses	Included in administration expenses
Non-operating activities	−1.4	16.1[a]	8.3	64.1[b]
Net profit	1.6	19.5	12.7	72.2
Total assets	35.9	185.8	178.2	494.3
Cash	5.9	14.1	4.5	32.2
Current	6.9	16.9	14.5	50.0
Investments	1.1	1.9	0	0
Property and improvements	35.9	185.7	133.7	273.4
Total liabilities	22.7	154.7	150.7	305.7
Current	9.8	20.2	23.5	37.9
Non-current	12.9	134.5	127.2	267.8
Net assets (member funds)	13.2	31.1	27.5	188.6
Repaid borrowings	0.4	5.9	31.3	1.2

[a]Government loan to MCC written off.
[b]Includes Government funds for MCG/Commonwealth Games redevelopment.
Source: Melbourne Cricket Club (1990–2005).

Wage efficiency ratios in football leagues

The Australian Football League (AFL) is Australia's premier professional sports league. It attracts more fans and has the most lucrative broadcast rights fees. It is also heavily regulated through a commission that imposes a salary cap and redistributes revenue to give clubs a guaranteed minimum income. At the same time, some clubs receive salary cap bonuses, while other clubs do not use up the full amount of their caps. In addition there are no controls over payments to coaching, medical, and support staff. As a result the total player and coaching and support wage bills vary between clubs.

Table 9.9 AFL 2005 Wage Efficiency Ratios

Club	League Points 2005	Total Football Department Wage Costs (AUD million)	Player Payments (AUD million)	Wage Efficiency Ratio
Adelaide Crows	68	11.6	7.5	171
West Coast Eagles	68	12.6	8.0	186
St Kilda Saints	56	10.4	7.4	186
North Melbourne Kangaroos	52	9.8	6.9	188
Melbourne Demons	48	10.7	7.1	223
Geelong Cats	48	11.0	7.2	230
Western Bulldogs	44	10.6	7.5	240
Sydney Swans	60	14.5	9.5	242
Fremantle Dockers	44	11.1	7.4	251
Port Adelaide Power	46	11.7	7.8	254
Richmond Tigers	40	10.3	7.6	256
Brisbane Lions	40	13.2	8.6	330
Essendon Bombers	32	12.1	7.9	379
Hawthorn Hawks	20	11.3	8.0	566
Carlton Blues	18	10.9	7.8	609
Collingwood Magpies	20	12.9	7.9	644

Source: Denham, G. (2006).

Sydney Swans had the highest wages bill in 2005 of AUD 14.5 million, while the North Melbourne Kangaroos had the lowest wage bill, which was AUD 9.8 million. When the wage bills are compared with the end of year League standing there are many interesting differences. The club with the highest wage/league standing (i.e. wage efficiency) ratio was the Collingwood Maypies. Whereas its wage bill of AUD 12.9 million was in the top quartile, it finished second bottom on the League ladder. Its wage efficiency ratio was 645 000, which means that for every League standing point it paid out AUD 645 000 in wage costs. The club with the best wage efficiency ratio was Adelaide Crows who only paid out $171 000 for each league standing point. Details of this are expanded in Table 9.9.

International sport associations

The international governing bodies for sport, otherwise known as International Sporting Organizations (ISOs), depend for their financial viability on the revenues they can secure from major sport events. Two of the most highly

Table 9.10 Financial Indicators for ICC

	2005 (USD million)	*2004 (USD million)*
Operating income	49.4	11.9
Event income	37.9	2.0
Member subscriptions	11.1	9.7
Operating expenses	29.8	19.4
Cricket development	7.2	8.2
Total assets	77.6	86.8
Cash assets	44.5	69.5
Total liabilities	61.0	79.9
Current liabilities	30.7	75.5

credentialed ISOs are the International Cricket Council (ICC) and the International Rugby Board (IRB).

The ICC, which has 96 member countries, runs two major competitions, the World Cup and the Champions Trophy. The Champions Trophy was last run in 2005, and its success is reflected in the sharp increase in its operating income. The ICC's financial indicators for 2004 and 2005 are listed in Table 9.10.

The IRB, which has 115 member nations, operates a similar financial cycle. The World Cup was conducted in 2003 in Australia, and by any measure was highly successful. In 2004, with no global competition, revenues contracted. Its financial indicators are listed in Table 9.11.

Table 9.11 Financial Indicators for IRB

	2004 (GBP million)	*2003 (GBP million)*
Operating income	19.5	72.2
Broadcasting	17.1	25.2
Sponsorship	0.2	12.1
Licensing	2.1	34.0
Operating expenses	14.5	29.0
Total assets	80.3	82.3
Cash assets	51.7	42.8
Total liabilities	3.9	4.9
Current liabilities	3.6	4.8

When measuring the comparative financial performances of the ICC and IRB, it is important to convert the figures to a common currency. In 2006 the average exchange rate was 1 GBP to 1.85 USDs. Both organizations have strong revenue streams, but bearing in mind the exchange rate, the IRB figures are significantly stronger. The IRB also has fewer liabilities and a higher level of net assets.

Questions to consider

1. Identify three reference points that can be used to build a model of financial analysis for a sport organization.
2. Identify three ways you can go about measuring profitability in a sport organization. Nominate the strengths and weaknesses of each method.
3. What does the level of working capital reveal about a sport organization's short-term financial health? How can the level of working capital be converted to a ratio?
4. How might the cash flow statement be used to reveal the level of liquidity of a sport organization?
5. Identify and explain two measures of operating efficiency.
6. How might you go about measuring the extent to which a sport organization depends on debt to fund it operations?
7. After examining the financial indicators of the MCC, how would you rate its financial performance over the last 15 years? What are its financial strengths and weaknesses?
8. What does the table of wage efficiency ratios for AFL clubs tell you about how well clubs convert their player wage bills into on-field success?
9. Compare and contrast the financial performance of the IRB and the ICC over recent times. How do you explain the fluctuations in operating income?

Further reading

For a broad-based generic review of financial ratios and what they mean, see Atrill, P., McLaney, E., Harvey, D. and Jenner, M. (2006). *Accounting: An Introduction*, 3rd Edition. Pearson Education Australia, Chapter 6 (Analysis and Interpretation). A basic, but comprehensive analysis of the use and abuse of financial ratios is provided in Hart, L. (2006). *Accounting Demystified: A Self Teaching Guide*. McGraw Hill, Chapter 14 (Prep-work), Chapter 15 (Profit Ratios), Chapter 16 (Liquidity), Chapter 17 (Cash Ratios), and Chapter 18 (Financial Ratios).

For a succinct account of how ratio analysis can be applied to the financial statements of non-profit organizations see Anthony, R. and Young, D. (2003). *Management Control in Non-profit Organizations*, 7th Edition. McGraw Hill, Chapter 4 (Analyzing Financial Statements).

An excellent sport-specific guide to financial performance evaluation is contained in Gerrard, W. (2004a). Sport Finance. In J. Beech and S. Chadwick (Eds.), *The Business of Sport Management*. Pearson Education, pp. 154–190. At the end of this chapter there is an extensive case study of the financial meltdown of Leeds United Football Club in 2002.

In Brown, A. and Walsh, A. (1999). *Not For Sale: Manchester United, Murdoch and the Defeat of BSkyB*, Mainstream, there is an impressive analysis of the rise and rise of Manchester United Football Club, and how it became the wealthiest sport club in the world.

An update of the commercial and cultural dominance of MUFC is contained in Gerrard, W. (2004b). Why does Manchester United Keep Winning? In D. Andrews (Ed.), *Manchester United: A Thematic Study*. pp. 65–86, Routledge. This chapter is particularly instructive in explaining how MUFC has been able to sustain its competitive advantage for so long. According to Gerrard it is all about the club's capacity to build its playing talent, fan goodwill, and organizational effectiveness (p. 66).

For an extensive analysis of the value and profitability of the Liverpool Football Club see Foster, G., Greyser, P. and Walsh, B. (2006). *The Business of Sports: Texts and Cases on Strategy and Management*. Thomson, Section 10 (Case 10.2 Liverpool Football Club: What is its Current Market Value?).

The ways in which Olympic sport clubs and associations go about measuring their economic and financial success, and how they are balanced against social and cultural measures, is examined in Chappelet, J. and Bayle, E. (2005). *Strategic and Performance Management of Olympic Sport Organizations*. Human Kinetics, Chapter 5 (Definition of Performance Management) and Chapter 6 (Measuring Performance).

PART THREE

Sport Funding: Financial Planning and Evaluation

10 Budgeting and costing

Overview

This chapter will discuss the crucial importance of budgeting for sport organizations, and explain the tools for controlling expenditure. An initial distinction will be made between operating budgets and capital budgets, and how each of them can be constructed. Operating budgets will be divided into line item, program, and performance, and their application to different sport situations will be discussed. Variance analysis will be explored as a means of monitoring expenditure and income. The use of break-even analysis (BEA) to assist the budget process will also be examined. The chapter will end with a brief analysis of capital budgeting and how it can be used to appraise the costing of sport venues and stadiums.

The basics of budgeting

Budgeting is a crucial part of the financial management process. It is one thing to construct some simple accounts and diagnose the financial health of sport clubs, associations, and leagues. It is another thing to make sure resources are available for allocation to the various parts of their operations. No matter how wealthy a sport organization is, its resource base will always be limited,

133

and decisions have to be made about not only where the resources are allocated (facility maintenance, player salaries, coaching staff, equipment upgrade), but also how much each operational activity will receive. Moreover budgets are finite, and the constraining factor will always be the amount of available funds.

Budgets are really financial plans that involve the allocation of funds to strategically important operations and activities. Budgets are essential for ensuring costs and expenses are contained, and do not exceed the planned revenue. Good budgets act as a constraint on spending, and also provide a clear picture of the anticipated sources of revenue. Budgets come in different shapes and forms but they all share the desire to control spending patterns and make sure the spending is grounded in an appropriate level of funding and support.

Benefits of budgeting

A good system of budgeting is crucially important for sport clubs and associations. As already noted, the sport world has become increasingly complex, and the need to manage money effectively is stronger than ever. In addition a well-planned budget is the basis for efficient management and ensuring viability over the long term. The benefits of budgeting are many. They can:

1. help anticipate the future and thereby assist the strategic planning process;
2. give a clear picture of resource needs and program priorities;
3. signal where there may be revenue shortfalls;
4. allow management to better manage and monitor spending;
5. communicate the club or association's financial plans to key stakeholders;
6. enable precise measures of financial performance to be made.

Types of budgets

As already noted, budgets indicate the spending limits on different activities over particular periods. On one hand there is the operational budget (which is sometimes called a recurrent budget), and on the other hand there is the capital expenditure budget (which is sometimes called an investment budget). Whereas an operating budget refers to spending on the day-to-day operations of the sport club, association, or league, a capital budget refers to spending on buildings, facilities and equipment, and other tangible assets.

Operational budgets

An operational budget is a statement of the anticipated levels of revenue for a period of time, and how the revenue will be spent. The figures are estimates only, since there will always be unforeseen circumstances that will change the financial parameters in which a club or association conducts its affairs. As a result, the financial projections that underpinned the budget figures may not be realized due to changing economic and social conditions. For example, a sponsor may want to renegotiate its agreement, membership income may fall because of poor on-field performance, and coaching and support staff costs may blow out because of an increased demand for skilled specialists.

An operational budget aims to accurately estimate the likely level of revenue that a club or association will have to play with, and the anticipated expenses associated with the earning of that income. For every sport club and association it is crucial to ensure that revenue and expenses will balance, and at best, work toward the generation of a healthy surplus. The following example illustrates what an operational budget will look like, and what items might be included.

The simple budget shown in Table 10.1 immediately reveals a number of important things. First it identifies the main items of revenue and spending. Clearly, in this fictitious case, the Pleasant Valley Darts Club (PVDC) is heavily dependent on the local sponsor which just so happens to be the main hotel in town. It also shows that the day-to-day administration expenses are significant, although it would be good to have a breakdown of this item, since it might reveal specific activities like marketing or office rental that need to be monitored. Second it also shows when the revenue is earned and the expenses are incurred. While this is a not a cash budget it does indicate possible times of cash flow problems. However, this is unlikely to be a problem here since most of the revenue is expected to arrive early in the year. The budget consequently allows the PVDC to monitor the balance between expense commitments and revenue collections for different parts of the financial planning period.

Table 10.1 PVDC Operating Line-item Budget

	March Quarter ($)	June Quarter ($)	September Quarter ($)	December Quarter ($)	Year Total ($)
Revenue					
Donations	500			1000	1500
Sponsor	6000				6000
Member fees	1400	200	200	200	2000
Gaming	1400	1300	1100	700	4500
Total	9300	1500	1300	1900	14000
Expenses					
General administration services	2000	2000	2000	2000	8000
Coaching					0
Event administration		1000	1000		2000
Travel		500	500	500	1500
Dart board supplies	2000				2000
Total	4000	3500	3500	2500	13500

Operating budgets can be organized in different ways as well. For example, an operational budget may be structured as a line-item budget which is illustrated in Table 10.1. This involves breaking down the spending and income into specific categories like administration, travel, marketing, and entertainment, and applying overall spending limits to each item. All of the different activities or programs in the organization will work to these limits. The PVDC budget uses the line-item method in setting its forecast figures.

A budget can also be organized as a program budget (Table 10.2). This involves allocating a designated amount of funds to each activity or program. Each program area is then allowed to spend on what they want, up to, but not beyond, the designated limit. For example, the PVDC may allocate funds to each of its junior, regional, and veterans league programs along the following lines. Each program manager can then decide how best to distribute the funds to each of its program activities.

Table 10.2 Program Budget for PVDC

	Junior League Program ($)	Regional League Program ($)	Veterans League Program ($)
Budget	4000	8000	2000

Program budgets can be converted into performance budgets without too much difficulty. The strength of a performance budget is that it links the budget to the club or association's strategic plan. It forces the program manager to not only work within the budget parameters, but also ensure that the funds are directed to the achievement of relevant outcomes. In the case of the PVDC, a performance budget could take the following shape (Table 10.3).

Table 10.3 Performance Budget for PVDC

Junior League Program	Regional League Program	Veterans League Program
Goal		
To provide activities that attract young children to the club	To provide activities that attract quality players through access to elite competition	To provide activities that balance social and competition darts
Anticipated outcome		
Increase in registered juniors	All teams finish in top half of league table	Viable competition
Budget ($)		
4000	8000	2000

Variance analysis

Budgets can not only be used to estimate crucial financial indicators, but to also provide a mechanism for monitoring and controlling revenue collections and spending.

Once the budget cycle has started it is important to compare the budget figure with the actual figure. This can take the form of a monthly report that lists first, the annual budget figure for revenue and expenses, second, the monthly equivalent (which is the annual figure divided by 12) and third, the actual monthly figure. These figures can then be used to calculate the variance between the budgeted figure and the actual figure. The variance can be used to identify areas on overspending, or revenue shortfalls.

Variance analysis is a simple but powerful technique for monitoring the financial progress of an organization. Variance analysis can only be undertaken if a budget has been constructed. It is essentially an after-the-event exercise where the actual revenue and expense figures are compared and contrasted with the budgeted items. The variance can be either favorable or unfavorable. For example, if a fun-run event recovered $3000 from entry fees, when the budgeted figure was only $2500, then the variance is favorable. That is, the entry fee revenue was greater than anticipated. Favorable variances are entered as a positive, while unfavorable variances are recorded as a negative figure. If the actual revenue was only $2000, then the variance is unfavorable. That is, the revenue was less than anticipated. The same principle can be applied to expenses. If for example, the actual fun-run security expenses exceeded the budgeted figure, the outcome would be unfavorable, but if the security budget was not fully spent, then the outcome would be seen as favorable. In the case of PVDC, a quarterly comparison could be made for actual and budgeted revenue and actual and budgeted expenses, as in Table 10.4.

The variance analysis immediately picks up items of revenue that have not been reached, and items of expenditure that are higher than anticipated. This provides a signal to take remedial action to prevent a budget blowout. In this particular case revenue collected is $700 below the budgeted figure, whilst expenditure to date is $1400 above the budgeted amount. This means that revenue may have to be expanded in the short term, while expenditure might have to be closely monitored over the next two quarters.

Capital budgeting

The capital budgeting process is different from the operating budget process. This is because decisions about capital involve significant investments which are intended to produce some level of financial return or public benefit. This return must be able to satisfy member or shareholder expectations, whilst also providing a surplus to meet any borrowing costs.

There are numerous tools for deciding what to invest in, and how much should be invested. Some are rubbery, while others are more methodologically exact. A useful rubbery method is the payback rule, which proposes that funds

Table 10.4 Variance Analysis for PVDC

	Year Total: Budget ($)	March Quarter: Budget ($)	March Quarter: Actual ($)	March Quarter: Variance ($)	June Quarter: Budget ($)	June Quarter: Actual ($)	June Quarter: Variance ($)	Year to Date: Budget ($)	Year to Date: Actual ($)	Year to Date: Variance ($)
Revenue										
Donations	1500	500	400	−100	0	100	100	500	500	0
Sponsor	6000	6000	3000	−3000	0	2000	2000	6000	5000	−1000
Member fees	2000	1400	1200	−200	200	800	600	1600	2000	400
Gaming	4500	1400	1500	100	1300	1100	−200	2700	2600	−100
Total	14 000	9300	6100	−3200	1500	4000	2500	10 800	10 100	−700
Expenses										
General administration services	8000	2000	2100	−100	2000	2100	−100	4000	4200	−200
Coaching	0	0	0	0	0	1000	−1000	0	1000	−1000
Event administration	2000	0	0	0	1000	1200	−200	1000	1200	−200
Travel	1500	0	0	0	500	1000	−500	500	1000	−500
Dart board supplies	2000	2000	1000	1000	0	500	−500	2000	1500	500
Total	13 500	4000	3100	900	3500	5800	−2300	7500	8900	−1400

Table 10.5 Payback Approach to Capital Budgeting

	Project 1: Merchandise Shop	Project 2: Sports Museum ($ Million)
Capital cost ($ Million)	3	2
Estimated annual Return ($ Thousand)	500	200
Payback period (Years)	6	10

should only be provided to those projects where the initial outlay can be paid back in the shortest possible time. For example, if it is found that one project has a payback period of 6 years, and the other 10 years, then the short payback investment will prevail. In the case in Table 10.5, Project 1 would be selected.

However the payback rule is not able to say if the project might also be viable in the long run. All it does is to indicate that Project 1 is less risky. Moreover, it says nothing about the returns after the payback period has elapsed.

A slightly more robust tool is the accounting rate of return (ROR), which is an estimate of the ratio of the expected average annual profits from the investment to its capital cost. Therefore an investment in a leisure center of $10 million with an average annual profit return of $200 000 would produce an average ROR of 2 percent. This could then be compared and contrasted with other projects to see where the largest return is.

The most systematic method for evaluating investment proposals is the Discounted Cash Flow (DCF) method. As noted in Chapter 4, DCF takes into account the time value of money which places greater weight on revenues and profits received in the early stages of the project, and less weight on revenues and profits received in the later stages of the project. That is, all expected returns are reduced to a present value which is then used to evaluate the proposed investment.

Mega-event budgeting

The principles for designing an operating budget for a mega-sport event like the Olympic or Commonwealth Games are no different from a community fun run. It is just the mega-sport event which is far more complex and logistically demanding. Take for example the Olympics. The Sydney Organising Committee for the Olympic Games (SOCOG) released the Sydney 2000 Olympic Games Budget in early 1997. The Games Budget represents the forecast of revenues and expenditures associated with the organizing and staging of the Sydney 2000 Olympic Games.

The budget forecasts a surplus of AUD 41 million, with revenue standing at AUD 2332 million and spending estimated to be AUD 2291 (Table 10.6).

Table 10.6 Sydney 2000 Olympic Games Pre-event Operating Budget

Games Budget	AUD Million
Revenues	
Sponsorship	829
Consumer products	61
Ticket sales	487
Television rights	955
Total	2332
Expenditures	
Accommodation, Olympic family, and medical	83
Ceremonies	37
Consumer products and creative services	26
Executive office and legal	61
Financial, risk, and project management	51
Human resources, communications, and community relations	54
Logistics	44
Media: press and broadcasting	184
Sponsorship and general marketing	135
Sport	78
Technology, premises, and administration	364
Ticketing	43
Torch relay, events, Olympic arts festivals	38
Transport and accreditation	53
Venue management and security	364
Venues and environment	284
Villages	198
Volunteers and uniforms	31
Contingencies	163
Total	2291

SOCOG also contributed AUD 370 million to the New South Wales (NSW) Government for rental of venues, construction reimbursements, and services, including security. The Budget was the result of detailed operational planning and review, and was subsequently approved by the International Olympic Committee (IOC).

Although the actual revenues and expenses subsequently exceeded the budgeted figures, the Games Budget provided a useful ballpark estimate of the sources and levels of revenue, and the scale of the main items of expenditure. In particular it provided a clear picture of what revenues were required to cover the costs of mounting the Games. One of the weaknesses of these figures was that they only covered operating revenue and expenses, and did not include capital investment figures. That is, it is an operating budget only.

The AUD 1100 million budget for the 2006 Melbourne Commonwealth Games made clear distinctions between capital and operating expenditures, but did not provide a detailed breakdown of core revenue and expenditure items. This led to a public concern that some expense items, particularly those covering security, were not fully identified and accounted for.

The London Organising Committee of the Olympic Games (LOCOG) has already produced an operating revenue budget for the 2012 Games. LOCOG Chair, Sebastian Coe, cited a budget figure of GBP 2000 million, which would be sourced from broadcast rights, sponsor income, ticket sales, and merchandising. He also noted that this amount would slightly exceed the expense budget, which is an optimistic but pleasing forecast.

Costing

When considering the costs of running a sport organization it is important to note that there are different ways of categorizing, managing, and controlling them. A distinction can be made between fixed and variable costs, and controllable costs can be contrasted with uncontrollable costs. It is therefore important to manage the costs of delivering sport services. A good starting point for controlling and managing costs is to contrast variable costs with fixed costs. Fixed costs are those costs that remain constant, and are independent of the level of activity, or numbers of spectators, clients, or users. Fixed costs included things like venue hire, equipment depreciation, most power and light costs, and core staff costs. Variable costs are those costs that change in direct relation to the number of spectators, clients, and users. For example, more users means more equipment supplies, more catering costs, more maintenance, and some additional staff. There are also costs that are called semi-fixed. These costs only change after some usage ceiling is met. A good example is the staffing costs in running a fitness or aerobics class (Figure 10.1).

Once costs have been sorted and classified, then it is possible to undertake Break-Even Analysis (BEA), which is a very effective way of working out just how many paying spectators, clients, and users are required to cover all costs and ensure a viable operation. So, what is BEA?

Break-Even Analysis

BEA, or as it otherwise known cost–volume–profit analysis, looks at how costs, revenues, and profits change in relation to changes in sales, membership, and attendance. BEA is a valuable budgeting tool, and helps in financial planning and decision-making. The break-even sales, membership, and attendance point occurs where total revenue equals total costs. Below that, point losses will be made, while above that point profits will result. BEA is particularly applicable to event management and sport service delivery. It answers the question: what attendance level or usage rate is needed to ensure a viable event or operation? It shows the changes in profits and losses that result from changing attendance or usage patterns, and changes in prices. As a result, it quickly shows if an event or operation is likely to be a commercial success.

There are a number of steps involved in identifying the break-even point. The first step involves dividing costs into fixed and variable. For example, for

141

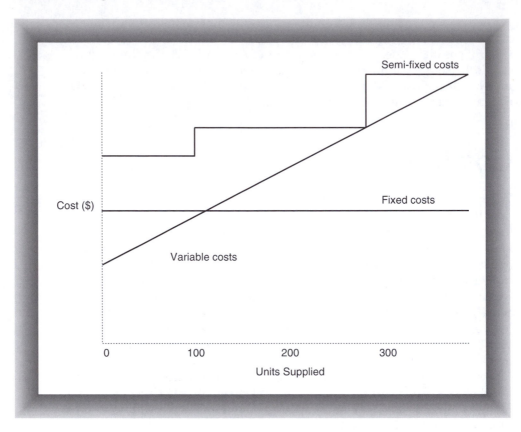

Figure 10.1 Variable, Fixed and Semi-fixed Costs

an event, fixed costs are those costs that remain constant as sales, membership, and attendance levels change. They include the venue hire, rental, guest speakers, light and power, insurance, and the cost associated with core or permanent staff. On the other hand, variable costs will vary directly with changes in sales, membership, and attendance levels. They include things like the use of casual staff, equipment, consumables, giveaways, and catering. The second step is to estimate anticipated revenues for every level of sales, membership, and attendance. The third step is to compare and contrast total revenue and total cost for every sales, membership, and attendance level. The following fictitious case gives a succinct picture of how BEA operates.

Budgeting for a sport management conference

Janet Jackass has been asked to do some budget figures for a sport management conference to be run next year. She has been asked to work out the minimum number of people attending to ensure a viable event. The first thing Janet does is to break down costs into fixed and variable. She finds out that the fixed costs include:

1. Light and power
2. Core staff
3. Venue hire
4. Guest speakers.

She estimates that total fixed costs equals $1000. This is the cost of setting up the event, and remains constant whatever the attendance level. Janet does the same for variable costs which is the additional cost incurred for every additional person who attends. She identifies three major variable costs items, which are:

1. Additional staff
2. Printing, stationery, and supplies
3. Food and drink.

She has calculated that variable costs are $60 per person, which becomes the average variable cost for the event. She then has to do some figures for the revenue that comes from each person attending the conference. The total revenue estimates will be based on:

1. The number of people attending
2. The registration fee per person.

Janet is considering a registration fee of $80 per person, which is the average admission charge. This $80 fee constitutes the additional revenue earned for every additional person who attends. Janet can then calculate the contribution margin which is the difference between average revenue (the registration fee) and average variable cost. The contribution margin is therefore $80 − $60 = $20. This means that every additional person attending will generate a profit of $20.

The break-even attendance point = fixed costs ÷ contribution margin (where contribution margin is the average revenue minus average variable cost). Consequently the break-even point is $1000 (fixed costs) divided by $20 (the contribution margin), which equals 50 attendees. In other words, if we assume that each person attending will be paying on average $80, then this will produce a profit of $20 per person. In order to cover the $1000 worth of fixed costs, 50 people are required, thereby providing the $1000 profit to offset the fixed costs.

If the attendance level falls below 50, then losses will occur, while for every attendee over the 50 cutoff, profits will increase. It should also be noted that any change in fixed costs, variable costs, or admission prices will change the break-even point. If for example it is decided to cut the admission fee to $70 then the contribution margin will fall to $10. As a result, 100 people will need to attend to break-even. A $90 registration fee would produce a contribution margin of $30 and as a result only 34 registrations would be required to break-even. However, it would be imprudent to cut admission prices to $50, since this would produce a negative contribution of $10. In this

143

case each additional person would increase the losses. Losses would consequently be minimized by having the lowest attendance possible. This would be an intolerable situation to create, unless of course the event was being subsidized to ensure the lowest possible registration fee.

Budgeting for a sport event

As noted previously, BEA can provide a clear picture of minimum required attendance levels for all sorts of events and programs. In this fictitious case, Barry Blockhead has been asked to run an indoor beach volleyball tournament for the local council using a local multipurpose recreation center. Barry is new to indoor sport programs, but has a few budgeting skills, one of which is the ability to undertake BEA for events and festivals. He is confident that the principles he learnt in the arts field can be easily applied to community sport activities. He has been given the financial data to work with as given in Table 10.7.

Table 10.7 Volleyball Tournament BEA Summary Results

Item	$
Tournament entry fee	90
Hall hire (fixed)	500
Security (fixed)	1500
Administration staff (fixed)	1000
Referee costs (per player)	5
Catering expenses (per player)	15
Insurance (public liability) (fixed)	1400
Insurance (professional indemnity for referees) (fixed)	600
Medical and massage expenses (per player)	50

Barry has to provide some recommendations to the local council as to the viability of running this event. He has been told that there is a 200-player ceiling on the tournament entries. Barry did a few sums and came up with the following numbers as given in Table 10.8.

Table 10.8 Volleyball Tournament BEA Summary Results

Total fixed costs	$5000
Average variable costs	$70
Average revenue (entry fee)	$90
Contribution margin	$20
Break-even player registrations	250

Barry remembered that the break-even attendance point was the number of participants required to cover all fixed costs. He noted the relatively large fixed costs, but also noted the handy contribution margin of $20. This meant that for every person that attended the tournament a profit of $20 would be secured. As a result 250 players were needed to break-even. The concern for Barry was that not only getting 250 paid-up participants would be a big ask, but the local council had put a 200-player ceiling on tournament entries. The only alternative was to increase entry fees. He noted, though, that if the tournament entry fee was increased to $110 the contribution margin would be $40 and consequently the break-even participation would now be around 138, which is a more realistic participation level. He advised council accordingly.

Questions to consider

1. What is the purpose of a budget?
2. What benefits arise from the budget process?
3. Contrast an operating budget with a capital budget.
4. What is a line-item budget and how does it differ from a program budget?
5. How can a program budget be converted into a performance budget?
6. What is variance analysis, and how can it assist the budget process?
7. Describe the simplest form of capital budgeting, and explain how it assists in making decisions about investment and capital expenditure.
8. What are costs?
9. How might costs be segmented to better understand how costs can vary in response to changes in the supply of a sports good or service?
10. What is BEA all about, and what does it aim to do?
11. Give an example of how a change in admission price levels for a sport event can impact on the break-even level of attendance.
12. Having read the Barry Blockhead volleyball tournament case, would you offer the same advice to council as Barry, or would you do things differently?

Further reading

For an extensive introduction to the budgeting process see Hoggett, J., Edwards, L. and Medlin, J. (2006). *Accounting*, 6th Edition. Wiley, Chapter 11 (Cost–Volume Profit Analysis) and Chapter 12 (Budgeting for Planning and Control). A detailed analysis of costing and budgeting processes, with an instructive review of BEA, is contained in Anthony, R. and Young, D. (2003). *Management Control in Non-profit Organizations*, 7th Edition. McGraw Hill, Chapter 6 (Measurement and Use of Differential Costs) and Chapter 10 (Budgeting).

For an introduction to sport-related budgeting processes and practices see Whitehouse, J. and Tilley, C. (1992). *Finance and Leisure*. Longman, especially Chapter 8 (Budgets and Budgetary Control) and Chapter 9 (The Concept of Cost). A sport-related discussion of budgeting is contained in Fried, G., Shapiro, S. and Deschriver, T. (2003). *Sport Finance*. Human Kinetics, see Chapter 7 (Approaches to Financial Planning). Another sport-related discussion of budgeting is contained in Horine, L. and Stotlar, D. (2004). *Administration of Physical Education and Sport Programs*, 5th Edition. McGraw Hill, Chapter 6 (Financial Management). A useful complementary summary of budgeting is contained in Sawyer, T., Hypes, M. and Hypes, J. (2004). *Financing the Sport Enterprise*. Sagamore Publishing, Chapter 4 (Budgeting).

11   Pricing

Overview

This chapter will examine the pricing of sport services and products from both a theoretical and a practical perspective. A number of different pricing models will be discussed, including cost-plus pricing, demand-based pricing, elasticity pricing, competition-based pricing, discriminatory pricing, premium pricing, and equity pricing. Each pricing method will be applied to sport leagues, sport events, and community sport activities to assess their impact on demand, revenue, and profits. The pricing of professional sport events will also be discussed.

Is there a right price?

Pricing is an important financial issue for sport organizations. Setting the right price can increase revenue, but it is not easy to establish just what the right price should be. If prices are too high then the demand for the good or service will be dampened, while a price that is too low will fail to secure any consumer surplus. Take for example, the 2003 Rugby Union World Cup (RWC) that was conducted in Sydney. The tournament was a success from many perspectives, as indicated in Chapter 12. A number of optimistic assumptions were made prior to the tournament about the number of international tourists who would visit Australia in 2003. However, the subsequent terrorist

147

alert cut the level of international tourism and as a result the demand for tickets was lower than anticipated. The high-price tickets (from AUD 80 to AUD 100) were especially slow to sell. In hindsight it may have been better to provide more discounted seat prices to both international visitors and local fans. In addition, lower prices could have been set for the early games, with prices increasing as the tournament entered the semi-finals stage. However, for mega-sport events like the RWC it is difficult to set a price that maximizes revenue since there will always be intervening incidents and events that shift the demand conditions for the events.

Pricing is not only linked to demand, it is also linked to cost. The ticket prices to the opening ceremony of 2006 Commonwealth Games in Melbourne ranged from AUD 40 to AUD 500. Part of the explanation for the high prices is the result of scarce seats (the 92 000 maximum seating of the Melbourne Cricket Ground (MCG) combined with high demand. The other explanation is the very high cost of staging the opening ceremony, which was estimated to be around AUD 20 million. As a point of comparison the opening ceremony at Sydney 2000 was nearer AUD 30 million with ticket prices ranging from AUD 20 to AUD 850. So, the question arises as to what constitutes effective pricing, and what specific strategy might be used to ensure both appropriate levels of revenue and the recovery of costs, while at the same time enabling broad community access.

High or low prices?

Setting prices for sport activities can be quite complicated. It is often difficult to balance the need to cover costs and make profits with the desire to give people access and not have prohibitively high entry fees and prices. At the same time in the sport industry there are a number of guiding principles values and principles that can be used to defend specific pricing policies and strategies. While commercial sport pricing usually aims to extract as much money from fans as demand conditions allow, there are many instances when there is a need to adopt pricing policies that provide access to all categories of participants and supporters. This is why discounted entry fees are arranged for people with disabilities, on low incomes, or unemployed. In the area of community sport and leisure, there is often an even more pressing need to price sporting services to ensure broad access. On the other hand, prices cannot be so low that the facilities are sustained only through massive local taxpayer subsidies. There are many arguments both for and against the setting of admission fees that cover the full costs of participation on one hand, or account for only a small part of the fee on the other.

Full cost recovery

There are a number of reasons for setting prices that recover the costs of providing the service. They apply equally to spectator sports where a multitude of fans are keen to see the sporting heroes on the field of play, and community sport where the focus is on enabling people to participate in a range of sporting activities. Specifically, a number of benefits arise from full cost recovery pricing.

First, it encourages commercial investment in sport-related activities. Private developers will be encouraged to put resources into sport facilities if they see an appropriate price incentive and can more easily replicate the successes of existing sport service providers. As a result the range and level of sport opportunities will be improved. Second, it provides funds for the ongoing development of sport facilities and services. Many facilities and programs could not be provided if fees were not charged. This applies not only to commercial operations but also to those non-commercial facilities and programs which have high overhead costs or which are provided by organizations with limited budgets. Third, it permits some costly, but socially beneficial activities to be subsidized. Facilities which can generate a profit allow the operator to deliver low demand, but socially desirable facilities and programs which could otherwise not be provided. For instance, the surplus from full cost recovery pricing in high-demand areas like aerobics and fitness training can be used to fund specialist services like massage for the disabled and remedial physiotherapy. Finally, it provides funds for service improvements. In particular, it enables continual equipment upgrade, and permits the employment of more and better trained staff.

Pricing below cost

On the other hand, there are persuasive arguments against having a blanket policy that says all fees and charges should be based on full cost recovery. Although in reality there must be some way of paying the cost of delivering sport activity experiences (i.e. someone has to pay), there may be occasions when a fee or charge well below the cost of providing the service will be appropriate. The first point to be made is that high fees and charges create privileged access where the use of the facility or access of the service is dependent on the income of the user. Where the right of use is assumed by a narrow base of participants it discourages other individual and community group use. In the most severe case, existing users may see themselves as lessees with the right to reject initiatives to diversify the program or lower the cost of participation. This is why community-based swim centers usually price their services below cost. It signals to the community that the facility is not only open to all, but also a priority activity that has a valuable social benefit (in this case a healthy local community). Second, high fees and charges can exclude the disadvantaged. The higher price may come with a few add-on services, but it also penalizes the young, the unemployed, the socially disadvantaged, and the elderly. And, it is these groups who gain most from participating in a properly supported physical activity program. Finally, fees and charges based on a strict cost recovery model often lack a rationale or proper costing process. As Chapter 10 indicates, budgeting for specific programs and activities are fraught with difficulty, and there is always a margin for error which can produce underestimates of revenue and overestimates of costs.

Pricing strategies

As indicated previously, pricing sport products can be a challenging exercise. Since most sport organizations are not-for-profit it is not essential to set prices that maximize profits. Some sport organizations have a charter to provide their services to as many people as possible and ensure price is not a barrier to participation. At the same time, price is both an important marketing tool, and the means by which revenue is raised. There is therefore a balance to be achieved, with community access and accessibility at one end of the pricing policy continuum, and the need to raise as much revenue as possible at the other end of the continuum. In practice, there are a multitude of ways to price a sport product, some of which are geared to providing access and equity, others that are centered on ensuring a competitive edge over rivals and others that are aimed at maximizing revenues. In short, there are a number of principles and strategies that can be used when pricing sport products. They are listed below.

Cost-plus pricing

In the vast majority of cases it will be necessary to set a price that not only covers the cost of providing the sport activity or competition, but also includes a margin that contributes to the overall profitability of the club, association, event, or league. In the commercial business sector different formulae are use to decide what level of markup will be installed. For example, large department stores will often set prices that are two times higher than the purchase cost of the merchandise to ensure that all selling costs are covered, leaving a relatively modest unit-profit. For professional services or consulting businesses, the rule-of-thumb is to bill clients at an hourly rate that is two to three times the hourly rate charged by the consulting team. The payment is subsequently broken down into three segments. The first segment aims to cover the business's overheads and fixed cost, the second covers the consultant's salary, while the final segment becomes the profit margin.

In sport the same approach can be adopted. For example, a costing study may have shown that the average cost of delivering a swim program to users is around $10 a person comprising $3 for the cost of using the facility, $1 for maintenance costs, and $6 for staff costs. A swim charge of $12 will therefore not only cover all the costs of delivering the service but also give a $2 profit margin per user. So, for every person that uses the facility a $2 profit will be made.

Equity pricing

150

Equity pricing is effectively the opposite of cost-plus pricing, since the aim here is to set a price that does not impede people on low incomes, or from socially disadvantaged communities, from accessing the product or service. As noted in the earlier section of this chapter equity pricing will most probably involve setting a price below the average cost of delivering the service. Equity pricing can only be sustained if there is a grant or subsidy to cover the funding shortfall. Equity price is often used in community sport, and is frequently used in local sport to enable access and opportunity to the whole neighborhood. Equity pricing is less frequently used in commercial sport where the need to break even is more important, and special funding support is not available.

Demand-based pricing

In some instances, prices are set around what the market will bear. There are many examples of this in sport particularly where spectators are involved. For most sport events there is a fixed supply. That is, there are a fixed number of seats which cannot be changed in the short run. If, however it is anticipated that demand will increase strongly because the event has a star performance, or it is crucial to the league standing, then it makes sense to increase the price in the belief that the stadium will still draw a capacity attendance because of the sharp increase in the demand for seats. This always occurs for grand finals and championship contests, and in any case where the contest matters. So, it is not unexpected that an Ashes test match between Australia and England will have a higher demand and hence higher admission price than a friendly game between New Zealand and the Netherlands.

Demand-based pricing, or variable pricing as it is sometimes called, is based on two assumptions about the relationship between supply and demand. The first assumption is that where demand is high it is reasonable to increase price in the knowledge that the level of usage or support will remain at roughly the same level. The second assumption is that when demand is low it is time to lower price to stimulate the level of participant use and spectator support.

There are a number of situations where the demand for sport products will be high, and prices can be increased. In the case of spectator sport, demand will be highest at the weekend rather than a week night, where there are a number of star players involved (the Bradman, Jordan, and Woods factors are at work here), where two high-performing teams are playing, and when the premiership race is tightly contested. On the other hand, prices should be lowered where these factors are not present. Demand will be particularly weak when two low-performing teams with few stars are playing in a weekday match that does matter much. Variable pricing is not common in professional sport leagues, where admission prices are fixed at the beginning of the season. It is used extensively though in community sport and leisure service provision. For example, in gymnasia and fitness centers the casual rate is always higher in peak periods (like late afternoon and early evening) and lower in off-peak periods (like mid-morning). The variety of situations where high demand can accommodate higher prices and low demand, lower prices are listed in Table 11.1.

Table 11.1 High- and Low-Demand Conditions in Sport and Leisure

High-Demand Situation	Low-Demand Situation
Weekend	Mid-week
Late afternoon	Mid-morning
Monday evening	Friday evening

Elasticity pricing

Elasticity pricing, like demand-based pricing, is based on the changing relationships between demand and supply. But, unlike demand-based pricing, it aims to set a price on the basis of estimations of how sensitive demand is likely to be a change in price. There are two possibilities to consider here.

First, demand can be sensitive to price change. For example, studies may have found that when the price of fitness center annual membership fell by 10 percent (from $200 to $180) the demand for memberships increased by 20 percent (from 300 to 360). This means that whereas total member receipts were $60 000 (300 × $200) at the higher price, it was $64 800 (360 × $180) at the lower price. In this instance demand is described as elastic, which means it is better to charge lower prices, since total receipts or revenue will increase as a result (Table 11.2).

Table 11.2 Relationship between Elastic Demand, Prices, and Revenue

Elastic demand	Demand is sensitive to price change	Price increase generates a fall in revenue	Price fall generates an increase in revenue

Alternatively, demand can be insensitive to price change. If for example, another study found that demand for fitness center memberships fell by a miniscule 3 percent (from 300 to 291) in response to a price increase of 10 percent (from $200 to $220) then demand would be price inelastic. That is, demand was relatively insensitive to a change in price. In this case the increase in memberships leads to an increase in total member receipts or revenue. Whereas the lower price generated revenues of $60 000 the higher price generated revenues of just over $64 000. In this case it therefore makes commercial sense to increase membership fees (Table 11.3).

Table 11.3 Relationship between Inelastic Demand, Prices, and Revenue

Inelastic demand	Demand is insensitive to price change	Price increase generates an increase in revenue	Price fall generates a fall in revenue

The same principle applies to ticket pricing for professional sport leagues. However, the evidence is ambiguous when it comes to deciding if the demand for stadium seats is price elastic or price inelastic. The intuitive response is to say that demand is price inelastic because sport fans have strong emotional attachments to teams. However, this is only partly true since not all fans are so passionate that they will attend despite any increase in admission prices. Many fans will attend if they expect good value for money, and may have a price threshold beyond which they are not prepared to go. In addition, price sensitivity may change with income levels. Fans on high incomes for instance may be insensitive to price while low-income earners may be far more price sensitive to different sport experiences.

Prestige pricing

When buyers want a special experience, their sensitivity to product features generally overrides their sensitivity to price. Owning an exclusive and high-status product gives some people not only confidence in their purchase but also security in their own sense of self. Highly priced products are more exclusive to own, and hence become more desirable to those who seek out status and prestige. Prestige goods can be used to authenticate success or economic power, and are sometimes called positional goods. This is because their prestige-value is contingent on them being relatively scarce, and available only to a select few.

Prestige pricing is particularly prevalent in the provision of sport stadium seats. Private boxes are highly priced and therefore only accessible to an exclusive few. This makes it very attractive to the fan who wants prestige and status in addition to a quality game experience. The provision of exclusive membership packages serves the same function. The high price comes with additional service benefits like gourmet meals, luxury seats, and free drinks, but the main benefit is the belief that the membership package is only available to a select few.

Quality-assurance pricing

In many instances, price can be used to reinforce a brand image of quality as exemplified in the slogan quality-comes-at-a-price. In this case the higher price is indicative of a superior product, and a low-price indicative of a lower-quality product. In other words, buyers believe that you get what you pay for, and therefore will pay more with the expectation of getting more. Simply put, a high price can enhance the perceived quality of a product when compared to substitutes. For example, when battery-run electronic clocks and watches first appeared on the market their low-initial price was seen as indicative of low quality. Sales soared when prices were raised to levels comparable to their mechanical substitutes. The problem created by the initial low price was that consumers did not believe they were getting more than they were used to paying for, largely because the cost and quality innovations were radical and not visibly apparent. Price can therefore be used to signal

153

that extra effort has been made to produce a superior product that will perform to the buyer's satisfaction.

Quality-assurance pricing is particularly relevant to sport. Mega-sport events use a quality-assurance model when they set prices for their tournaments. In Australia, an international sport fixture in any code of football will always attract a premium price. Whereas a local interclub game, even when involving two high-quality professional teams, will have a price between AUD 15 and AUD 50, a game involving the national team will attract an admission price of AUD 100 to AUD 500. In 2006 the Australian world football team played Greece at the MCG, and on the expectation of a quality game featuring Australia's best players, tickets were marked from AUD 50 to AUD 600. The game was a sellout. A similar situation arose at the 2006 Commonwealth Games, when the opening ceremony confirmed the expectation that it would be quality experience by setting ticket prices in the AUD 40 to AUD 500 range.

Discriminatory pricing

Discriminatory pricing, or differential pricing as it is sometimes called, involves charging different prices to different market segments and product users. The underlying assumption behind this approach to pricing is that different groups of people have different capacities to pay, and that the greater the capacity to pay, the higher the price to be charged. Capacity to pay is in turn linked to the income levels of consumers. As a result, this model of pricing concludes that professional workers like company directors, lawyers, doctors, and academics will be able to pay higher prices than teachers, clerks, and nurses for the similar good or service. At the other end of the socioeconomic spectrum the unemployed and students will have a very low capacity to pay, and will thus be repelled by high prices for anything but essential products like food, drink, and rent.

Discriminatory pricing operates at two levels. First, it aims to maximize revenue by adopting a high-price threshold for high-income earners where demand is not choked, but receipts are maximized. Second, it targets low-income earners with the bait of low prices to ensure a higher level of demand. By segmenting the market on the basis of capacity to pay, it is anticipated that total revenue will be optimized, and certainly higher than if a single price was charged to everyone.

This is a common feature of sport pricing at both the participant and spectator level. Low prices are charged for unemployed and people on disability pensions, while a discount is also provided to students. A higher price is charged for adults, while a special price is charged for family groups. The family price is usually a middle ground price which provides an average family member charge that is somewhere between the adult entry and the student entry.

Competition pricing

In this instance prices are placed in line with competitors. This is done to first ensure that prices are not so high that potential purchases will shift their spending to competitor's products. The second reason is to ensure that price is not so low that while it attracts new purchasers, it fails to secure any available consumer surplus.

This device is frequently used in sport. At the community level one of the first things a sport and fitness center does is compile a list of competitor prices as a means of setting a benchmark price for its services. While this can quickly establish a pricing band (which sets a minimum and maximum fee or charge) it can also squeeze the potential for profits by not taking the cost structure of competitors into account. For example, if a swim center finds that the average entry fee for its competitors is $8 it may want to set a competitive entry fee of $9. This seems reasonable, but it might find that while the average operating costs of its competitors is around $7, its own operating costs are $10. If it also aims to break even on its operations then a $9 entry fee will not be sustainable.

Penetration pricing

Penetration pricing occurs when price is initially discounted, and then set below cost. The aim is to build market share and earn profits from future repeat sales. A business can offer a penetration price in several ways. At the extreme, a company selling new pharmaceuticals will introduce them at a zero price through free sampling. Computer software is also often given away to opinion leaders. Penetration pricing can be a very effective pricing strategy for the following reasons:

1. It results in faster adoption and market penetration. This can take the competition by surprise.
2. It creates an early-adopter goodwill, which results in more word-of-mouth adoptions.
3. It creates cost-reduction and cost-control pressures and this creates the condition for productivity improvements and high levels of efficiency.
4. It discourages the entry of competitors by signaling to others that it has sustainable, cost-competitive advantages.

Penetration pricing has the potential for use in some sport situations, and in particular where a new sport league has been introduced, or new gymnasium program offered. Penetration pricing can also be usefully employed in attracting new members to community sport clubs and leisure centers where the level of service and facility quality is similar between competing organizations. In this case the probability of creating a value-for-money experience is high and word-of-mouth can elicit a second swell of interest, even if prices are increased for this group of users.

Price skimming

Price skimming is the opposite of penetration pricing, since it sets a relatively high level to attract a threshold of buyers who value the product most highly. Its aim is to set a price above its competitors so as to ensure a high surplus for a limited demand. Like premium pricing it requires a loyal market where quality is valued over price. It is also best used when supply is limited. In sport it can be applied to luxury stadium seating and exclusive gymnasium facilities. It can be combined with premium pricing to capture high-income consumers who put high value on positional goods like an opening ceremony at a mega-sport event.

Pricing strategies in professional sports leagues

Despite the growth of sporting sponsorship and broadcasting rights fees, game tickets sales are still an important source of revenue for professional sport leagues and clubs. Although it has fallen in relative terms (in the 1970s it comprised between 50 and 70 percent of club revenues), it is still in the top four revenue streams for most large sport clubs and leagues.

Pricing is a crucial component of revenue collection for two reasons. First it establishes the contribution that each paying fan will make to league and club finances, and second it also impacts on the demand for tickets. Research has shown that in USA professional sports league fans cite the cost of attending games as the single most important factor influencing their preparedness to attend. Whereas only 14 percent of fans said that a change in team performance would impact on their decision to buy a ticket, 57 percent said that increasing ticket prices would influence their pattern of attendance (Howard and Crompton 2004:39). This begs the question as to how ticket prices are determined in professional sport leagues. On the basis of the earlier analysis of pricing it would be logical to adopt pricing strategies that in the first instance cover costs, secondly compare favorably with the price of rival leagues and competitors, and third, reflect demand conditions.

Pricing strategies

In a study of ticket pricing in to America's National Football League (NFL) it was found that team performance was the single most important factor. In other words, when teams were winning more than they were losing ticket-pricers wanted to increase ticket prices. Behind this view is the assumption that a winning team would attract more fans who would be prepared to pay more for a winning experience. Other important factors included the need to secure more revenue, general economic conditions, and the level of fan identification. The least important factors were the expected television coverage, access to the game, weather conditions, and the presence of star players. A list of the factors and their relative importance are included in Table 11.4.

156

Table 11.4 Factors Influencing Ticket Pricing in the NFL

Description	Most Important (%)	Not Important (%)
Team performance	43	11
Revenue needs	37	11
Average price	32	21
Economic factors	21	21
Market price toleration	21	16
Fan identification	16	16
Public relations	16	11
Capacity of facility	11	21
Competing entertainment	11	37
Condition of facility	11	64
Average income	6	43
Population	0	64
Schedule	0	85
Television media coverage	0	85
Accessibility	0	90
Star players	0	95
Weather conditions	0	100
Racial composition	0	100

Source: Reese, J., Mittelstaedt, R. (2001).

However, the research should not be taken as confirmation that sports' pricing is systematic and based on firm costing principles. In fact, when it comes to ticket pricing, some critics believes that sport managers operate "by the seat of their pants" (Howard and Crompton 2004:356). According to some sport economists, the pricing of tickets in the USA is nothing more than "best informed guesses" (Quirk and Fort 1992:144). The rough rule-of-thumb for most sport event organizers is to set prices that first generates an appropriate cash flow, second compares favorably with related sport events, and finally takes into account any threshold price that fans would baulk at paying. In other words, they charge the going rate. The going rate is a safe and conservative approach, but there is no guarantee that they will cover costs. Tickets may alternatively be priced to ensure it covers all event or operating costs. In some instances it may be necessary to set a price that aims to recover both the capital repayment cost as well as operating costs. At the other extreme, ticket prices may be set below the operating cost to stimulate club membership and fan interest.

The problem of escalating admission prices

As noted previously, price performs a number of essential functions for sport organizations. First, it is the basis of every revenue stream. Sponsorships, league and club merchandise, and media rights all have a price, and at the most fundamental level, membership, and game admission both come at a

157

price. Second, it is a tool for extracting revenue from different corporate, member, and fan segments. Sport marketers have developed sophisticated techniques for dividing up the sport experience into a variety of categories, and pricing each category on the basis of the different benefits that are provided. Club memberships and sport stadium seating are good cases in point. Third, price can be used as a policy tool by setting high fees or charges for one group of members or fans, and using the surplus to fund a low or indeed below-cost fee for low income earners or some other disadvantaged group.

For the fan, price is simply part of the cost of obtaining a sport experience. It can be a source of attraction insofar as it represents a bargain, or just value for money. On the other hand, it may have the effect of excluding some fans, and privileging others. So, what can we say about the pricing of sport events, and the changes that have occurred over recent years. And how might we explain these changes? In the first place, the price of attending elite sport events has escalated over recent times. There are two inflationary forces. The first is administrative salaries and player payments. In the Australian Football League (AFL), for example, the average player salary has increased from AUD 50 000 in 1990 to AUD 150 000 in 2005. In National Rugby League (NRL) a similar explosion of player wages occurred. The second factor is stadium construction and maintenance costs. During the 20th century major stadium redevelopment took place in the USA, Europe, and Australia, with the construction cost frequently exceeding USD 300 million (Foster, Greyser and Walsh 2006).

According to Howard and Crompton (2004) investment in sport stadia and arenas have increased exponentially over the last 10–15 years. Furthermore the actual cost of constructing the facility can sometimes be less than 50 percent of the total project costs. In one stadium development costing more than USD 470 million, land purchase and site preparation cost USD 100 million, relocating transport infrastructure cost another USD 65 million, and the establishment of parking facilities cost another USD 10 million (Howard and Crompton 2004:52). While these additional costs are necessary, they put additional pressures on the game admission prices.

There is also an additional factor that needs to be addressed. This complicating factor is the revenue that leagues and clubs obtain from the corporate world. Television rights, merchandising income, and sponsorship fees now provide a dominant contribution to their revenue base. This non-admission charge revenue source can not only add to profits, but also be used to subsidize admission charges and membership fees. The AFL claims that the full cost of maintaining the national competition is around AUD 40 per person attending. However, the sponsorship and other corporate funding enables the AFL to currently charge no more that AUD 20 per person attending on a walk-up basis. Table 11.5 shows a relatively modest increase in standard AFL ticket prices between 1990 and 2005.

Despite the size of the corporate subsidy, the pressure on ticket prices has been severe. As a result, the general level of admission prices for professional sport leagues has risen substantially over the last 10 years. When this is combined with the replacement of terrace-based grounds with all seat stadia, there was pressure to seek out affluent fans who were prepared to pay something extra for a quality experience. In other words, a new type of fan

Table 11.5 AFL Base Admission Charges (AUD) to Home and Away Games

1990	1995	2000	2005
10	13	14	20

was targeted at the expense of the old. The traditional working class fan has been marginalized, while the more affluent professional middle class supporter has been more strongly targeted (King 1998). In the USA, this trend caused one commentator to conclude that professional sport had gone through a process of white-collarization. Table 11.6 shows the scale of the change in ticket prices between 1991 and 2003.

Table 11.6 Costs (in USD) of Attending Major League Sporting Events for a Family of Four

League	1991	2003
MLB	77	145
NBA	139	255
NFL	153	290
NHL	133	240

Source: Howard, D. and Crompton, J. (2004).

A similar trend occurred in English professional sport in general and English Premier League (EPL) in particular. In 2006 a standard seat at Chelsea's Stamford Bridge stadium cost GBP 45 to GBP 50. By contrast a seat in 1995 cost GBP 10. The pressure to increase ticket prices in EPL was compounded by the Glazer family buy-out of Manchester United Football club in 2005. In order to help cover GBP 650 million in loans acquired to purchase the club, plans were made to increase ticket prices by over 50 percent over the next 5 years. The movement in EPL ticket prices over the last 15 years is listed in Table 11.7.

The quality experience that professional sport now provides its fans has come at a cost. The all seat stadium that offers superior sightlines, greater

Table 11.7 EPL Standard Ticket Price (GBP) Trends 1990–2005

1990	1995	2000	2005
10	16	25	35

comfort, a weatherproof playing surface, extensive food and drink, protection from the rain, and even the occasional retractable roof, has ensured a quality spectator experience. However, it also comes with a stiff ticket price. Many low-income supporters have been priced out of regular attendance, and in their place has sauntered middle class, white-collar families. Television is now the medium by which most fans watch their favorite professional sport team. Live attendance is now all about capacity to pay, and paying for the privilege.

In the short term, a pricing strategy that customizes the needs of fans around the capacity to pay will boost revenue. In the long term, the benefits may be undermined by two factors. First, ticket prices may exceed the price threshold of many fans. Second, many fickle theatre-goers may decide to direct their discretionary spending to some newly fashionable leisure experience. This begs the question as to whether loyalty and passion has been subordinated to preparedness to pay as the primary link between fans and professional sport leagues? And, if it has, will professional sport maintain its mass appeal?

Questions to consider

1. Why is pricing so important to the financial viability of sport organizations?
2. What is meant by full cost recovery pricing?
3. Contrast full cost recovery pricing with pricing below cost. Under what circumstance would it be possible and proper to price below cost for a sport service? Where does equity pricing fit into this context?
4. Give examples of cost-plus pricing in sport.
5. How does demand-based pricing work in sport?
6. Give examples of sport products that might have a low-price elasticity of demand, and those sport products that might have a high-price elasticity of demand.
7. How does prestige pricing work in sport, both at the low and high end of the market? And, how is quality-assurance pricing linked to prestige pricing?
8. How does discriminatory pricing work in sport? Give examples from community sport and recreation, and professional sport leagues.
9. Contrast penetration pricing with skimming pricing. Under what conditions would one approach be used over the other?
10. How important is competition pricing in sport?
11. What are the pressures on ticket prices in professional sport?
12. Is there any evidence that higher ticket prices for professional sport league games are threatening attendance levels?

Further reading

An extensive analysis of different pricing regimes, including full cost pricing, market-based pricing, subsidized pricing and free pricing, is provided by Anthony, R. and Young, D. (2003). *Management Control in Non-profit Organizations*, 7th Edition. McGraw Hill, Chapter 7 (Pricing Decisions).

For a concise introduction to the pricing of services (including sport-related services) see Hoffman, K. and Bateson, J. (2001). *Essentials of Services Marketing*, 2nd Edition. South Western, Chapter 7 (The Pricing of Services), which includes a discussion of the distinction between cost, price, and value.

A useful introduction to the pricing of sport products is contained in Mullin, B., Hardy, S. and Sutton, W. (2001). *Sport Marketing*, 2nd Edition. Human Kinetics, Chapter 9 (Pricing Strategies). For an extensive analysis of the economics of pricing in the sport and leisure see Tribe, J. (2004). *The Economics of Recreation, Leisure and Tourism*, 3rd Edition. Elsevier.

In Howard, D. and Crompton, J. (2004). *Financing Sport*, 2nd Edition. Fitness Information Technology, there is an extensive analysis of pricing and ticketing in USA professional sport leagues. See Chapter 9 (Ticket Sales and Operations).

In Foster, G., Greyser, S. and Walsh, B (2006). *The Business of Sports*. Thomson, there is a succinct analysis of how ticket prices for USA professional sport leagues are packaged and tiered. See Section 7 (Local Revenue Enhancement and Ticket Pricing).

12 Cost–benefit analysis

Overview

This chapter will examine the application of cost–benefit analysis to sport organizations and events. Cost–benefit analysis has become an essential tool for measuring the costs and benefits that accrue to cities and communities from hosting sport events. The chapter will commence with a detailed review of economic impact statements, and the ways in which they are constructed. Particular attention will be given to their validity and how they can be manipulated to give exaggerated results. This will be followed by a discussion of the relationship between economic impact statements and cost–benefit analysis, and how non-economic benefits and costs may be measured.

Economic impacts in sport

State governments, cities, and local councils around the world put many resources into securing major sport events. They argue that running a sport event is a good investment because it provides a major economic boost to the local economy. At the same time there are many consultants who claim to be

Table 12.1 Attendance and Visitor Profiles for Selected Sport Events in the UK

Event	Host City	Attendances (Thousand)	Out-of-Town (Percentage)
1997 World Badminton	Glasgow	22	62
1997 Cricket Cornhill Test Match	Birmingham	73	92
1997 Women's British Open Golf	Sunningdale	50	99
1999 European Show Jumping	Hickstead	40	55
1999 World Judo	Birmingham	16	87
2000 Flora London Marathon	Gateshead	300	57
2001 World Half Marathon	Bristol	15	45
2003 World Cup Triathlon	Manchester	31	85

Source: UK Sport (2004).

experts in producing economic impact statements for major sport events. These statements are used to either convince a government that an event will produce a significant economic impact, or that it has produced an impact. In both cases the figures can be easily exaggerated for a number of reasons that will be discussed in a later section of this chapter. It is therefore essential that sport administrators understand what economic impact statements are all about, and the theory that underpins their construction. So, where do we begin?

Economic impact statements work on the principle that people who go to an event directly spend money in and around the event. This money is then circulated in the local economy, and, because of a ripple effect, creates indirect and additional levels of spending, income, and employment. As a result it is argued that sport events that can attract a large attendance will make a positive impact on the local economy. However, this argument is only partly true, since the real impact comes from people attending from out-of-town. In other words, locals who attend merely shift their spending from the suburbs to the inner-city or just from one suburb to another. In addition, it is also important to recognize how many people may leave town in order to get away from the event (the avoiders). There is also the problem of identifying people who changed their itinerary to come to town for this event rather than another (the time-switchers), and those people who were in town anyway, and just happened to attend the event (the casuals). There is also the confounding problem of using attendance figures to establish the number of out-of-towners who came for the event. A 100 000 attendance looks good to the event organizers, but is not so attractive to civic leaders if only 10 percent come from outside the host city. On the other hand a crowd of 50 000, 80 percent of whom are from outside the city, will provide the greater economic impact. Therefore attendance figures alone are a poor indicator of an event's economic impact. Table 12.1 lists a sample of sport events held in the UK from 1997 to 2003, and shows the breakdown of local and out-of-town visitors.

163

Another important thing to note is that whereas a sport event may incur an operating loss it may still produce a net benefit to the host city if it attracts sufficient out-of-towners to compensate for the loss. This state of affairs has regularly occurred with the Formula 1 Grand Prix held in Melbourne every March. It is a costly event to run, since it not only involves setting up the facilities and providing a safe track, but also involves the payment of a multi-million dollar fee to the event owner. While revenues from the event have rarely covered expenses, the Victorian State Government and City of Melbourne continue to support the event on the grounds that it attracts thousands of visitors from interstate and overseas who not only stay for up to one week each, but also spend extravagantly during their stay.

Non-economic impacts

It is also important to understand that major sport events produce more than economic benefits. They can also produce many social, environmental, and cultural benefits for the host city including a strengthening of civic pride, a beautification of the surrounds, a stronger international image, and urban renewal through the stimulus to inner-city infrastructure. On the other hand it can also come with substantial economic, social, and environmental costs. There are not only the costs of building the sports' infrastructure to support the event, but also the expenses of running the event, the loss of amenity and convenience, inner-city congestion, and an increasing cost associated with ensuring a secure climate for players, officials, and spectators. This wider approach is called benefit–cost analysis. In some cases the economic benefits may be overwhelmed by social and environmental costs. In other cases the economic benefits may be complemented by social and environmental benefits.

The rationale for public support of sport events

It is one thing to claim that a sport event is an integral part of a community's cultural fabric, and should be supported because it can attract an audience, get people talking, and make them feel better about themselves. It is another thing to convince a government official that it is sufficiently important to warrant a subsidy, grant, or some other form of taxpayer support. This issue arises frequently in sport in the USA, where cities are prepared to build, at taxpayers' expense, multi-million dollar stadia to attract a professional football, baseball, basketball or ice-hockey franchise (Euchner 1993). So, how do they justify the spending of scarce community resources on the construction of a stadium or arena for the use of an often privately owned sports team?

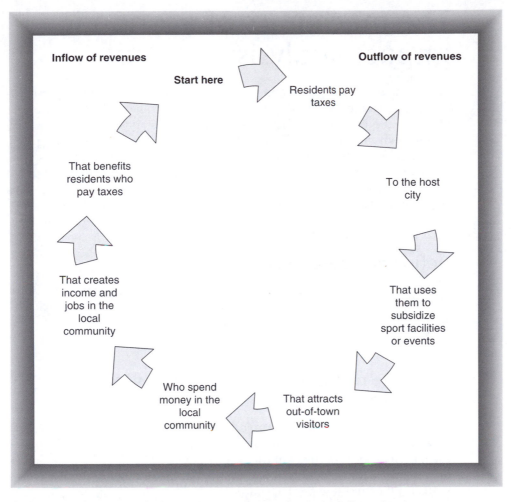

Figure 12.1 The Rationale for Taxpayer Support of Sport Stadia and Events

The same question arises when one examines the hosting of large-scale sport festivals like the Olympic and Commonwealth Games, where the combined capital and operating costs can exceed AUD 3000 million. The answer is embedded in the proposition that the investment of taxpayers' funds will yield a return that makes the whole community better off. The scale of the return is dependent on the number of visitors attracted to the event, and the amount of money they spend during their stay in the host city. This relationship between taxpayer subsidies, event impact, and community payoff is illustrated in Figure 12.1.

This outflow of funds to generate a consequent inflow of revenue can be viewed as a "virtuous cycle of community development" Howard and Crompton (2004:105). However the cycle becomes virtuous only when the flow of revenue and associated benefits exceeds the flow of funds into the event or stadium.

The mechanics of economic impact analysis

The mechanics of doing an economic impact statement are reasonably straight-forward once the jargon is deconstructed and the steps identified. Fundamentally the key to an effective analysis is to establish first, how many out-of-town visitors have come just for the event, second, how long they stayed for, third, how much they spent on average per day, and finally how much of their spending stayed within the host city, and how much leaked to other places and regions. The following fictitious case illustrates the steps required to undertake an economic impact analysis for a sport event.

Define and describe the event

I will examine the Berwick City Master's Tennis Classic, a tournament for club tennis players aged 35 years and over. The location is the Berwick City Tennis Club. The event was held from the 10 to 15 April.

Calculate number of visitors to Berwick for event

I will count the number of occupied hotel or motel rooms and beds, and breakfast accommodation, and count the number of registered participants. I will exclude local participants: they are not visitors. I will also exclude visitors not there for the tennis. It was found that the number of tennis visitors is 1000, although there are 1200 participants. The number of out-of-towners who participated in the event is consequently 1000.

Survey a representative sample of visitors

I will use the survey of out-of-town participants (i.e. visitors) to establish average number of days stayed, and average spending per visitor. The average number of days stayed per visitor is estimated to be 5 days. The average spending per visitor is estimated to be $150 per day, which equals $750 per tennis visitor.

I will check to see if extreme spending by some visitors skews the average upward. That is, the average or mean ($750) may be higher than median spending ($600). The median is the figure that splits the visitor spending 50 percent above and 50 percent below. In this case, the majority of visitors spend less than $750. I will also ensure that different visitor types are accounted for: overseas, interstate, nearby city, and nearby town. Overseas visitors generally spend more than nearby visitors.

Calculate total visitor expenditure

I will calculate total visitor expenditure by multiplying the number of out-of-town visitors by average spending during visit. That is, $1000 \times \$750 = \$750\,000$.

Calculate any time-switching factor

I am aware that time-switching relates to the number of people who intended to visit Berwick earlier but changed their schedule to fit in with the tennis tournament. The survey found that 10 percent (i.e. 100 visitors) were time-switchers (equal to $100 \times \$750 = \$75\,000$ visitor expenditure).

Calculate net visitor expenditure (NVE)

Time-switcher spending is subtracted from total visitor expenditure ($750\,000$ less $75\,000$). This gives the net visitor expenditure (NVE) of $675\,000$.

Use a multiplier to account for the ripple effect from spending on accommodation, food, entertainment, transport, and personal services

I also note that multipliers are used to estimate the overall impact of spending on community income and employment levels. Multipliers are calculated from input–output tables that economists construct in modeling regional economies. Multipliers can vary between industry sectors – where 2 is high, and 1 is low. The higher the spending leakage to suppliers outside the host city, the lower is the multiplier. The regional leisure multiplier for this event is 1.5.

Calculate the economic impact of the Berwick City Autumn Tennis Classic

The NVE of $675\,000$ is multiplied by 1.5 to generate a $1 million addition to aggregate community income. This is the economic impact. These eight steps provide an estimation of the economic impact only. However, it can be converted to a broader benefit–cost calculus by working through the following four steps.

Calculate costs of staging event

I understand that the event costs can be divided into capital and operating costs, where capital costs included clubhouse refurbishment of $500\,000$, court resurfacing of $200\,000$, landscaping of $100\,000$, which produces a total capital cost of $800\,000$. The facilities are an asset, but are also a lost opportunity. That is, they could have been used to deliver other benefits (e.g. school or health center).

Operating costs/expenses comprise wages and staff payments of $100 000; promotions of $50 000; and general administration of $50 000. Total operating costs are therefore $200 000.

Calculate event revenues

I note that the revenues comprise entry fees of $50 000, sponsorship of $50 000, and a government grant of $100 000. Total revenue is therefore $200 000.

Calculate net economic benefit (NEB)

To ensure a broader compilation of benefits and costs, I added total revenues to the $1 million economic impact. I also subtracted the operating costs and share of the capital costs from the gross economic benefit. The net economic benefit (NEB) is therefore $800 000 comprising $1 million economic impact less $200 000 share of capital cost (allocated 25 percent amortization in Year 1 of 4 years) less $200 000 operating cost, plus $200 000 event revenue. Had I allocated the total capital cost to this year's event, the NEB would have been only $200 000.

Benefit–cost ratio

A benefit–cost ratio can be calculated by dividing total benefits by total costs. That is, $1 million plus $200 000 of benefits is divided by $200 000 plus $200 000 of costs to produce a ratio of 1.2/0.4 = 3:1.

Proceed with caution

In summary, undertaking an impact analysis, a number of important tasks need to be undertaken and in the above example it begins with a brief description of the event and ends with the calculation of the economic impact flowed by estimations of additional benefits and costs. But beware that the figures are subject to error, and there are also non-economic benefits and costs to consider to obtain a broad overview of benefits and costs.

Margins for error

At first glance the figures that come out of an economic impact analysis look impressive. For the most part they are conducted by consulting businesses with experience in the field, and are supported by a conceptual framework. There is also a strong internal logic to the results, and this gives a study of this type instant credibility. However, the figures are also subject to a high degree of error, and in most instances should be treated with caution. Indeed, some critics argue that a high proportion of impact statements exaggerate the results by a factor of 5 to 10 (Howard and Crompton 2004:109). The pressures to stretch the numbers were exemplified in a Dallas USA 2012 Olympic Bid Committee claim that the Games would produce a USD 4000 million benefit.

These exaggerations are not difficult to make because at each stage of the impact methodological uncertainties arise. First, the out-of-town visitor numbers are calculated from samples of accommodation estimates, the responses of people who attend the event, and in-bound tourist statistics. These databases provide strong ballpark figures, but in no way constitute accurate figures.

Second, the average expenditures per visitor per day are also subject to error. They are collected through questionnaires distributed to a sample of relevant informants. However, it is never easy to secure a representative sample of visitors, and this is a problem since spending between visitor types can vary considerably. Moreover, when people are invited to record their recollection of how much they spent and what they spent it on, the responses can be quite unreliable. On the one hand, some spending may have been forgotten, or deliberately hidden to avoid embarrassment, while other spending may have been topped-up to confirm one's self-importance.

Finally the weight of the multiplier may be inappropriate. While multipliers are tested and validated through various forms of input–output analysis, and statistical benchmarking, they are often used incorrectly. It is never clear exactly how much initial spending is recirculated in the host city or town, and how much is redirected or leaked to external businesses and employers. In some instances the multiplier can be as high as 1.8 (i.e. for every dollar of visitor spending there is a $1.80 increase in overall economic activity) or as low as 1.1 (i.e. for every dollar of visitor spending there is only a $1.10 increase in overall economic activity. The problematic use of multipliers for sport event impact statements is discussed in detail in Howard and Crompton (2004) and Li, Hofacre and Mahoney (2001).

Problems in doing impact statements

As indicated previously, there are a number of crucial steps involved in putting together an economic impact statement. In this section attention will be paid to three important activities. The first activity is to establish a framework by which to classify events so that useful comparisons and contrasts can be made once the results have been tabulated. The second activity is to set up a process for collecting data on the number of out-of-town visitors for the event. The third activity is to design methods for estimating visitor expenditure. The final activity is to agree on a reasonable method for calculating the final impact, being careful to distinguish between expenditure, output, and employment.

Table 12.2 Typology of Sporting Events

Frequent	Community Tennis	(Australian) National Rugby League Game
Infrequent	Sydney-city-to-surf fun run	Formula 1 Grand Prix
	Participant-based	Spectator-based

Typologizing sport events

There are many ways of distinguishing between different types of sport events but when looking at their impacts the following typology is useful. First, events can be classified because of their regularity or frequency. That is, they are held on a regular basis, which could be every week (in the case of a sport league) or every 4 years, (in the case of the World Rugby Union Cup). Second, they may be mainly spectator events, or alternatively participant-based events. These two differences can be illustrated in Table 12.2.

It is also possible to add a third dimension by using a bubble chart to signal the scale of the event and its likely economic impact. A large bubble indicates a large impact, while a small bubble indicates a marginal to slight impact (Figure 12.2). It is therefore technically possible for an irregular participant-based event (bubble 2) to secure a larger eco-impact than a regular spectator-based event (bubble 3).

Estimating the number of out-of-town visitors

As indicated previously the scale of any economic impact for a sport event is directly related to the number of visitors who are in town to attend the event. This raises the issue as to how to best calculate this figure. Generally speaking a composite number is generated from hotel reservations, and tickets purchased by interstate and international visitors. The numbers can be refined by identifying specific categories of visitors, including athletes, officials, and media representatives.

However the task of calculating just how many people came just for the event, and how many people went elsewhere because of the event, can become quite messy. There are a number of different visitor and home-resident movements during the event that need to be identified.

It is also important to discard all those visitors who would have visited anyway, but rescheduled their visit to coincide with the event as well as those people who just happened to be visiting when the event was running.

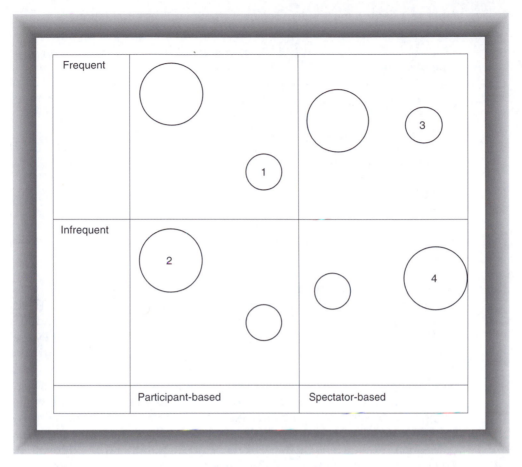

Figure 12.2 Possible relationships that could result. 1: Monthly basketball tournament; 2: London Marathon; 3: English Premier League game and 4: Cricket test match

It should also be noted that attendance levels are not a good proxy for the number of out-of-town visitors, since a significant proportion will usually be local residents. There are also some negative visitor movements which involve local residents deciding to leave the host city for the duration of the event. In fact there are eight issues to deal with here.

First it is not just a matter of counting the number of people who came to the city only because the event was on. These event-fan visitors are clearly important, because they directly increase the amount of spending. However, they constitute only one segment of people affected by the staging of the event. A second segment, as previously noted, is the casuals. However since casuals are defined as tourists who would have been in town, even if the games had not been held, they should not be included in any extra-spending calculation. A similar problem exists with time-switchers, the third segment who would have visited the city at another time, but changed their itinerary to coincide with the event. They too, should not be included in the

Table 12.3 Visitor and Resident Segments for Sport Event Evaluation

Type of Group	Demographic Weight	Impact on Host City Spending
Event-fans (visitors)	XXX	Positive
Extensioners (visitors)	XX	Positive
Home-stayers (residents)	XX	Positive
Casuals (visitors)	XX	Neutral
Time-switchers (visitors)	XX	Neutral
Runaways (residents)	XX	Negative
Changers (residents)	X	Negative
Avoiders (visitors)	X	Neutral

Source: Based on research by Preuss (2004).

extra-spending calculation. A fourth segment is the extensioners, who would have come anyway, but extend their stay because of the event. These people should clearly be included in the calculation of additional spending. Similarly home-stayers the fifth segment, should be included since they are defined as people who may have taken holidays elsewhere, but chose to stay home and attend the event instead. A sixth segment are the avoiders, who would have visited the host city had the event not been on. The seventh segment, the runaways, are residents who leave the city during the event, while changers, the eighth segment, effectively do the same thing by deciding to shift their out-of-town holidays to the event time. These final three segments consequently take spending away from the host city, rather than adding to it. The spending impact of each of the above eight groups can be illustrated in Table 12.3.

Visitor spending

It is one thing to calculate the number of people who came to town in order to attend the event, and who would not have otherwise visited. It is another thing to collect reliable data on their spending patterns. It is therefore important to design a comprehensive but clear questionnaire that can capture the proper levels of visitor expenditure. There are two crucial steps to be taken when designing a questionnaire. The first is to breakdown visitor spending into a number of categories, being careful to distinguish between event-related spending and other spending. An example of how this can be done is listed in Table 12.4.

The second is to segment the visitors into specific types. This allows the results to show not only what type of visitors predominated, but also how much each visitor type spent. Research has shown that competitors spend less per day than officials. The heaviest spenders are media representatives. An

Table 12.4 Categories of Visitor Expenditure

Type of Expenditure	Amount Spent During Visit ($)
Admission/entry fees to event	
Food and beverages at event	
Food and beverages not at event	
Night clubs and bars (charges, drinks, etc.)	
Retail shopping (clothing, souvenirs, gifts, etc.)	
Accommodation expenses (hotel, motel, etc.)	
Motor vehicle expenses (fuel, oil, repairs, parking fees, etc.)	
Rental car expenses	
Event-related merchandise	
Other expenses	

English study found that whereas a typical competitor spent GBP 55 to GBP 65 per day, media people spent from GBP 100 to GBP 125 per day (UK Sport 2004).

Non-economic benefits and costs

In assessing the impact of a sport event or the host city or region, nearly all of the space is given to the economic benefits, which, as noted previously, centers on visitor expenditure and its spending, employment, and tax collection spin-offs. When challenged, the impact statement proponents will cautiously review the financial costs incurred in securing the economic benefits. While this allows for a more effective analysis of the net benefits flowing from the event, it does not tell the full story. In reality there are often a clutch of non-economic benefits and costs that are relegated to the fine print at best, or ignored at worst. These benefits and costs may not have the same weight as the economic outputs, but they are sufficiently important to demand attention. These additional factors are listed in Table 12.5.

The legacy

Another way of viewing the impact of a sport event on the host city is to compile a list of its expected legacy which is concerned more with long-term tangible and intangible benefits arising from the event. It can be subtle but significant, like an expanded sense of community pride and confidence that is a catalyst

173

Table 12.5 Non-Economic Benefits and Costs Associated with Sporting Events

Factor	Benefit	Cost
Traffic congestion and increase in travel time		X
Loss of amenity due to event occupying space or facility		X
Increase in community and civic pride through identification with successful event	X	
Homeless and low-income residents move out-of-city in order to accommodate visitors		X
Environment cleaned up to impress visitors	X	
Increase in security associated with fall in crime rate	X	
Marginalized groups use event to protest and disrupt commuters and visitors	X	X
Inner-city crowding encourages vandalism		X

for social development. It can also take the form of an increase in the skills of young people because of their previous event management experiences. It may be exemplified in a remaking of the physical environment through large-scale landscaping and land reclamation. Additionally it can be the result of a building program that left a base of quality facilities for use by elite athletes, spectators, and community groups. It can also take the form of large-scale urban renewal, as occurred in both Kuala Lumpur and Manchester in their preparation for the 1998 and 2002 Commonwealth Games respectively. Consequently the breadth and scale of the legacy can vary considerably. For example, while the host city may have delivered an array of sport facilities, they may have been located in an inconvenient place, required heavy maintenance, and subject to low usage. In a worst-case situation the costs of maintaining the facilities may regularly exceed the revenues gained from their use. In other words, not only was a capital cost incurred, but ongoing operating losses have to be met by the community into the future.

Comparing the economic impact of mega-sport events

It is now commonplace for sport events to be evaluated with specific reference to its economic impact in particular, and its overall benefits and costs in general. As seen in Table 12.1, the impacts of some recent sport events held in the UK are listed. It can be readily seen that some events have a major economic impact, while others do not. The differences can in the main be explained by the scale of the event as measured by the number of players, officials, and spectators, the length of time occupied by the event, and the length of the visitor stay.

174

Table 12.6 Estimate of Economic Impact at Selected Australian Sport Events

Event	Attendance (Thousand)	Out-of-Town Visitors (Thousand)	Average Visitor Expenditure (AUD)	Total Visitor Expenditure (AUD Million)
Formula 1 Grand Prix	150	50	1200	60
Australian Open Tennis	450	30	720	26
Masters Games	25	10	1200	12
Spring Horse Racing Carnival	490	50	1500	75

The impacts between events vary enormously. At one end of the spectrum are mega-sport events like the Olympic Games, world-football World Cup, Commonwealth Games, Asian Games, and Grand Slam tennis tournament events, while at the other end are community-based sport festivals, mass participation fun funs, and sport competitions. In each case though, the tools for measuring the impacts are the same. It is just the scale of the operation that varies. Table 12.6 lists the estimated impact of a sample of Australian sport events.

Again there are significant differences between events. The figures also confirm that it is not raw attendances that drives the scale of the impact, but rather the number of out-of-town visitors that are attracted, the time spent in the host city, and the amount of money they spend. While the economic impact is always promoted with a degree of authority it must be remembered that it has a margin of error and should not be confused with a benefit–cost ratio.

The 2003 Rugby World Cup

Rugby Union is one of the world's oldest team sports, having been codified in the 1860s in England. It spread around the world, and become particularly popular in English-speaking colonies like Australia, New Zealand, and South Africa. It also developed a strong presence in the Pacific Islands, parts of South America, France, and Italy. It subsequently emerged as a major international sport, with around 90 countries affiliated with its governing body, the International Rugby Union Board (IRB).

The inaugural Rugby World Cup (RWC) competition was held in Australia and New Zealand in 1987, and has subsequently became a major international sport event. RWC 1987 was broadcast to 17 countries and had a cumulative audience of 300 million people while the tournament finished

Table 12.7 Rugby World Cup Tournaments: 1987–1999

Year	Place	Total Match Attendance (Million)	Cumulative Television Audiences (Million)	Gross Commercial Income (GBP Million)	Net Surplus (GBP Million)
1987	Australia/ New Zealand	0.6	0.3	3.3	1.0
1991	England	1.0	1750	23.6	5.0
1995	South Africa	1.0	2670	30.3	17.6
1999	England	1.7	3000	70.0	47.0

Source: URS Consulting (2004:2).

with a net surplus of GBP 1 million after accumulating gross commercial income of GBP 3.3 million. Since then there has been a consistent increase in match attendance, world television audiences, commercial income, and net surpluses for each of the tournaments, as Table 12.7 indicates.

By any measure RWC has been a success, and has secured itself a top five international sports festival position. The host country consequently has an opportunity to exploit the tournament as a catalyst for economic and cultural development.

Tournament organization

The 2003 RWC was hosted by Australia and a total of forty-eight games were played involving forty pool matches and eight finals. Games were spread across eleven venues in ten cities (Adelaide, Brisbane, Canberra, Gosford, Launceston, Melbourne, Perth, Sydney, Townsville, and Wollongong). The semi-finals and final were played in Sydney at Telstra Stadium. Twenty nations contested RWC 2003, divided into four pools of five teams. All eight quarter-finalists from RWC 1999 qualified automatically. They were Argentina, Australia, England, France, New Zealand, Scotland, South Africa, and Wales. The remaining twelve teams were Fiji, Samoa, Japan, Canada, Uruguay, Ireland, Italy, Georgia, Romania, Namibia, Tonga, and the USA. The tournament drew large attendances, and attracted thousands of overseas visitors. There was general agreement that it had a strong economic impact on the host nation.

Visitor numbers

A number of surveys were undertaken and it was estimated that a total of 65 000 international visitors came to Australia primarily as a result of Australia hosting RWC 2003. The breakdown of total visitor numbers is indicated in Table 12.8.

Table 12.8 Estimated Number of International Visitors

RWC Visitors/Supporters	Media Visitors	RWC Corporate Visitors	Total
60 000	2500	2500	65 000

Source: URS Consulting (2004:3).

The majority of international visitors were from the UK and Europe. While the remainder came from New Zealand, Pacific Islands, South Africa, and the Americas. Rugby fans accounted for just over 60 000 visitors, while media and corporate each accounted for an additional 2500 visitors.

Visitor expenditure

Visitors from UK/Europe were found to have the highest per-visitor expenditure of all visitors at AUD 8300 followed by visitors from the Americas (AUD 6740), Africa (AUD 6260), and New Zealand (AUD 3150) providing a total-trip spend for all visitors of AUD 401 million. Details are provided in Table 12.9.

Table 12.9 Average Spending by International Visitors

Region	Total Number of Visitors	Average Spend per Visit 2003 (AUD)	Average Length of Stay (Nights)	Average Total Daily Spend (AUD)	Total Trip Spend (AUD Millions)
UK–Europe	31 794	8300	36	230	256
New Zealand/ Asia	19 413	3150	15	210	59
Africa	10 638	6260	24	260	65
Americas	3155	6740	22	306	21
Total	65 000				401

Source: URS (2004:8).

Main expenditure items

Table 12.10 indicates the breakdown of expenditure for international visitors. Key spending items of international visitors were accommodations, food, and drink along with airfares, packaged tours, and retail shopping.

Table 12.10 Expenditure by Item for International Visitors

Item	Total Expenditure (AUD Million)
Packaged tours	79
Organized tours	12
International airfares	104
Domestic airfares	3
Self drive transport	6
Petrol	3
Other motor vehicle costs	6
Other transport	8
Shopping	45
Food, drink, and accommodation	87
Gambling	5
Entertainment	6
Communications	6
Other	31
Total	401

Source: URS (2004:9).

The impact

The impact of WRC 2003 can be summarized around three dimensions. They are first event audience, second visitor expenditure, and finally economic impact.

Audience levels

Audience levels were spread over forty-eight matches spread across eleven venues in ten cities around Australia. In addition the event was broadcast to an estimated global cumulative audience of 3400 million. Finally, total RWC ticket sales exceeded 1.8 million and were valued at nearly AUD 200 million.

Visitor spending

Around 65 000 international RWC visitors from UK/Europe, Asia Pacific, Africa and the Americas traveled to Australia, and they spent a total of AUD 401 million. An estimated 49 percent of visitors traveled from the UK/ Europe, nearly 13 percent came from New Zealand/Asia, 16 percent from Africa and 5 percent from the Americas. In addition these international visitors spent AUD 6308 each and stayed in Australia for around 3 weeks. It was also found that locals (Australians) purchased RWC tickets valued at AUD 137 million and made nearly 180 000 interstate trips to attend RWC matches. They collectively spent AUD 142 million.

Economic impacts

By any measure, RWC 2003 had a significant economic impact. It generated AUD 494 million in additional industry sales in the Australian economy, and also created an additional 4476 full and part time jobs. At the same time the Commonwealth Government secured an additional AUD 55 million in revenue, while an additional AUD 289 million was added to Australia's Gross Domestic Product. Finally an additional AUD 27 million in longer-term tourism sales was estimated to have occurred in 2004 and 2005.

However, like all other studies of this type, the data should be treated with caution. It should be remembered that the above data focuses on visitor expenditure only and does not take into account the costs of running the event, or the non-economic costs and benefits. In addition, when compared to the Sydney 2000 Olympic Games, RWC 2003 had a lesser impact. Whereas RWC 2003 attracted 65 000 international visitors, Sydney 2000 attracted nearly 100 000 international visitors.

The case of the Big-City Open Tennis Championship

So, what is an appropriate model for working through the economic impact of a sport. In the following fictitious case assume then you have been appointed to the event assessment team of the Great Exaggerations Sport Marketing Group (GESM). One of your first tasks is to write up an economic impact statement for the Big-City Open Tennis Championship (BCOTC). You are expected to produce a benefit–cost report as well as provide a succinct statement on the economic impact of the event on the host city. You have been given the following information to work from.

The case details

1. Surveys showed that 100 000 separate people or visitors attended the BCOTC, many of whom went three or more times. Around 78 000 (or just under 80 percent) of these people came from metropolitan areas.
2. The BCOTC also attracted a cumulative at-ground audience of 450 000. This is in marked contrast to the 220 000 fans that attended the one-day international cricket matches over the summer period.
3. Of the 22 000 visitors who came from out-of-town, 16 000 were from interstate, and 6000 were from overseas.
4. Around 1000 interstate visitors and another 1000 overseas visitors said they would have traveled to Big-City irrespective of the BCOTC being played at this time.

5. Visitor surveys showed that the interstate visitors spent on average $1000 during their stay in Big-City, while overseas visitors spent an average of $3000 per visitor.

6. The survey also found that 500 foreign media representatives were in town for the BCOTC. On average, they each spent $4000 while covering the event. These media types were not included in the previous visitor figures.

7. Coincidentally, an international convention of Southern Ocean Fish Life researchers was held at the Big-City Convention Center at exactly the same time as the BCOTC. They accounted for an additional 5000 visitors. They also paid $200 to attend a forum on Fishing as a Religious Experience. It was estimated that this event produced an economic impact of $10 million.

8. You were also provided with an income and expenditure multiplier. You were no economist, but you understood that the inclusion of a ripple effect arising from the initial expenditure was needed to calculate the overall economic impact. A consulting economist provided you with an expenditure multiplier figure of 2.0. This seemed excessive, but the economist suggested that there were only going to be small leakages from the subsequent rounds of spending.

9. The BCOTC received massive media exposure. Just over 150 hours of live television was broadcast to 90 countries, including the USA and most of Western Europe.

10. Unfortunately there was also massive traffic congestion in Big-City for the entire tournament. Many commuters were late for work, and many fans were late for matches.

11. The ticketing arrangements turned out to be a fiasco. People often had to wait up to 50 minutes to make their telephone and Internet bookings. Moreover collection points were often under-serviced. Queues were sometime up to 500 meters long.

12. Some very expensive landscaping around the new city square added to the general attractiveness of the area leading up to Big-City Park.

13. GESM was also advised that $20 million had been spent on a facility upgrade. It was clear that these figures must be included in any benefit–cost analysis, and it was also noted that the facility had an operating life of 10 years. Not only was the upgrade expensive, but it also cut severely into adjoining parkland. Many 100-year-old elm trees were destroyed in the process.

14. The scheduling of the BCOTC also coincided with the opening of the Big-City Aquarium. It was found that this new attraction boosted the number of out-of-town visitors by a further 5000.

15. A follow-up survey of Big-City residents (including business owners) found that 90 percent of respondents believed that the event was well run, and felt that it enhanced the status of Big-City as a truly international and cosmopolitan city. They also felt it demonstrated the ability of Big-City to mount premier sport events.

Big-City therefore not only secured substantial benefits from this event, but it also incurred a number of costs. However it needs to be remembered that

Table 12.11 Visitor Expenditure at Big-City Open Tennis Championship (BCOTC)

	Total Visitors	*Average Expenditure ($)*	*Total Visitor Expenditure ($ Million)*
Interstate visitor expenditure	15 000	1000	15
Overseas visitor expenditure	5000	3000	15
Foreign media visitors	500	4000	2

any cost–benefit analysis is prone to error and there is also the added difficulty of quantifying in tangible impacts. There is also the problem of deciding how many people came from out-of-town just to attend the event? And, who decides the value of the multiplier, and, is our sample of visitors really representative, and, how accurate are the visitor estimates of their daily expenditure? Finally many non-economic impacts are ignored by event promoters, who want to put the best spin on the event's impact. So, just what net gains did Big-City get out of this event?

Model answers

Once the dust had settled it was found that 15 000 interstate visitors came just for the event, 5000 international visitors came just for the event, while 500 foreign media also attended. The amount of visitors' expenditure is shown in Table 12.11.

Overall the gross impact was $64 million. When the amortized facility upgrade cost is subtracted this leaves a net impact of $62 million.

At the same time the non-economic impacts need to be evaluated. There has been noise and congestion and a loss of trees and flora. But there was also a high level of international exposure and a swell of civic pride. Despite the build-up of non-economic costs, it can only be concluded that the tennis championships were good for Big-City. So long as it attracts a significant pool of visitors from interstate and overseas it will be worth the cost and the time.

The case of the Pleasantville Special Games

In this fictitious case the Pleasantville Organizing Committee for the Special Games (POCSG) keep telling us that the 2007 Special Games provided a variety of benefits, particularly to the city of Pleasantville. This is possibly quite true, but the whole Special Games experience also involved significant costs.

A number of studies have attempted to sort out these costs, and to balance them against the benefits. There are two serious problems, to consider when doing this type of analysis. The first is to ensure that all the costs and benefits are taken into account. The second is to quantify them, but this is not as easy as it sounds. For example, just what costs and benefits are attributable to the event? For example, Pleasantville had more tourists during the Special Games, but do we know exactly how many of these tourists came just for the event? And, how do we put a number on the environmental improvements associated with the Swamplands site, or the congestion that came with the crowds? In other words, how do we measure some of these costs and benefits?

Anyway, you have been invited to compile an inventory of the costs and benefits of the Special Games. You also need to say something about the social impact of the Games by noting that some people from low-cost accommodation and housing were forced out onto the streets. And, where do we fit the euphoric community feeling associated with the torch relay and the Special Games themselves? Is this a legitimate benefit, and if so, what do you call it and how do you quantify it? Can it be quantified? There is some data available, a lot of which is useful, and a bit of which is not. A selection of useful material is listed below:

1. Total cost of all sporting facilities for the Special Games is about $1000 million. They were purpose built: that is, without the Games they would not have been built.
2. About 50 000 out-of-town tourists came to Pleasantville just for the Special Games, including 20 000 from interstate.
3. Another 20 000 people came from out-of-town, and just happened to be in Pleasantville during the Special Games.
4. All up, 20 000 athletes and officials came from overseas.
5. As usual, the media circus also came in big numbers. There were 500 from Pleasantville, and 10 000 from overseas.
6. On average, tourists spent 30 days in Pleasantville. Athletes and officials spent 20 days, while media spent 25 days.
7. The media were the biggest spenders at $600 a day. Next were the overseas tourists at $500 a day, interstate tourists at $400 a day, and finally athletes and officials at $200 a day.
8. The expenditure multiplier is estimated to be 2.0.
9. Queues increased for many inner-city services. Waiting time was up by 30 minutes, and it impacted on around 500 000 people for about 20 days. The average hourly income for these people was estimated to be $40.
10. POCOG total operating revenue from the Special Games was $2500 million.
11. POCOG total operating expenditure on the Special Games was $2700 million.
12. It was generally agreed that these were the best ever Special Games. We all felt proud about not just our own athletes' performance, but also the very positive image projected to overseas visitors and television viewers.
13. The Swamplands site looked great. It got a very good rating from various environmental groups.

Model answers

The answers have been divided into three parts. They are first, visitor expenditure; second, Net Economic Benefit (NEB); and finally, the non-economic benefits and costs.

Visitor expenditure arising out of the Special Games

Visitor expenditure has been segmented on the basis of tourists being first, from overseas, second, from interstate, third, visiting athletes and officials, and finally overseas media (Table 12.12). Having aggregated the different segments of visitor expenditure, total visitor expenditure is calculated to be $920 million.

Table 12:12 Visitor Expenditure on the Special Games

Visitor Type	Numbers	Ave Spent per person ($)	Total Visitor Expenditure ($ Million)
Overseas tourists	30 000	15 000	450
Interstate tourists	20 000	12 000	240
Athletes/officials	20 000	4000	80
Overseas media	10 000	15 000	150

Net economic benefits (NEBs) from the Special Games

The total visitor expenditure of $920 million produces a gross economic benefit of $1840 million after application of the multiplier of 2.0. The NEB however will also take into account the total capital cost of the venues, and the operating revenue and operating loss on the event. The numbers are listed in Table 12.13.

Table 12.13 Net Economic Benefit from the Special Games

	($ Million)
Gross benefit	1840
Less capital cost of venues	1000
Less operating loss	200
Net benefit	640

Following on from these calculations, the NEB arising from the Special Games is calculated to be $640 million. However, two points need to be made. First the full capital cost is included in the calculation, whereas it would have been appropriate to include only the amortized cost for Year 1. Second, the multiplier of 2.0 is very generous, and may be excessive.

Non-economic benefits and costs from the Special Games

The non-economic costs were significant, and included congestion which was quantified at $200 million, and the homeless problem. On the other hand there were some additional benefits which included a good Greenpeace rating on the environment, civic pride (the feel-good factor), the international television audience (broader awareness), and infrastructure impacts through the addition of a number of high-quality sport venues.

On balance, Pleasantville secured substantial benefits for the Special Games. However, when the full costs are taken into account, the net benefit is not quite so impressive. However as with the Big-City case in the previous section of this chapter, the significance of the impact is primarily dependent on the number of out-of-town visitors and the money they spend in and around the host city. There is also the tendency to highlight the material benefits whilst ignoring the capital cost, and many of the less intangible social and cultural impacts.

Questions to consider

1. Why are tourists and visitors an important part of a sport event?
2. When people talk about the economic impact of a sport event on the host city, what do they mean?
3. What are some of the non-economic impacts on sport events?
4. How might the economic impact argument be used to secure government funds for a major sport event?
5. How is total visitor expenditure of an event calculated? What are the difficulties involved in calculating this figure?
6. How is an economic multiplier used to calculate the economic impact of a sporting event? And, what values are usually given to the multiplier?
7. List the main difficulties in securing accurate measures of economic impacts of sport events.
8. What is the difference between an economic impact statement and a cost–benefit analysis of a sport event? Which is better for deciding where funds should be allocated to obtain the best outcome for a district town or city?
9. Compare and contrast the economic and other costs and benefits that resulted from the BCOTC and the Pleasantville Special Games. Identify the items that are essential for constructing an economic impact analysis

as well as those items that are extraneous to the exercise. In particular, how do you deal with the capital costs associated with the event?

Further reading

An overview of economic impact analysis in sport is provided by Brown, M. and Zuefle, D. (2005). Economic Impact. In Gillentine, A. and Crow, B. *Foundations of Sport Management*, *Fitness Information Technology*, pp. 55–56. For an extended discussion of the topic see Howard, D. and Crompton, J. (2004). *Financing Sport*, 2nd Edition, Fitness Information Technology, Chapter 4 (The Principles of Economic Impact Analysis).

For a succinct review of a study on the impact of an event on a local community see Turco, D. and Navarro, R. (1993). Assessing the economic impact and financial return on investment of a national sporting event, *Sport Marketing Quarterly*, 2(3), pp. 17–23. A useful discussion of how multipliers are constructed, and the distinction between direct, indirect, and induced impacts is contained in Li, M., Hofacre, S. and Mahoney, D. (2001). *Economics of Sport*, *Fitness Information Technology*, Chapter 7 (Economic Impact of Sport).

For an analysis of the distinction between impact analysis and cost–benefit analysis see Kessene, S. (2005). Do we need an economic impact study or a cost–benefit analysis of a sport event? *European Sport Management Quarterly*, pp. 133–142. An examination of the costs and benefits of attracting a professional team-sport club to a city, an providing it with a city-funded stadium, is contained in Leeds, M. and Von Allmen, P. (2005). *The Economics of Sports*, Pearson, Chapter 7 (The Costs and Benefits of a Franchise to a City).

For a detailed coverage of the short and long term impacts of the Olympic Games on various host cities see Preuss, H. (2004). *The Economics of Staging the Olympics*, Edward Elgar especially Chapters 5 (Technique of Measuring), Chapter 6 (Tourism and Exports) and Chapter 7 (Investing in the Reconstruction of a City).

For a general discussion of the economic impact of various sport events in the United Kingdom see UK Sport (2004). *Measuring Success: The Economic Impact of Major Sport Events*, UK Sport.

For a detailed analysis of the impact of the Rugby World Cup 2003 see URS Finance and Economics (2004). *Economic Impact of the Rugby World Cup on the Australian Economy*, New South Wales State Government, Department of Industry, Tourism, and Resources.

For an examination of the social impacts of sport events see Lenskyi, H. (2002). *The Best Olympics Ever? The Social Impacts of Sydney 2000*, SUNY Press.

13 Feasibility studies

Overview

This chapter will discuss the ways in which feasibility studies can be used to evaluate the viability of major sport projects. The main steps involved in undertaking a feasibility study, or as it is sometimes called, a project evaluation, will be identified and explained. Special attention will be given to market analysis, the concept plan, location and environmental impact, capital costs and funding sources, and estimates of operating revenue and expenditure.

The scarce resources problem

In the world of sport people come up with many imaginative ideas about what would be good for their sport, and what would be good for the community they serve. In a perfect world every local community would have a swimming pool, indoor sport center, fully equipped gym, golf course, multi-purpose sports fields, bush orienteering course, cycle path, jogging circuit, and rock-climbing wall. It would provide great choice and convenience, and encourage participation in some form of physical activity. This would not only benefit individuals who use the facilities, but also build social capital and improve the community's general level of well-being. However, every idea for a new sport facility comes with a price-tag. There is also the opportunity cost whereby the allocation of more resources to one particular facility, activity, or program, will mean fewer resources being available to some other facility, activity, or program.

In the above examples, the costs of setting up the facilities may be steep, and there is the additional issue of where the funds are going to come from. Not only that, it does not make sense to invest heavily in projects where the usage is low. In other words there are a lot of questions that need to be asked before local taxpayers' or private investors' money is called on. It is therefore important to establish a method for working out both the initial costs and ongoing costs and benefits that flow from translating these great ideas into practical outcomes.

The same questions arise when deciding about the construction of sport stadiums and arenas. In these cases the design and construction costs can be massive. For example, the rebuilding of the Wembley Stadium in London (which will be ready for play in 2007) cost more than GBP 2000 million, while the redevelopment of the Melbourne Cricket Ground (which was completed in 2006 in time for the Melbourne Commonwealth Games) was around AUD 450 million. If the government is funding stadium development, it will want to have an assurance that it will be used extensively, and attract both international standard sport events and large crowds. A private investor will want an assurance that the stadium will generate a return, and provide a stream of income sufficient to cover both the cost of funds borrowed to finance the stadium's construction, and its subsequent operation. For community sport facilities and large sport stadiums there is the compounding problem of the non-financial benefits and cost associated with the investment. As indicated in Chapter 12, the community may secure stronger neighborhood involvement in community activities, and it may end up with an attractive landscaped environment that attracts out-of-town visitors. On the other hand, the architecture may be ugly, and the concentration of facility users may lead to chronic traffic congestion. In the case of the stadium there may be an increase in civic pride from having a professional sport team located in the region, but on the other hand, it may occupy land that was previously highly valued public space. So, if the facility may be costly to set up, or run at a loss, it may be the price to pay to secure some additional benefits. Or, if it was likely to break-even, its success may be undermined by recurring social costs. This begs the question as to what conditions would need to exist for a sport venue or center to be run at a loss in the interests of the community. The next question to consider is who would then pay the difference.

Therefore, before any good idea about running an event or constructing a facility is put into practice, it is prudent to ask a number of questions. The key question is "Is this event, or facility viable and does it constitute an efficient use of scarce resources?" That is, can it be properly funded, will it meet a significant community need, and will it generate enough revenue to cover its costs of operation? And if it cannot be operated profitably, should it be dropped, or should be subsidized or supported in some other way?

The capital investment issue

It should be remembered that the funding of sport facilities is a significant capital investment decision, and in order to get the best outcome, a systematic way of making the decision should be developed. In this context it is important to note that the key feature of business investment decisions is that they are linked to the long-term strategic goals of the organization and the benefits that are likely to flow from the investment. The allocation of resources to large-scale projects is a significant decision, and the construction of facilities and the purchase of assets require long-range planning and a systematic assessment of the associated project's benefits, costs, and risks.

The issue of capital investment decision-making is particularly relevant to the construction of sport stadiums and arenas, where there is an element of risk or uncertainty in predicting what the future return will be. These decisions also have significant impacts on key stakeholders including sponsors, broadcasters, players, fans, and participants. Moreover, the success of a new sport facility will require not only frequent consultation with these stakeholders but also require their continued role in contributing streams of income. The risk of failure and loss of investment will therefore be minimized if ongoing consultation with key stakeholders is maintained, and people with appropriate skills are driving the project. Good planning requires an in-depth analysis of all the factors that will contribute to its success or failure. So, what has to be done, in practical terms, to ensure good planning and sound investment in the field of sport facility development? The most effective way of securing a sustainable future for sport stadia, sport arenas, and events, is to undertake a project evaluation or feasibility study. But, what is a feasibility study?

What is a feasibility study?

A feasibility study can be defined as the systematic design, collection, analysis, and reporting of data and findings relevant to a specific project being considered by an organization. This will involve a careful consideration of the product being offered, the market it will be sold to, and the physical, financial and operational requirements of creating it, and obtaining all the necessary approvals and finance to bring it into existence. It is also an assessment of the financial return which is likely to accrue to the investor, be that government or private business.

In addition, a feasibility study must provide the information and analysis that allows a reasoned decision. It will cover all relevant factors and issues that will affect the viability of the new facility. It will include not only a market and financial analysis, but also examine the context in which the study is being conducted, the anticipated aims to be achieved, a clear and succinct description of what to project involves, and a recommendation on whether the project should proceed.

Taking a critical look at the concept

Feasibility studies are necessary because they provide third-party confirmation of the viability of the proposal, and also because they provide credibility that is necessary to obtain funding. However, although feasibility studies might be accurate when they are conducted, market conditions are often dynamic and circumstances can change very quickly. In the case of sport, this can take the form of major venue redesign issues, a decline in public interest, and the loss of a major tenant or provider. Because a feasibility study is a snapshot of current conditions, investors must consequently accept the risk that these conditions might change. At the same time, the typical project evaluation is framed by optimistic expectations and hidden political agendas. For example, feasibility studies are often commissioned to protect investors from criticism, and secure broad public support.

Who should undertake a feasibility study?

A project evaluation in sport will usually be compiled by a team because the process requires input from several disciplines. It is important that a number of specialists are utilized, including:

1. Consultants with experience in sport facility management who understand the importance of sport consumer needs and the delivery of sports services.
2. Marketing specialists who can undertake market analysis.
3. Architects who understand design trends.
4. Financial analysts who can formulate a detailed capital budget and operational plan of revenues and expenditures.

The team leader has a crucial role in the project evaluation, as this person has the responsibility of integrating the input from these various specialists. The team must map out a plan for the study, and must be prepared to coordinate and review both its own work and the work of other consultants whose input is required at various stages of the study. The team must also be aware of the financial parameters of the study. The team will have clear schedules and timelines, and must be conscious of the need for communication among both team members and with the investors who have commissioned the study. There should also be contingency plans for any problems and delays that might arise. The team leader should be capable and knowledgeable in the field, and thus able to make well-considered judgments. It also means they will be impartial and assertive enough to prepare a fair and independent report.

The fundamentals of a feasibility study

A feasibility study can be a complex activity, but when distilled to its fundamentals, involves three crucial activities.

First, it is important to undertake a broad market audit. This involves the use of demographic and economic data like population levels and density, occupational profiles, income levels, age, and gender breakdowns to establish the level of potential market demand for the facility.

Second, market analysis should be used to generate detailed estimates of customer usage. A significant proportion of a feasibility study's resources should be used to estimate the demand by different consumer segments for the services provided by the facility. In the case of a sport stadium it will be important to identify the tenants, what games they intend to schedule, the anticipated attendances, the revenues that will be associated with these attendances, and its capacity to generate a steady stream of sponsor income. Caution is needed here however, since calculations on likely income streams can often be nothing more than inspired guesses and optimistic forecasts without much supporting evidence.

Third, it is vital to undertake detailed financial analysis that can be used to establish the overall viability of the project, and whether it is financially sustainable. It should be noted at this point that financial sustainability has two components which need to be systematically addressed. They are a capital funding component and a recurrent funding component. Taking the above discussion into account, a comprehensive feasibility study will:

1. Explain the development concept in the context of a generalized problem or need and its long-term viability.
2. Identify likely market demand through in-depth analysis.
3. Enable the necessary finance and government approvals to be obtained with minimum delay.
4. Define strategies for dealing with stakeholders.
5. Identify the capital costs and how they will be sourced.
6. Prepare estimates of operating revenues and expenses.

A 10-step process

In order to reinforce the principles underlying feasibility studies, and to give a clear picture of what needs to be done to ensure a best possible outcome, the following 10-step process model has been developed. It not only lists the nature of each step, but how they can be best completed. The steps to determine feasibility follow.

Locate the proposal within a strategic framework

1. Identify the problem or issue to be resolved.
2. Specify the project brief by answering the question: what have we been asked to do?

Develop the need or demand for the facility or event

1. Start with a short discussion of the main stakeholders and their expectations.
2. Establish the size of the potential market.
3. Conduct surveys of potential users (questionnaires and focus groups are particularly appropriate).
4. Identify their recreational needs and preferences.
5. Construct a demographic profile of anticipated users.
6. Quantify the anticipated level of usage, making sure to break usage into demographic segments.

Prepare a concept design or plan

1. Describe features and/or functions in context of other options.
2. Provide detailed specifications, architectural plans, and graphics.
3. Identify possible locations, ending with a ranking of sites.
4. List the range of benefits expected to flow from the facility or event.

Identify regulations, rules, and by-laws that must be observed

1. Make sure all appropriate permits can be obtained.
2. Seek advice from all relevant parties.

Calculate the impact of the event or facility on the surrounding environment

1. Consider the economic impact.
2. Consider the social impact.
3. Consider the environmental impact.

Make an estimate of capital cost and funding

1. Calculate capital cost (land acquisition, site preparation, consultant fees, construction costs, equipment costs).
2. List capital funding arrangements and the sources of funds (listing figures for each source).

Estimate the anticipated operating revenues

1. Identify any annual grants.
2. Calculate income from users (fees and charges, membership, weekly usage, income from each user group) whilst ensuring that it is consistent with data market demand.
3. Estimate sales of merchandise.
4. Identify any equipment hire.
5. Identify revenue to be secured from sponsors, local philanthropists, or benefactors.
6. Divide revenues into fixed and variable. The more fixed revenue, for example, sponsorship, the better, since it is not dependent on usage levels.

Calculate operating costs

1. Provide line items for staffing costs, office and administration, utilities, phone, gas, maintenance costs, marketing costs, and incidentals.
2. Divide costs into fixed and variable if appropriate.

Do profit projections

1. Design different scenarios by varying assumptions on usage rates, prices and charges, other revenues, and costs. Examine some what-if situations.
2. Include some break-even analysis in what-if scenarios.
3. Evaluate options.

Make recommendations

1. The first question to consider is: can we afford it?
2. The second question to consider is: what is the best option?
3. All the costs and benefits (both tangible and non-tangible) should be considered.
4. So, is it a goldmine or a white elephant, or somewhere in between?

Doing a feasibility study

The following fictional case provides an evaluation of a go-cart track proposed for a university starved of sporting facilities. The context for the case is a lack of sport and recreation facilities at one of the university's regional campuses which is a nationally recognized provider of sport management education. The university (which goes under the name of Blairstone) is concerned that its Howard Heights campus is poorly resourced, and is keen to give the Howard Heights campus a competitive edge by building some unique recreational services that can be used to not only increase the sporting options of the local community, but also attract quality students, and provide them with internships. A consultant was given the brief of coming up with a proposal that was both imaginative and viable. The go-cart option is presented below.

Strategic overview

The Howard Heights campus has a mandate to improve the recreational services to students and the local community which are currently substandard. It is also important to work with the local council to create a facility that can be jointly funded and managed.

Needs analysis

The market for a new recreational facility can be segmented into various categories with each category representing a specific user group. The segments, together with their demographics, are listed in Table 13.1.

Table 13.1 Go-Cart Survey – Market Segments

Segment	Market Size
Primary school students	3000
Secondary school students	4000
University students	3000
Local community	30 000
Total market size	40 000

Market survey

A random survey was conducted amongst a group of people that included students, teachers, and the local community. The response was positive. Nearly 80 percent of respondents claimed an additional recreational facility was needed. Moreover, 97 percent of residents aged between 15 and 25 years desired a facility that went beyond the traditional activities of track and field, football, and cricket. The survey results also indicated that 50 percent of people were willing to use the facility at least twice a week, while 90 percent of respondents in the 15–25-year age group said they would be prepared to take out a membership package.

In order to establish the type of facility that was most strongly requested, respondents were asked to rank the most desirable from a mini-golf center, an orienteering circuit, an outdoor court, an indoor gymnasium, and a go-cart track. Concept designs were shown to respondents. The results are outlined in Table 13.2.

Table 13.2 Respondent Rankings of Facilities

Type of Facility	Percentage of Respondents Who Ranked Facility as a Priority
Mini-golf	5
Orienteering	10
Court	15
Gymnasium	30
Go-cart	60

The concept

The go-cart track will occupy 5 hectares of land situated on the edge of the Howard Heights campus. It will be 300 meters long, with full bitumen surface. Surrounding land will be landscaped, and the track will have full safety barrier protection.

Capital cost

194

Based on the construction of a similar facility in the Bushville District the following estimates have been provided (Table 13.3).

Table 13.3 Capital Expenditure for Go-Cart Track

Capital Expenses	($)
Construction of track	120 000
Safety nets	5000
Sand	2000
Safety barriers	10 000
First aid and fire equipment	3000
Storage and office facility	40 000
12 × high performance go-carts	12 000
Go-cart spares	4000
Tools	4000
Total capital cost	200 000

Source of capital

It is anticipated that capital funds will be sourced as outlined in Table 13.4.

Table 13.4 Anticipated Sources of Capital Funds for Go-Cart Facility

Source	Amount ($ thousand)
Local council	60
University	80
Naming rights sponsor	30
Long-term bank loan	30
Capital total	200

Revenues

It is proposed that the revenue for the facility will come from a number of different sources, the main ones being daily users, members, sponsors, and operating grants.

Pricing structure

Separate price schedules have been set for students, teachers, the public, and concession card holders. Casual prices are for 15 minutes of track time.

Membership will allow the holder to unlimited track time for the duration of that membership. Memberships are sold for 3-, 6-, and 12-month periods. Table 13.5 identifies the prices.

Table 13.5 Pricing Structure for Go-Cart Facility

	Casual Rate ($)	3-Month Membership ($)	6-Month Membership ($)	12-Month Membership ($)
Students	10	120	200	250
Teachers	20	130	250	350
Public	15	130	250	350
Concession	15	120	230	300

Revenue projections

Revenue projections are based on minimum weekly casual visits of 100 and 150 annual member packages during Year 1. Sponsorships have been guaranteed for Years 1 through to Year 4. A 4-year revenue projection is provided in Table 13.6.

Table 13.6 Revenue Projections for Go-Cart Facility

	Daily Visits ($ thousand)	Memberships ($ thousand)	Sponsorship ($ thousand)	Total ($ thousand)
Year 1	55	45	20	120
Year 2	60	50	20	130
Year 3	65	55	20	140
Year 4	70	60	20	150

Operating expenses

Expense projections combine variable and fixed costs, and include full-time staff, full maintenance and servicing costs, depreciation on go-carts, and interest payable on bank loan. A 4-year projection can be seen in Table 13.7.

Table 13.7 Expenses for Go-Cart Facility

Expense	Estimated Cost Year 1 ($ thousand)	Estimated Cost Year 2 ($ thousand)	Estimated Cost Year 3 ($ thousand)	Estimated Cost Year 4 ($ thousand)
Advertising	12	10	10	10
Insurance	8	12	15	20
Staffing	60	80	85	85
Maintenance	8	8	8	8
Repairs (go-carts)	5	5	5	5
Depreciation (go-carts)	3	3	3	3
Sundry expenses	2	3	3	3
Bank charges (interest on loan)	2	2	2	2
Fuel	10	11	14	14
Total	110	134	145	150

Profit forecasts

Profit forecasts use the revenue and expense projections identified previously to construct estimates of future profits. This best-case scenario has the track making a small profit in Year 1, a loss in Year 2, a loss in Year 3, and breaking even in Year 4 (Table 13.8). It also assumes ongoing support from local sponsors.

Table 13.8 Four-Year Profit Forecast for Go-Cart Facility

	Operating Expenses ($ thousand)	Depreciation Expenses ($ thousand)	Total Expenses ($ thousand)	Revenue ($ thousand)
Year 1	107	3	110	120
Year 2	131	3	134	130
Year 3	142	3	145	140
Year 4	147	3	150	150

These forecasts suggest that the project is sustainable even without an operating grant. But a loss of sponsor support and a decline in membership will impact severely on operating profits. On balance though the proposal to construct and operate a go-cart track on the perimeter of the Howard Heights campus is sound and should not only meet a widespread community need, but also provide full cost recovery with a small surplus over the first 4 years of operation.

Questions to consider

1. What is a feasibility study and what does it aim to do?
2. Where should you begin when conducting a feasibility study?
3. Why is it so important to undertake a detailed market analysis as part of a feasibility study?
4. What is a concept plan, and where does it fit into a feasibility study?
5. Why is it so important to distinguish between capital costs and running or operating costs when doing a feasibility study?
6. What goes into the construction of operating revenue and expense estimates?
7. How might you go about constructing different scenarios for the financial projections of a feasibility study?
8. Review the strengths and weaknesses of the proposal to build and operate a go-cart track.

Further reading

For a discussion of where feasibility studies fit into the general field of project management see Pinkerton, W. (2003). *Project Management.* McGraw Hill, Chapter 5 (Pre-Project Planning).

For a sport-specific review of the role of feasibility studies in guiding in the development of sport facilities see Fried, G. (2005). *Managing Sport Facilities.* Human Kinetics, Chapter 4 (Facility Planning).

A detailed analysis of the feasibility study process is contained in the Ministry of Sport and Recreation (1995). *How to Undertake a Feasibility Study for a Proposed Sport of Recreation Facility.* Western Australia Government. For a useful introduction to the topic from a hospitality perspective see Baker, K. (2002). *Project Evaluation and Feasibility Analysis for Hospitality Operations.* Hospitality Press.

For a comprehensive and broadly structured approach to the development of a feasibility study see NGF Consulting (2001). *Feasibility Study for the Proposed Town of Norfolk Golf Course,* Florida, http://www.virtualnorfolk. org/public_documents/NorfolkMA_documents/towndocs/F000193C3/ S00441E80.-1/ngf1128.pdf accessed July 2006. A detailed approach to needs analysis is provided by Global Leisure Group (2004). Kaitaia Swimming Pool Feasibility Study, http://www.fndc.govt.nz/parks/feasibility_study_ kaitaia_pool.pdf accessed July 2006.

PART FOUR

Sport Funding: Financial Futures

14

Sport funding and performance measurement in the future

Overview

This chapter will examine some emerging issues that sport organizations will have to deal with over the next few years. They include the development of public–private partnerships (PPPs), a greater reliance on debt finance, a move to privately-owned sport teams and leagues, a greater concern for corporate social responsibility (CSR), and the ways in which environmental constraints affect the financial sustainability of sport.

Financing options

As the previous chapters of this book have indicated, large parts of sport have become a complex operation that combines large-scale infrastructure with the delivery of sophisticated entertainment experiences. They all come at a cost however, and this raises the issue as to how they may be financed and operated.

For any major sport project there are a number of developmental and operational stages to be completed. Moreover for each stage there are a number of decision-making options. The first stage is to decide upon who will be driving the project. The next stages involve deciding on the location of the facility and the funding required to secure control and/or ownership. The next stage involves the design of the facility after consulting with various stakeholders. Following this, is the decision about who will be responsible for construction of the facility. The next stage is to decide upon an arrangement for operating and maintaining the facility. The final stage is to put in place arrangements for securing and delivering sporting and related events.

There are a range of possibilities which include the government as the sole driver, or a private consortium driving the project. Another option may include a mix of both involving a government agency and private or not-for-profit consortium in partnership with the government. Each approach has its own strengths and weaknesses. The strength of a government-controlled model is that it is not compromised by a commercial imperative for high profits and it can also provide for more community access and equity. The weakness is that there are insufficient incentives to ensure a reasonable level of efficiency, and accountability particularly with respect to the construction and management of the facility. Whereas the strength of a privately driven arrangement is that the government now has a lower financial risk exposure, and because of its business focus, (that is, long-term profitability) it will have a greater concern for cost containment, efficiency, and innovative practices. However, the major problem of a fully privatized arrangement is the lack of attention likely to be given to social benefits and community accessibility. That is, less emphasis will be given to low-cost facilities and indifferent response to low-income potential users. One way of overcoming the weaknesses of the above models, whilst maintaining their strengths is to create some type of Public Private Partnership (PPP) where government and the private sector jointly drive the project.

There are also a number of models for financing major projects. At the simplest level the government can fund the entire project which can start with purchase of the land and include all design and construction costs and all management and maintenance costs. The government might also wish to fully manage the facility and deliver its services. At the other extreme all of these costs may be borne by a private business or consortium. However, there are a variety of schemes or arrangements that allow the public sector to fund some aspects of the facility development and the private sector to develop other aspects of the facility development. For example, the government might fully finance the land purchase, capital design and construction costs, and the management, maintenance, and the day-to-day operations may be contracted out to a private business. With respect to funding sources a fully public-funded facility will be funded predominantly from government revenue, that is taxpayers' money or from external borrowings. If on the other hand the facility was funded mainly by the private sector, the funds can be sourced from either shareholders' funds, that is equity finance, or from private borrowings and bonds. With respect to borrowed funds, governments are usually able to borrow at a lower rate which consequently reduces the overall cost of the project. However, the disadvantage of high dependency on government borrowings is that the costs are borne by future generations of taxpayers. A PPP allows for a financing package that spreads the financial risks whilst securing the lowest-cost borrowing arrangements. As a result funds can be raised through a combination of government (taxes), private borrowings, sponsorship, and shareholders' funds.

Take for example, the location of a flagship sport stadium. The first thing to do is to decide upon the specific location. There are a number of factors to be considered at this point. One option is to locate the stadium in an inner-city precinct as part of an urban renewal program. However, this can be costly and will clearly involve significant government support and direction, but one of the benefits will be easy access and proximity to public transport. The other option is to scan the outer suburbs and find a large piece of real estate that can be used to create an appropriate facility. This has the advantage of a likely lower purchase price and no negotiations around preservation of heritage buildings and the like. On the other hand, there is the problem of distance and accessibility for the sporting public. Another option is to redevelop an existing facility. This has the potential benefit of minimizing the land purchase price. The limitation however is the constraints of the existing facility and the space that it occupies.

From a design perspective a fully publicly designed facility will be more sensitive to the needs of stakeholders and as a result aim to meet the needs of minority groups and therefore provide for a diversity of usage needs. A fully privatized model is more likely to only accommodate design features that will deliver long-term profits. On the other hand, a PPP is more likely to identify design features that combine the capacity to cross-subsidize high-profit delivery outcomes with design features may be difficult to run at a profit.

A government-driven construction model will generally provide for stable employment over the short to medium term and less likely to contravene workplace, and health and safety legislation. On the other hand, there are fewer pressures to be efficient and provide a timely completion. A privately driven construction will be guided by the need to ensure a favorable return on shareholders' funds, and as a result timelines and construction budgets are more likely to be more strictly adhered to. A PPP will ideally combine the best of both the above models.

The issue of the use of a fully public, a fully private, or some mixed management system is particularly relevant to the operation and maintenance of sports' facilities. In particular Australian local governments have a history of contracting out the management and operation of sporting facilities to a private management group or consortium. On the other hand, large-scale Australian sport stadia generally are owned and operated by government or its agency in the form of a trust. Government provision will allow for stable employment and where possible price the services at a level to ensure broad-based community use. On the other hand, the private sector tends to only provide services which provide full-cost recovery. This will most likely reduce the range of activities and programs. Private providers will also have a tendency to minimize maintenance and cleaning costs as a way of ensuring efficiency and cost containment. At the same time, private providers are less likely to be constrained by traditional practices and the pressures of conservative stakeholders. To this end they are more likely to be flexible and innovative in operating the facility. However, with respect to sporting fields and ball courts the delivery is the responsibility of a particular tenant who effectively leases the facility for a particular period of time.

Conceptually, there are a broad range of models for delivering sport activities. Government and its agencies can theoretically deliver sporting activities and this can apply to community leisure centers where government employees plan and manage programs. The primary benefit arising from government delivery of sport is its continuity and reliability. However, this may come at the expense of innovation and new forms of delivery. However, in most situations sport services are delivered by members of not-for-profit sporting clubs and associations. The great strength of this model is its direct link with the user since clubs and associations are for the most part run by the members themselves. This is to say, collectively the members will often both deliver and use the service. At the same time there can also be private providers who plan and deliver a sporting activity with a profit expectation. A good example of this model would be a privately managed, operated, and delivered rock-climbing facility. The benefit of private delivery is they are not constrained by traditional practices and customs. The limitation though is that only those services that can ensure financial viability will be provided. Overall there are many public–private sector combinations for the planning and delivery of sport facilities, and they are illustrated in Table 14.1.

At each of the seven stages of the project there are three possibilities. As a result the combinations are extensive, and indeed a bit daunting, although in practice the decision to go one way or the other is taken with a solid base of knowledge. Whereas in the past most of the seven stages of sport facility development have been dominated by the public sector over recent years the tendency has been to go for more PPP involvement in Step 2, and more private sector involvement in Steps 6 and 7.

In short there are a variety of approaches that can be used to drive, fund, locate, design, construct, operate, maintain, and deliver sporting outcomes. They all have their benefits and costs, and while the traditional models have tended to be either public or private, there is a growing trend to PPPs. Ideally a partnership will combine the strengths of each of the collaborating

Table 14.1 PPP options

Steps of project	Mainly public involvement	Public–private partnership (PPP)	Mainly private involvement
1 Project driver			
2 Project funding			
3 Land acquisition			
4 Facility design			
5 Facility construction			
6 Facility management			
7 Service delivery			

organizations, and negate their weaknesses. For example, the public sector will in the main have access to a bank of land from which the preferred location can be identified. It can also borrow capital at lower interest rates, and therefore reduce the cost of funds and the risk of non-repayment. It also has the opportunity to waive any taxes and charges that may impede the development of a facility. Finally, it will have intimate knowledge of zoning regulations and planning permits which should enable proposals to be appropriately framed and defended. The private sector also brings many strengths to the table. The primary strength is its management expertise. This comes through not only a broad base of experience where the pressures to be decisive and efficient are high, but also extensive industry knowledge. As noted in Chapter 2, this is especially important in sport, where volunteers are crucial to getting things done, where fan loyalty and attachment drives so much revenue collection, and where cooperation and competition go hand-in-hand. The private sector can also deliver lower labor costs through a combination of incentives, contract and casual workers, and fewer restrictive work practices to deal with. This model of labor supply can also deliver more flexibility by placing more workers on short-term contracts, which is particularly important with mega-sport events that require a large pool of labor for a short period of time.

Corporate social responsibility

Businesses are often criticized for thinking only of the profits they make, and ignoring the social consequences of their strategic decisions and the outputs they deliver. This dilemma is particularly striking in the case of tobacco companies. On one hand there are profits to be made, but on the other hand there is a pile of evidence that links smoking cigarettes to lung cancer and heart disease. Sport has for many years had a close relationship with tobacco producers, who have provided millions of dollars of sponsor funds to both community and professional sport.

There is now growing pressure from both government and the public in general for businesses to move beyond the bottom line and take into account the effect their decisions have on the wider community. This idea has given rise to the concept of triple bottom line accounting, which gets business to consider their contribution to not just economic prosperity, but also social justice and environmental quality. While the measurement of social justice and environmental quality is fraught with danger, the overall aim is to see profits and net worth as just one measure of the performance of an organization. Triple bottom line accounting consequently provides for three measures of how a business contributes to society, with each measure being geared around the value-added concept. These measures are:

1. economic value-added,
2. social value-added,
3. environmental value-added.

This way of measuring performance presents many challenges for sport organizations. It has already been noted that sport organizations are motivated by more than money. For a national sporting body the growth of the sport may be equally important, and for a professional sports club the dominant goal may be on-field success. However, despite the primacy of these goals, sport organizations can equally make decisions and produce outputs that have negative consequences for society in general. The heavy use of tobacco companies as sponsors may have secured a valuable source of funds, but the subsequent association of tobacco products with glamorous sport stars was instrumental in convincing young people that smoking was socially desirable, even if it might kill them in the long run. In some sports heavy drinking of alcohol products is part of the club culture, and in these cases no success is seen as complete without a long binge-drinking session. Similarly, in professional sport leagues, where neo-tribalism is strong, groups of rival supporters will resolve their antagonism with a wild brawl. Football hooliganism in Britain is the archetypal model in this respect. All of these outputs have negative social consequences, and it therefore makes sense to encourage sport clubs, associations, and leagues to measure their overall performance in terms of their social and environmental impact as well as their participation impact, win-loss impact, or revenue-raising impact.

Recently a number of global businesses with the support of the United Nations developed a program called the Global Reporting Initiative (GRI). The mission of GRI is to design and promulgate sustainability reporting guidelines for each of the economic, social, and environmental outputs identified above. Organizations that sign up to GRI are expected to enact reporting systems that are transparent and accessible, provide quality and reliable information, and include information that is relevant and complete. GRI has also compiled a list of factors under each of the economic, social, and environmental headings that indicate specific issues that require addressing. A sample of factors particularly relevant to sport organizations is provided in Table 14.2.

The GPI model of performance management is complex, and will force sport organizations to be more systematic in the way they build their stakeholder relations. It will also enable them to go beyond revenue growth and on-field success and evaluate the contribution they are making to the wider society, and monitor their impact on the physical environment. This can only be a good thing.

Where to from here?

When viewed collectively, PPPs and CSR highlight the increasing importance of working with core stakeholders to secure long-term financial sustainability. It also demonstrates the benefits that can accrue from building strategic alliances with other organizations, and in particular using those alliances to secure more revenue, equity funds, and long-term borrowings. Moreover, it shows that working toward the public good is more than winning

Table 14.2 Global Reporting Initiative performance indicators

Performance category	Performance measures
Direct economic impacts	Sales to satisfied customers Purchases from suppliers Employees hired Taxes paid Dividend and interest paid
Product responsibility	Safety and durability Truth in advertising and product labeling
Work practices	Health, safety and security Training, education and consultation Appropriate wages and conditions
Social practices	No bribery and corruption Transparent lobbying Free from collusion and coercion
Human rights	Non-discriminatory hiring practices Free from forced labor
Environmental impacts	Efficient energy use Appropriate water recycling Controlled emissions Waste management Maintenance of biodiversity

another premiership, securing a better broadcast rights deal, or building a new sport stadium.

Questions to consider

1. What is the benefit of having a mainly public funded and managed sport facility?
2. What is the benefit of having a mainly privately funded and managed sport facility?
3. How do you explain the shift over recent years to more PPPs in the field of sport facility development?
4. What is meant by the term CSR and how does it relate to the concept of triple bottom line accounting?
5. How can CSR be applied to sport?
6. How did the GRI originate, and what does it hope to achieve?
7. How can the GRI model be applied to sport clubs, associations, events, and leagues?

207

8. In what ways might the development of strategic alliances and partnerships in sport sustain its financial viability?
9. Discuss the different funding scenarios that sport will face in the future.

Further reading

The different financing options that face sport organizations in the future (including a review of the strengths and weaknesses of equity/shares and loans/bonds) is examined in some detail by Fried, G., Shapiro, S. and Deschriver, T. (2003). *Sport Finance*, Human Kinetics, Chapter 8 (Obtaining Funding), Chapter 9 (Capital Stocks) and Chapter 10 (Bonds).

For an overview of the shifting balance between public and private funding of sport stadia in the USA see Crompton, J., Howard, D. and Var, T. (2003). Financing Major Sport Facilities: Status, Evolution and Conflicting Forces. *Journal of Sport Management*, 17, 156–184. For a more detailed review of the different ways that PPPs can be built, see Howard, D. and Crompton, J. (2004). *Financing Sport*, 2nd edition, Fitness Information Technology, Chapter 8 (Implementation of Public–Private Partnerships).

There is a useful discussion of PPPs and their underlying ideology in Thibault, L., Kikulis, L. and Frisby W. (2004). Partnerships between Local Government Sport and Leisure Departments and the Commercial Sector: Changes, Complexities and Consequences. In T. Slack (Ed.), The *Commercialization of Sport*, Routledge, pp. 119–139.

For a broad overview of recent trends in public sector financing of sport development in the UK see Kovalycsik, K and Karver, R. (2005). Sport Finance: The Cost of Success. *PANSTADIA International*, 43.

An introductory discussion of CSR and triple bottom line accounting is contained in Atrill, P., McLaney, E., Harvey, D. and Jenner, M. (2006) *Accounting: An Introduction*, Pearson Education Australia, Chapter 15 (Trends and Issues in Accounting). For a detailed review of CSR see Hancock, J. (2004). *Investing in Corporate Social Responsibility*, Kogan Page.

For a revealing analysis of how strategic alliances work in sport, and how they can be used to build brand equity and financial sustainability, see Gladden, J., Irwin, R. and Sutton, W. (2001). Managing North American Major Professional Sport Teams in the New Millennium: A Focus on Building Brand Equity. *Journal of Sport Management*, 15, 297–317. The ways in which alliances can be used to develop more creative funding arrangements is examined in Mahoney, D. and Howard, D. (2001). Sport Business in the Next Decade: A General Overview of Expected Trends. *Journal of Sport Management*, 15, 275–296.

For a detailed discussion of sport's impact on the environment, and how sport practices can be made more sustainable, see Chernushenko, D. (2002) *Sustainable Sport Management: Running an Environmentally, Socially & Economically Responsible Organisation*, Earth print.

Bibliography

Australian Football League (AFL) (1981–2005), *Annual Reports*.

Allison, L. (2005). *The Global Politics of Sport: The Role of Global Institutions in Sport*. Routledge.

Amis, J. and Cornwell, T. (2005). *Global Sport Sponsorship*. Berg.

Andrew, W. and Staudohar, P. (2002). European and US Sports Business Models, in C. Barros, M. Ibrahimo and S. Szymanski (Eds.), *Transatlantic Sport: The Comparative Economics of North American and European Sport*. Edward Elgar, pp.23–49.

Andrews, D. (Ed.) (2004). *Manchester United: A Thematic Study*. Routledge.

Anthony, R. and Young, D. (2003). *Management Control in Non-profit Organizations*, 7th Edition. McGraw Hill.

Atrill, P., McLaney, E., Harvey, D. and Jenner, M. (2006). *Accounting: An Introduction*. Pearson Education, Australia.

Baker, K. (2002). *Project Evaluation and Feasibility Analysis for Hospitality Operations*. Hospitality Press.

Barney, J. (1991). Firm Resources and Sustained Competitive Advantage. *Journal of Management*, 17, 99–120.

Barney, R., Ween, S. and Martyn, S. (2002). *Selling the Five Rings: The International Olympic Committee and the Rise of Olympic Commercialism*. University of Utah Press.

Beck-Burridge, M. and Walton, J. (2001). *Sport Sponsorship and Brand Development: The Subaru and Jaguar Stories*. Palgrave Macmillan.

Beech, J. and Chadwick, S. (Eds.) (2004). *The Business of Sport Management*. Prentice Hall.

Brown, A. and Walsh, A. (1999). *Not For Sale: Manchester United, Murdoch and the Defeat of BskyB*. Mainstream.

Brown, M. and Zuefle, D. (2005). Economic Impact, in A. Gillentine and B. Crow (Eds.), *Foundations of Sport Management*. Fitness Information Technology.

Business Review Weekly (2006) March 16–22.

Chappelet, J. and Bayle, E. (2005). *Strategic and Performance Management of Olympic Sport Organizations.* Human Kinetics.

Chernushenko, D. (2002). *Sustainable Sport Management: Running an Environmentally, Socially & Economically Responsible Organisation*, Earthprint.

Cousins, L. (1997). From Diamonds to Dollars: The Dynamics of Change in AAA Baseball Franchises. *Journal of Sport Management*, 11, 11–30.

Crawford, G. (2004). *Consuming Sport: Fans, Sport and Culture.* Routledge, London.

Crompton, J., Howard, D. and Var, T. (2003). Financing Major Sport Facilities: Status, Evolution and Conflicting Forces. *Journal of Sport Management*, 17, 156–184.

Davies, G. (2005). *A History of Money from Ancient Times to Present Day.* 3rd Edition. University of Wales Press.

Deloittes (2006). *Survey of Professional Football.*

Denham, G. (2006). Swans Blue Blood Ethic Pay Off. *Sunday Age*, April 9.

Dobson, S. and Goddard, J. (2001). *The Economics of Football.* Cambridge University Press.

Downard, P. and Dawson, A. (2000). *The Economics of Professional Team Sports.* Routledge.

Euchner, C. (1993). *Playing the Field: Why Sports Teams Move and Cities Fight to Keep Them.* John Hopkins University Press.

Ferrand, A. and Torrigiani, L. (2005). *Marketing of Olympic Sport Organizations.* Human Kinetics.

Fleisher, A., Goff, B. and Tollison, R. (1992). *The National Collegiate Athletic Association: A Study in Cartel Behavior.* The University of Chicago Press.

Forster, J. and Pope, N. (2004). *The Political Economy of Global Sporting Organisations.* Routledge.

Foster, G., Greyser, P. and Walsh, B. (2006). *The Business of Sports: Texts and Cases on Strategy and Management.* Thomson.

Fried, G. (2005). *Managing Sport Facilities.* Human Kinetics.

Fried, G., Shapiro, S. and Deschriver, T. (2003). *Sport Finance.* Human Kinetics.

Gerrard, W. (2004a). Sport Finance. In J. Beech and S. Chadwick (Eds.), *The Business of Sport Management.* Pearson Education.

Gerrard, W. (2004b). Why Does Manchester United Keep Winning? In D. Andrews (Ed.), *Manchester United: A Thematic Study.* Routledge.

Gerrard, W. (2005). A Resource Utilization Model of Organizational Efficiency in Professional Team Sports. *Journal of Sport Management*, 19(2), 143–169.

Gillentine, A. and Crow, R. (Eds.) (2005). *Foundations of Sport Management.* Fitness Information Technology.

Giroux, G. (1999). *A Short History of Accounting and Business.* http://acct.tamu.edu/giroux/Shorthistory.html (accessed July 2006).

Gladden, J., Irwin, R. and Sutton, W. (2001). Managing North American Major Professional Sport Teams in the New Millennium: A Focus on Building Brand Equity. *Journal of Sport Management*, 15, 297–317.

Global Leisure Group (2004). Kaitaia Swimming Pool Feasibility Study, http://www.fndc.govt.nz/parks/feasibility_study_kaitaia_pool.pdf (accessed July 2006).

Gratton, C. (2000). The Peculiar Economics of English Professional Football, in J. Garland, P. Malcolm and M. Rowe (Eds.), *The Future of Football*. Frank Cass.

Green, M. and Houlihan, B. (2005). *Elite Sport Development: Policy Learning and Political Priorities*. Routledge.

Hancock, J. (2004). *Investing in Corporate Social Responsibility*. Kogan Page.

Hart, L. (2006). *Accounting Demystified: A Self Teaching Guide*. McGraw Hill.

Healey, D. (2003). *Sport and the Law*, 3rd Edition. University of New South Wales Press.

Hess, R. and Stewart, R. (Eds.) (1998). *More than a Game: An Unauthorised History of Australian Rules Football*. Melbourne University Press.

Hoffman, K. and Bateson, J. (2001). *Essentials of Services Marketing*. 2nd Edition. South Western.

Hoggett, J., Edwards, L. and Medlin, J. (2006). *Accounting*. 6th Edition. John Wiley and Sons.

Horine, L. and Stotlar, D. (2004). *Administration of Physical Education and Sport Programs*. 5th Edition. McGraw Hill.

Horngren, C., Harrison, W. and Bamber, L. (2002). *Accounting*. 5th Edition. Prentice Hall.

Howard, D. and Crompton, J. (2004). *Financing Sport*. 2nd Edition. Fitness Information Technology.

Hoye, R., Smith, A., Westerbeek, H., Stewart, B. and Nicholson, M. (2006). *Sport Management: Principles and Practice*. Elsevier.

Ibsen, B. and Jorgensen, P. (2002). The Cultural and Voluntary Development of Sport for All, in L. DaCosta and L. Mirigaya (Eds.), *Worldwide Experiences and Trends in Sport for All*. Meyer and Meyer.

J.League. www.j-league.or.jp (accessed June 2006).

Kessene, S. (2005). Do We Need and Economic Impact Study or a Cost-Benefit Analysis of a Sport Event? *European Sport Management Quarterly*, pp.133–142.

King, A. (1998). *The End of the Terraces*. Leicester University Press.

Kovalycsik, K. and Karver, R. (2005). *Sport Finance: The Cost of Success*. PANSTADIA International.

La Feber, W. (1999). *Michael Jordon and the New Global Capitalism*. WW Norton.

Leeds, M. and von Allmen, P. (2005). *The Economics of Sports*, 2nd Edition. Pearson.

Lenskyi, H. (2002). *The Best Olympics Ever? The Social Impacts of Sydney 2000*. SUNY Press.

Li, M., Hofacre, S. and Mahoney, D. (2001). *Economics of Sport*. Fitness Information Technology.

Mahoney, D. and Howard, D. (2001). Sport Business in the Next Decade: A General Overview of Expected Trends, *Journal of Sport Management*, 15, 275–296.

Manchester United Football Club (2005). *Annual Report*, 2004–2005, Financial Statement.

Mauws, M., Mason, D. and Foster, W. (2003). Thinking Strategically About Professional Sports. *European Sport Management Quarterly*, 3, 145–164.

Melbourne Cricket Club, *Annual Reports*, 1990–2005.

Miller, T., Lawrence, C., McKay, J. and Rowe, D. (2001). *Globalisation and Sport.* Sage.

Ministry of Sport and Recreation (1995). *How to Undertake a Feasibility Study for a Proposed Sport of Recreation Facility.* Western Australia Government.

Morris, D. (1981). *The Soccer Tribe.* Jonathon Cape.

Mullin, B., Hardy, S. and Sutton, W. (2001). *Sport Marketing.* 2nd Edition. Human Kinetics.

NGF Consulting (2001). *Feasibility Study for the Proposed Town of Norfolk Golf Course.* Florida, http://www.virtualnorfolk.org/public_documents/NorfolkMA_documents/towndocs/F000193C3/S00441E80.-1/ngf1128.pdf (accessed July 2006).

Oakley, R. (1999). *Shaping Up.* Commonwealth Government of Australia.

Pinkerton, W. (2003). *Project Management.* McGraw Hill.

Pound, R. (2004). *Inside the Olympics.* Wiley.

Preuss, H. (2000). *Economics of the Olympic Games: Hosting the Games 1972–2000.* Walla Walla Press.

Preuss, H. (2004). *The Economics of Staging the Olympics.* Edward Elgar.

Quirk, J. and Fort, R. (1992). *Pay Dirt: The Business of Professional Team Sport.* Princeton University Press.

Reese, J. and Mittelstaedt, R. (2001). An Exploratory Study of the Criteria Used to Establish NFL Ticket Prices. *Sport Marketing Quarterly*, 10(4), 10–22.

Rosner, S. and Shropshire, K. (2004). *The Business of Sports.* Jones and Bartlett.

Rosson, P. (2005). SEGA Dreamcast: National Football Cultures and the New Europeanism, in M. Silk, D. Andrews and C. Cole (Eds.), *Sport and Corporate Nationalism.* Berg.

Sandy, R., Sloane, P. and Rosentraub, M. (2004). *The Economics of Sport: An International Perspective.* Palgrave Macmillan.

Sawyer, T., Hypes, M. and Hypes, J. (2004). *Financing the Sport Enterprise.* Sagamore Publishing.

Sheard, R. and Bingham-Hall, P. (2005). *The Stadium Architecture for the New Global Culture.* Pesaro Publishing.

Slack, T. (2004). *The Commercialization of Sport.* Routledge.

Smart, D. and Wolfe, R. (2000). Examining Sustainable Competitive Advantage in Intercollegiate Athletics: A Resource-Based View. *Journal of Sport Management*, 14(2), 133–153.

Smith, A. and Stewart, R. (1999). *Sport Management: A Guide to Professional Practice.* Allen and Unwin.

Stewart, R., Dickson, G. and Nicholson, M. (2005). The Australian Football League's Recent Progress: A Study in Cartel Conduct and Monopoly Power. *Sport Management Review*, 8(2), 145–166.

Stewart, R. (1984). *The Australian Sport Business.* Kangaroo Press.

Stewart, R., Nicholson, M., Smith, A. and Westerbeek, H. (2004). *Australian Sport: Better by Design? The Evolution of Australian Sport Policy.* Routledge.

Szymanski, S. (2004). Is there a European Model of Sports? in R. Fort and J. Fizel (Eds.), *International Sports Economic Comparisons.* Praeger, pp. 19–38.

Szymanski, S. and Kuypers, T. (2000). *Winners and Losers.* Penguin.

Thibault, L., Kikulis, L. and Frisby W. (2004). Partnerships between Local Government Sport and Leisure Departments and the Commercial

Sector: Changes, Complexities and Consequences. In T. Slack (Ed.), *The Commercialization of Sport.* Routledge, pp. 119–139.

Thompson, P., Toolczko, J. and Clarke, J. (Eds.) (1998). *Stadia, Arenas and Grandstands: Design, Construction and Operation*, E and FN Spon.

Tribe, J. (2004). *The Economics of Recreation, Leisure and Tourism*, 3rd Edition. Elsevier.

Turco, D. and Navarro, R. (1993). Assessing the Economic Impact and Financial Return on Investment of a National Sporting Event. *Sport Marketing Quarterly*, 2(3), pp. 17–23.

UK Sport (2004). *Measuring Success: The Economic Impact of Major Sport Events.* UK Sport.

URS Finance and Economics (2004). *Economic Impact of the Rugby World Cup on the Australian Economy.* New South Wales State Government, Department of Industry, Tourism, and Resources.

Wann, D., Melnick, M., Russell, G. and Pease, D. (2001). *Sport Fans: The Psychology and Social Impact of Spectators.* Routledge.

Westerbeek, H. and Smith, A. (2003). *Sport Business in the Global Marketplace.* Palgrave Macmillan.

Whitehouse, J. and Tilley, C. (1992). *Finance and Leisure.* Longman.

Index

Note: Page numbers in *italics* refer to figures and tables.